Investing in the Age of Sovereign Defaults

Investing in the Age of Sovereign Defaults

HOW TO PRESERVE YOUR WEALTH IN THE COMING CRISIS

Peter T. Treadway with contributions
from Michael C. S. Wong

WILEY

John Wiley & Sons Singapore Pte. Ltd.

Other Wiley Editorial Offices

John Wiley & Sons, 111 River Street, Hoboken, NJ 07030, USA

John Wiley & Sons, The Atrium, Southern Gate, Chichester, West Sussex, PO19 8SQ, United Kingdom

John Wiley & Sons (Canada) Ltd., 5353 Dundas Street West, Suite 400, Toronto, Ontario, M9B 6HB, Canada

John Wiley & Sons Australia Ltd., 42 McDougall Street, Milton, Queensland 4064, Australia

Wiley-VCH, Boschstrasse 12, D-69469 Weinheim, Germany

ISBN 978-1-118-24721-1 (Cloth)
ISBN 978-1-118-24724-2 (ePDF)
ISBN 978-1-118-24723-5 (Mobi)
ISBN 978-1-118-24722-8 (ePub)

Typeset in 11/13 pt, ITC New Baskerville by MPS Limited, Chennai, India.
Printed in Singapore by Ho Printing Pte. Ltd.

10 9 8 7 6 5 4 3 2 1

*I would like to dedicate this book to my late mother,
Dorothy Treadway, who always supported and
encouraged me in the world of
learning and intellect.*

Contents

Acknowledgments

I would like to express my appreciation to my colleague Dr. Michael Wong, who encouraged me to write this book and who provided research assistance.

I would also like to thank Rudy Beutell of Scarsdale Equities LLC for his invitations to his firm's regular lunches. These lunches, attended by fund managers as well as economists and strategists, gave me the opportunity to exchange ideas with investment practitioners.

Preface

Why Another Book on the Financial Crisis?

A mass of sovereign defaults, broadly defined, is looming on the horizon as the global financial crisis that began in 2008 lumbers on. The primary objective of this book is to come up with some answers for investors who, by and large, will be the ones defaulted on. Worse than that, governments desperate for money will look to the so-called "rich" and the more advanced in age, aka the investor class, to plug the yawning gaps in government budgets. In all countries affluent elders will be pitted against their or somebody else's children. In some countries, affluent investors from "elite" racial groups or castes will be pitted against different and allegedly downtrodden castes or racial groups. The reelection of Barack Obama and Democratic control of the Senate will accentuate this process in the United States.

A simple observation was the spark that created the incentive to write this book. Today the world's richest, best educated, most democratic—can we say most *civilized*—countries are headed for bankruptcy and default. Nobody is surprised when poor countries with their imperfect institutions, corrupt leaders, and low levels of education go bankrupt. But the rich, advanced countries? *This was not supposed to happen.*

This observation immediately raised two questions, which this book will try to answer. One, how did this happen? And two, how can investors preserve their wealth through the chaos ahead?

The terrible experience of German fixed-income investors in the early 1920s was deep in my mind. These investors constituted the solid bourgeois rock upon which German society rested. They were wiped out, and we know the history. The 1920s were followed by the 1930s, with the Great Depression and rise of Adolf Hitler. In the case of Germany, from 1914 on it was one *black swan* after another—that is, an unexpected event with a profound impact. This book is written for both institutional investors and for private investors who think they are affluent today but must live off their investments. Investing is never easy, but in times of historically unprecedented and unpredictable cataclysmic shifts in the economic landscape, investing comes close to being *mission impossible*. Nevertheless, investors have no choice. They must try. Every private investor today must harbor a fear in his or her heart that some terrible shift will occur—call it a black swan or whatever you like—that will reduce his or her real net worth to zero. For younger people, these shifts can be opportunities. But for older, retired, or semiretired people for whom investment income may be their only income and for whom starting over to take advantage of new opportunities is not an option, this can be a death sentence. For institutional investors, the penalty for failure to see the shifts coming is simply that they lose their jobs. That may be incentive enough.

Overview of Contents

Chapter 1 takes on the question of why the advanced, civilized countries are on the way to being broke and in default. The answer given is that in democracies there is an inexorable tendency toward populism by which the electorate attempts to make an end run around what the free market would provide and votes for politicians who provide the electorate with benefits, entitlements, and socialized risk. All these accumulate over time and become ultimately unaffordable. In other words, it is democracy itself that harbors this fatal predisposition to fiscal profligacy. As a part of this process, the governments gradually assume risks formerly borne by the market. Government demand management and manipulation, intellectually justified by Keynesianism and monetarism, becomes an integral part of this process and provides the intellectual cover for fiscal and monetary excess.

In some countries—the United States in particular—differences in observed income and educational performance among racial and ethnic groups exacerbate the problem. This is obviously a sensitive subject. The less successful groups, often with a sense of historical grievances, exhibit strong demands for government to overrule the market and exhibit greater dependency on the government.

It may surprise some readers to learn that the American Founding Fathers, notably James Madison (the so-called Father of the US Constitution) and Benjamin Franklin, had a profound distrust of democracy. They preferred a republic where only men of property would vote for representatives who would make the decisions for society. Yes, they were so dead-white-male and uncool in their attitudes. But they worried that in a democracy the less-affluent majority would vote to confiscate the property of the affluent minority. The word *democracy* cannot be found once in the US Constitution. No accident! The American Founding Fathers would not be surprised at the near bankrupt state of today's advanced countries. In fact, they virtually predicted it.

I am arguing that populism in democracies inevitably drives democracies to default. I hope that the word *inevitably* proves to be an exaggeration. I want to be proved wrong, or at least partly wrong. We do have the experience of democratic Scandinavia and Switzerland, as well as (almost) democratic Singapore, where affluent democracies are not going broke. Note, however, that these countries are all small and largely devoid of underperforming minority groups demanding special treatment. Maybe small *is* beautiful.

Is it possible that a sweep by fiscal conservatives in the recent US elections would have enabled the US to avoid default? I would say impossible since default, defined in a broad sense as used in this book, must happen for the country to move forward again. All of the entitlements that have been promised cannot be honored. But a conservative sweep could have prevented a messier type of default, either via inflation or outright rejection of US government debt by the bond markets. This book, in coming out right after the 2012 American elections, cannot be considered a political tract. I'm not asking you to vote for anybody. The election is over. The verdict is in. Investors lost.

Complicating all this is the coming demographic revolution in virtually all advanced countries. Birthrates have plummeted everywhere. Worker/entitlement recipient ratios are going south and that just exacerbates the fiscal problem. Is the *birth dearth,* as it has been called, a product of democracy and populism? Although I don't want to push this too far, I would argue yes. In days prior, children were the average family's social security program. Today, the state in part provides old-age security, thus replacing a family's own children. Of course, for society as a whole, the children of today will be paying for the entitlements of tomorrow. But most citizens don't make this connection. The state—in reality, the children of other people—will provide for their old age. Therefore, there is no need to have children. *Let George do it.*

Chapter 2 reviews the parlous fiscal state of the so-called advanced countries, including those of Western Europe, the United States, and Japan. This is a very fluid situation, and by the time the reader sees this book things may have changed somewhat. Then again, perhaps Italy, Greece, Portugal, and Ireland may have gone into full-scale default. (This is not a forecast but it is a possibility.) The just-held American elections, for example, were probably the United States' last chance for an economically sensible solution to the country's fiscal problems. A sweep by fiscal conservatives could have made this book seem too pessimistic. Unfortunately, the near sweep of Obama and his statist, soak-the-rich allies, ensures the US fiscal situation will worsen. Pardon the unsophisticated language but investors will get screwed.

Chapter 3 takes a detour to review China and India. These countries are not rich or "advanced" in the usual sense of the word. And China is not a democracy. So it doesn't suffer so much from the fatal democratic defect of populism. But the Chinese model has other problems, including protectionism, excess export dependency, overinvestment, a deliberately undervalued currency, and in general a massive misallocation of resources. India, by contrast, is a democracy and suffers from an overdose of populism, which is exacerbated by its caste system.

Chapter 4 looks at the current international monetary system. The gold standard—which operated, let's say, from 1880 to 1914—worked very well. Economic growth was strong, inflation was close to negligible. WWI destroyed the system. But it could never be put back in place properly after the war because governments had discovered the possibilities of demand management via monetary and fiscal policy—and because their post-WWI universal suffrage electorates could not endure the discipline of an anonymous metal. Slowly, the gold standard disappeared, going from the post-war gold exchange standard to the gold standard "lite" of Bretton Woods to the (manipulated) fiat money float of the current system. Creeping populism made the gold standard unwanted, no matter how successful it had been. The intellectual arguments against gold were in time duly provided by economists brought up in the new Keynesian/monetarist demand management schools.

Chapter 5 reviews the historical record of fiat money. Default by inflation is one of the favorite choices of fiscally bankrupt nations. Historically, massive money printing has led to inflation, and paper currencies have greatly depreciated in value or become worthless. The historical record is horrendous, starting with eleventh-century Sung Dynasty China, where fiat paper money was invented. Northern invaders threatened, the Dynasty printed more paper money to finance the defense, and the money became worthless. Today's populist-addled governments with quantitative easing of various stripes are doing exactly that. In the past, it was mainly wars that brought about this need for default by inflation and excess printing of fiat paper money. Today, the cumulative demands of populism and declining birthrates are the culprits.

Chapter 6 attempts an overall look at the trends affecting the current investment climate. Several things stand out. So far, the massive money printing implied by the various attempts at quantitative easing around the world has not resulted in inflation. Instead, the world is suffering from oversupply in the majority of categories of goods and services and a crimping of aggregate demand thanks to the global deleveraging that is a hangover from the prior boom. Investors face a world of deflation/disinflation now and inflation later. Today's smart fixed-income investment could turn into tomorrow's loser. Investors also face a world where advanced-country governments—desperate for money as they are—will try to pick investors pockets via higher taxes and financial repression.

My basic forecast is deflation (or more properly disinflation) first followed by inflation (which will be one method of government default). How long the deflationary/disinflationary period will last is anybody's guess, and that is one factor that will make investing so difficult. Nobody is going to ring a bell when the world flips from the current deflation to inflation. This "flip" could be years off. It could be next year. Right now, the world seems in oversupply on mostly everything. The Chinas, the Indias, the Brazils of the world are turning out a plethora of goods in a globalized economy that is benefiting from technology-driven increased productivity. The governments can print all the money they want, but it just sits in the central banks as excess bank reserves. Europe is in recession, China is slowing down, and the United States is barely above a recessionary growth path.

But there is one long-term positive of which investors should be aware. That is the continued acceleration of technology, which I believe is an integral part of human evolution and is an immense force for good. Globalization is but one manifestation of this technology acceleration and is a definite positive for investors and the human race overall. Jet planes, computers, fiber optic cables—the list goes on—make globalization unstoppable. Improvements in health and the quality of life are on the horizon, and investors will want to be in on these trends. I am a big fan of futurist Ray Kurzweil's ideas on technology and progress, which are found in his *Age of Spiritual Machines.* His law of accelerating returns is a law of accelerating technology. (You don't have to accept his views on artificial intelligence machines being the next stage of human evolution.)

Although the reader might not get this impression from reading the earlier chapters, in the long run, the optimists, not the pessimists, will prevail. But I admit it could be a long wait. Look back at history. Mankind and progress have been on a continuous upward trend over the long run. But there have been some bad years. And some bad centuries. We can hope that it will finally dawn on the well-educated inhabitants of the advanced democracies what their real problem is and that they will undertake real structural/supply-side reforms, as was done after the Asian crisis of 1997–1998. Real reforms mean dismantling the welfare state and its overbearing taxes and regulations and reducing unpayable obligations by defaults. This may seem like a contradiction, but certain types of defaults—particularly in the entitlements areas but also on sovereign debts—may be part of the reform process.

Chapter 7 gets to the theme raised by the title of the book—investing in an age of sovereign defaults. A review of various asset classes is undertaken starting with cash.

The book offers alternatives to investors who don't want to take risk and who want to hide in cash. But even cash is not a simple decision. Whose cash, is the question? Specifically, what currency are we talking about? US dollars, euros, Japanese yen? If inflation strikes these countries, cash denominated in their countries' currencies may indeed be trash. What about alternatives like the Singapore and Hong Kong dollars?

Gold as an alternative currency is also worth a look. But I firmly believe that the upside potential of gold is limited, simply because governments, to protect their monopoly over money, will go out of their way to limit the profits of gold investors. If you own gold, pray that gold goes up, but not by too much.

Long-run investing strategies, which include the major US and non-US (nonfinancial) global corporations, which are driven by technology and globalization make sense to me. Their governments may go broke but they will carry on and eventually rally, as did the big German corporations during and after the hyperinflation of the early 1920s. In my opinion, the frequently maligned but technology-driven global corporations are like the monks in their monasteries who carried on the tradition of learning in the Dark Ages. (Let's hope any coming Dark Ages don't last five hundred years, like the last one.)

As far as the global banks go, there we have a problem. Unless too big to fail is dropped—and that seems unlikely to me—the banks will become more like utilities. Global finance will have to be done in part by nonbanks that don't show up in the regulatory radar.

I have been writing a regular essay for several years called *The Dismal Optimist*. This essay deals with global macro and investment issues. *The Dismal Optimist* started out being e-mailed to clients and friends but its distribution list has grown gradually, essentially by word of mouth. A version of this essay is also sent out in China to clients of my colleague and author of the Appendix in this book, Dr. Michael Wong. Michael had suggested for some time that these essays be compiled into a book. This book, in a broad sense, is based on ideas expressed in *The Dismal Optimist*.

Finally, **Appendix A** is an important essay produced by Michael Wong. Michael provides a quantitative approach to model and identify sovereign risk and predict problem countries.

Democracies' Fatal Attraction of Populism

When national debts have been accumulated to a certain degree, there is scarce, I believe, single incidence of their having been fairly and completely paid.
—Adam Smith, *The Wealth of Nations*, 1776

Democracy is two wolves and a lamb voting on what to have for lunch.

When the people find that they can vote themselves money, that will herald the end of the republic.
—Benjamin Franklin

The United States shall guarantee to every State in this Union a Republican form of government.
—United States Constitution, Article 4, Section 4, Paragraph 1

I think when you spread the wealth around it's good for everybody.
—Barack Obama

The central theme of this book is that the so-called advanced nations are rapidly moving toward a broadly defined "default" on the many obligations they have accrued over the last hundred years. This defaulting is not some kind of historical accident but results from the underlying fatal attraction of populism in democracies with universal suffrage. This broadly defined default along with supply-side/structural reforms will be necessary for the advanced nations to reestablish themselves on the path of human progress.

Let's start with a definition of *populism*. Look it up and you will find a variety of definitions. The majority defines the word as policies benefiting the common people at the expense of the rich or the elite. But as a free market economist, I have my own definition, which is the meaning of the word the way it is used in this book. *As used here, populism is a political strategy ostensibly targeting the wealth and income of the affluent elite and based on a calculated appeal to the interests or prejudices of ordinary people regardless of the economic rationality of this strategy.* As an investor, you are categorized as belonging to the rich or the elite. So populism basically is a set of programs that are ultimately aimed at reducing your wealth.

Now back to our theme. Government defaults are an old story going back to antiquity. But the susceptibility of modern advanced democracies to default may come as somewhat of a surprise to most of us for whom democracy is truly a sacred concept. The idea, that democracy with universal suffrage may at times be inefficient but in the end the people always "get it right," is embedded in Western— indeed, global—political DNA. Suggesting that democracy has any serious faults is blasphemy. But the current reality is that, at least when it comes to fiscal probity and managing fiat paper money, the people *don't* always get it right.

This chapter will present a theory of why democracies with universal suffrage and well-developed political institutions will tend to eventual bankruptcy and default and why lenders in particular will be at risk. My reasoning will draw, in part, on many thinkers, including those as diverse as James Madison, the Father of the American Constitution, and Hyman Minsky, whose financial instability hypothesis has come from obscurity to receive much attention in recent years.

I want to be clear. This book is not advocating alternatives to democracy. Like Winston Churchill—who famously said (Churchill said many things) that democracy was the worst form of government devised, except for all the others—I am not suggesting a better idea. I will discuss, however, that America's Founding Fathers were afraid of universal suffrage democracies and preferred a more limited suffrage *republic.*

Default, an Expanded Definition

In its strict legal sense, *default* means the failure to perform a legal obligation specified in a contract or by law. Countries have frequently legally defaulted on their debts over the course of the centuries.

But the text of this book uses the word *default* in the broader sense of a sovereign government failing to meet any formal promise or obligation. In the sense used in this book, a default could be:

1. A legal default under the legal system of the borrowing country or a recognized international legal system such as that of the United States.
2. A restructuring of outstanding loans on a "voluntary" basis.
3. A situation where a loan can only be repaid or serviced with the assistance of bailout money coming from an external entity like the International Monetary Fund (IMF).
4. A reneging on promised entitlements, including those for medical or pensions for retirees. This type of default will actually be good for investors. Unless of course they are also recipients. Call it a *benign* default.
5. A default by inflation whereby a defaulting country prints money and destroys the value of its currency, which happens to be the currency in which it has incurred the obligation.
6. Financial repression whereby a sovereign nation takes measures that essentially confiscate money from its financial system via excess reserve requirements on its banks, interest rate caps on savers, and prohibitions on investments outside the home country.

All these types of defaults are on the horizon for advanced countries, with the exception that countries that can borrow in their own currency (e.g., the United States will choose the option of printing money and inflation rather than legally defaulting on their government debt).

From investors' viewpoint, default on promised entitlements is a good thing. This type of default reduces tax burdens. If investors are also relying on one or more government programs that are being defaulted on, then as beneficiaries they will feel some pain.

Debt Default in History—A Recurring Theme

"Countries don't go bust," famously remarked by Walter Wriston, a famous CEO of Citibank.[1] But they do. And often. According to Carmen Reinhart and Kenneth Rogoff in their now classic work

This Time Is Different, Eight Centuries of Financial Folly,[2] countries have been going bust as long as there have been countries. Way back in the fourteenth century, England's Edward III defaulted on his debt, contributing substantially to the demise of the Italian Bardi and Peruzzi banks who were his lenders.

Many countries at one time or another have been repeat offenders (i.e., *serial defaulters,* in the words of Reinhart and Rogoff). Greece, the current poster child for bankrupt sovereign debt, was in default more or less continuously from 1800 to the end of WWII. As Reinhart and Rogoff have so meticulously recorded, the list of sovereign defaulters is a long one and, going back over the last five hundred years, includes the majority of countries on earth. Reinhart and Rogoff record at least 250 sovereign external default episodes over 1800–2009 and at least 68 cases of default on domestic public debt.[3]

This book will not recite this list. Anyone seriously interested in this subject should read Reinhart and Rogoff's book, which is probably the definitive historical record on this subject.

However, contrary to the views of some American politicians, the United States is no exception. It has defaulted on more than one occasion. Three instances deserve special mention. First, the American states. A number of American states defaulted in the 1840s and again after the American Civil War in the 1860s. Second, in 1933 the United States refused to honor its obligation to pay in gold on its bonds held by US citizens. Third, in August 1971 the United States defaulted on its obligation under the Bretton Woods Agreement to redeem in gold dollars presented by central banks. (The Bretton Woods Agreement, along with the entire international monetary system, will be discussed in Chapter 4.)

With such a record, one might ask why anyone or any institution in their right mind would loan money to a government. History repeatedly shows that governments regularly default, then they promise never to do it again, then lenders lend once again, and governments default again. Incurable recidivist behavior on both sides is the norm.

Nobody Likes a Lender

Historically, investors and lenders have gotten little sympathy. Money lenders, as the hapless Jew Shylock in Shakespeare's *Merchant of Venice* can attest, are generally depicted as the bad guy. Lending at interest was banned by the medieval Christian Church in Europe and is still banned today under prevailing interpretations of the Koran. Jews in Europe, as nonbelievers, were confined to moneylending as an occupation. It turns out that moneylenders tend to get rich.[4]

The nineteenth century success of European Jews in this profession was to evoke the jealousy of their *goy* neighbors and serve as a foundation of Hitler's murderous National Socialist anti-Semitism. The Rothschilds, in particular, who played a major role in financing the British victory in Waterloo and had gone on to become the preeminent banking family in Europe, were the epitome of evil Jewish money lenders and the object of hatred by various non-Jewish deadbeats and defaulters. Alexander G. McNutt, governor of Mississippi, a US state that defaulted on its Rothschild-owned loans in the 1840s, said of Baron Nathan Rothschild: "The blood of Judas and Shylock flows in his veins."[5] McNutt went on to say that the Rothschilds might hold a mortgage on "the Sepulcher of our Savior" but "they will never hold a mortgage on our cotton fields or make serfs of our children."[6]

But it's not just Jews who have been singled out. Any group that specializes in lending and making a return on capital will not win a popularity contest. In South India, there is a group called the Chettiars who for centuries have specialized in moneylending and finance. Modern scholars have concluded that the Chettiars were important innovators in banking and that they financed the creation of a modern economy in several territories of the then British Empire, notably Burma and Ceylon, as they were then called. But in Burma, when the worldwide Great Depression came, the Chettiar lenders operating under British law foreclosed on property that had been pledged as collateral for loans in default. As a result, the Chettiars came to be hated by the indigenous population as well as the British colonial administrators. In bad times, when defaults rise, the underlying dislike of lenders rises to the surface.

Interestingly, intergovernmental institutions such as the International Monetary Fund (IMF) and now the European Central Bank (ECB) refuse to accept defaults on their troubled loans. Just why they should be in this preferred position is unclear. Private lenders somehow are always judged less noble than their governmental counterparts, and from time to time they must take haircuts on bad debts. Hedge funds and banks are bad guys; the IMF and the ECB are, at least in their own estimation, the good guys. This is a problem, for example, in the case of Greece, where the IMF and the ECB own a substantial portion of Greek obligations. In the case of default, a disproportionate share of the default burdens therefore has fallen on the private holders.

Looking at the history of debt, what you see, in the words of anthropologist David Graeber, is "profound moral confusion . . . the majority of human beings hold simultaneously that 1) paying back money one has borrowed is a simple matter of morality, and 2) anyone in the habit of lending money is evil."[7] Graeber is a scholar of somewhat leftward leanings. (He's a self-described anarchist who managed to get himself unhired as a member of the Yale faculty. Imagine, an American academic institution kicking out a professor for being too far left!) Graeber goes on in his five-hundred-page book *Debt, The First 5000 Years* to argue that not paying back money one has borrowed can be okay. (Graeber even goes so far as to express sympathy for the "non-industrious poor."[8]) President Barack Obama now seems to be in agreement, at least with regard to mortgages and student loans.

Congratulations to Students Who Can't Pay

The Obama administration, with Congress's cooperation, has proposed a form of debt relief for student loans that is unique in that it disregards market signals in favor of what could be called government signals. We will discuss government versus market in this chapter. The government signals, of course, are rooted in populism. Obama is essentially proposing to require that debt collectors let student-loan borrowers make payments based on what they can afford, rather than on the size of their debt. According to the financial media, the US Education Department, which hires private collectors, said it would mandate that the companies use a standard form to gather debtors' income and expenses. If borrowers protest, they would be offered an income-based formula, which can result in payments as low as $50 a month for an unmarried person with $20,000 in income and $20,000 in loans.

This effectively discriminates against brighter, more ambitious students who go to the top schools and/or choose fields of study that will lead to jobs that bring them higher incomes. On the one hand, these students will be forced to repay their loans. On the other hand, less-bright, less-focused students or students who choose fields of study that lead to jobs with lower remuneration will be favored. This is an interesting policy, given that the Obama administration has spent time lamenting the fact that American students are avoiding the sciences and related "hard" subjects. A purely private student loan program based on market signals would, of course, favor students who were most likely to pay back their loans.

Forgiveness of debts—another way to define *default*—is a theme that goes back in antiquity. *Clean slates* is an alternative way some scholars have characterized this phenomenon. The various civilizations of ancient Mesopotamia and the Middle East offer numerous examples of general forgiveness of debts and clean slates. Forgiveness of debt seemed to be necessary to prevent indebtedness from totally overwhelming and essentially enslaving predominantly agricultural communities that were vulnerable to bad harvests.

The word *jubilee* is popular in Occupy Wall Street circles. The Old Testament book of Leviticus has now become the favorite scripture of the atheistic left. In Leviticus 25, God tells Moses to forgive certain debts every Jubilee year, or once every fifty years. It's as if human societies have an irresistible tendency toward overindebtedness and the debt meter has to be set back to zero every once in a while.

As we will argue, universal suffrage democracy simply provides a channel to amplify this irresistible tendency. It is the will of the people that their governments overborrow. Democracy, more than any other form of government, expresses the will of the people.

Leviticus and the Mesopotamian records do not make easy reading. Plus, anyone doing serious work better be fluent in the original languages. Hebrew for starters and then Akkadian, Eblaite, Elamite, Phoenician, Semitic, and Sumerian. You don't run into people with that knowledge *and* a grasp of economics every day. (Actually, most days you don't even run into people with a grasp of economics.) No matter. Interpretations of ancient texts usually primarily reflect the views of the interpreter and the people reading the texts. Occupy Wall Street types have seized on Leviticus and the clean slates as somehow conferring the approval of the ancients on defaulting on such things as student loans and mortgages. The message here to investors and lenders seems to be: *God is not on your side.*

The ancient texts have provided grist for twenty-first-century economists, who certainly have their own axe to grind. For example, Michael Hudson is a former Wall Streeter himself and properly certified PhD economist who has defected from economic orthodoxy. Hudson, writing about clean slates in antiquity, is of interest because of his knowledge of and antipathy toward standard neoclassical economics. According to Hudson, in antiquity there was no concept of Adam Smith's deist god, "designing the world to run like clockwork." Nor was there a god of modern monetarist fundamentalism "who gave up trying to protect the poor and decreed instead that the economy's wealth and revenues should pass into the hands of the richest and most aggressively self-serving members rather than administered in a spirit of altruism." Hudson writes that to have adopted such an idea would have to been to let debts pile up and imposed a "widespread loss of family members, crop rights and ultimately land rights."[9]

Take that, Milton Friedman and Goldman Sachs! Take that, investors and lenders who have been taught since they entered their first expensive MBA class that aggressive and self-serving pursuit of wealth would benefit not only them but society as a whole. The invisible hand has been amputated.

The concept of debt forgiveness can also be found in classical Greece. In the sixth century BCE, the Athenian lawmaker Solon instituted a set of laws called *seisachtheia,* which canceled all debts. What a fine role model for the current Greek rulers, whose nation is completely bankrupt and will be, in our opinion, one of the first in a long line of countries forming a new wave of sovereign defaulters.

Interestingly, there are no such tales of debt forgiveness emanating from ancient China. Nobody ever accused Confucius and his tiger mom disciples of being soft-hearted! However, as we will discuss, a form of governmental default did occur in Imperial China. The Chinese, having invented paper money almost a thousand years ago, went on repeatedly to demonstrate how its value could be destroyed.

Cultural differences do matter. It shouldn't be forgotten that in response to the 1997–1998 Asian crises, Koreans, whose culture has a Confucian gene imbedded in its DNA, donated their jewelry to help their country through its crisis. This is a far cry from rioting Greeks.

With its $3.3 billion in what are essential foreign IOUs (excuse me, foreign reserves), China shapes up as a huge loser in any jubilee. *Jubilee* is not going to be a favorite word in Zhongnanhai (the residence of the Chinese leadership in Beijing.)

You don't have to be an expert in ancient civilizations to see the point of all this. Are these historical references mere curiosities, or do they represent an underlying theme in human civilization that every now and then, humans (including their governments) collectively get over their heads in debt and mass default becomes inevitable? Do democracies with universal suffrage turn out to be a perfect mechanism for expressing this unfortunate bad habit of the people?

This book will answer yes to these questions.

Populism, Democracy, and the Road to Default

History is replete with examples of clean slates, sovereign defaults, and associated asset bubbles that end in defaults of one kind or another. Sovereign defaults, bubbles, and personal bankruptcies are an old story, at least for anyone who bothers to study history. It is not our purpose to recite all this history here. As mentioned, this history is well documented in Reinhart and Rogoff's *This Time Is Different* and elsewhere, for those who care to look.

But to repeat, the central thesis of this book is that the coming wave of sovereign defaults of the advanced countries is, in fact, *unique*. It is a product of democracy itself and its irresistible populist urges, as experienced in so-called advanced Western nations. (The term *Western* here always includes Japan, who in this context has the dubious distinction of being an "Honorary Westerner.") The coming defaults represent the end point of a process that has been building for at least the last hundred years.

Democracy is *the* sacred political belief. Even dictatorships acknowledge this by giving themselves grandiloquent-sounding democratic names like "The German Democratic Republic." For Francis Fukuyama and his widely acclaimed *The End of History and the Last Man*, democracy is the end point in human political evolution.[10]

Once again, I am not coming up with or advocating an alternative type of government. At least not in this book. If I did, I know I would be burned at the stake. The book's ultimate goal is to preserve wealth and maybe come up with some useful advice to governments. But democracy, in my opinion, does have some inevitable fiscal consequences. The coming default wave is one.

Democratic societies with universal suffrage have successfully demanded that their governments do two things: First, redistribute income to the more numerous less affluent majority, and second, at the same time, try to protect the economy as a whole from the economic pain and risk of the business cycle—that is, socialize risk. Noble as these objectives may appear, no good deed goes unpunished. These goals have proven to have a huge fiscal downside.

The results of governments attempting to achieve these objectives will show up in the future in a tsunami of defaults by advanced countries. Greece and Iceland are just the first. These countries have overborrowed and overpromised in order to satisfy these deep-seated populist urges of their voter citizens.

First, consider redistribution. There will always be more less-affluent people than affluent people in any society. Under universal suffrage, which has now become the norm, the more numerous, less-affluent groups find it in their interest to vote for politicians who will, via taxes, confiscate the earnings and sometimes wealth of the less-numerous affluent. The politicians will redistribute the confiscated earnings and wealth to the less affluent in the way of immediate benefits and/or deferred entitlement programs, where true costs are hidden or unknown. *We vote for you, you reward us, the rich will pay* sums up the process. Once the public is hooked on the entitlements, these become virtually untouchable, and, in fact, get significantly expanded as time goes on.

Note that I did not use the term *poor people*. In the advanced affluent societies, even the bulk of the so-called poor citizens are relatively affluent, at least by global standards. It is in the advanced, affluent societies where the prospect of major defaults now lies ahead. Poorer countries, at least until recently, have always been defaulting. That should come as no surprise. But in rich countries, rising incomes bring with them over time a rising sense of entitlements.

The issue of the less-affluent voting to take wealth and income of the affluent was very much on the minds of America's founding fathers. James Madison, known as the Father of the American Constitution, wrote the following in 1787:

> The right of suffrage is a fundamental Article in Republican Constitutions. The regulation of it is, at the same time, a task of peculiar delicacy. Allow the right exclusively to property, and

the rights of persons may be oppressed . . . Extend it equally to all, and the rights of property or the claims of justice may be overruled by a majority without property, or interested in measures of injustice . . . In a just & a free, Government, therefore, the rights both of property & of persons ought to be effectually guarded. Will the former be so in case of a universal & equal suffrage? Will the latter be so in case of a suffrage confined to the holders of property?[11]

The affluent—persons of property, in Madison's terms—of course resist. Their greater wealth and income gives them an influence on public policy disproportionate to their numbers. One way of resisting is to make sure some of the redistribution is directed back to themselves. The entire system of US farm supports, including ethanol subsidies, is one example of this. The affluent are most successful when they succeed in getting a special program passed that benefits them and evokes little interest from the general public. Economists have spent a great deal of time talking about this process and about how voters are "rationally uninformed" about special programs benefiting a few.

The affluent benefit in other ways. Unless benefits are means tested, the affluent usually qualify along with everyone else for the entitlements they have been taxed to provide. The irrationality of taxing the affluent to support the affluent apparently has eluded politicians and the electorate.

But the major resistance of the affluent comes in the form of opposition to tax increases. The affluent get some sympathy from the politicians and the public on this, since there is general recognition that, at least at some level of taxation (never defined) on the affluent, economic growth becomes impossible. Unfortunately quantification of this is a matter of politics, not economics. President Obama and some European politicians talk about the rich paying their "fair share." This is an odd comment, considering that the percentage of Americans who don't pay income taxes is almost 50 percent of US potential taxpayers. It turns out the rich pay the bulk of income taxes. You might ask, how can the rich not be paying their fair share when they already pay the bulk of all taxes and 50 percent of the people don't pay any income taxes at all? If you pay the bulk of the taxes, how can your fair share be greater than that?

Supply-side economists like Arthur Laffer preach that at some point, tax rate increases bring in *less* tax revenues. But there is no formula that pops out an optimal tax rate.

The primary impetus for the coming sovereign defaults lies not with special favors for the affluent but in the political process responding to the wishes of the less-affluent majority. The politicians have found they cannot fund all the promised benefits from taxes. Therefore, politicians have resorted to borrowing and/or printing money to fund government expenditures. Politicians in the post–Bretton Woods, post–gold standard world since 1971 have had more latitude in this regard since all currencies are now fiat currencies whose supply is at the arbitrary and ultimately politically controlled discretion of central banks.

Second, there is governments' duty to protect their citizens from the risks and vagaries of the business cycle. This is a twentieth-century duty. In the nineteenth century, governments weren't responsible for every rise and fall in the economy. Autonomous metallic monetary regimes (gold after 1880, gold and silver before) determined monetary policy. Most countries had no central banks and there really was no such thing as macroeconomics or countercyclical macroeconomic policies. *Whatever you may think of Keynesianism or its archrival monetarism in theory, both can be viewed as demand management tools of populist-leaning governments attempting to dampen downturns in the business cycle.*[12]

During recessions, government spending is expected to fill in for shortfalls in consumer spending and keep the financial system afloat at all costs. Governments should borrow whatever it takes, and central banks are expected to print limitless quantities of high-powered money (i.e., the monetary base) out of thin air. And, as I will discuss, under our current international monetary system, countries other than the United States, notably those in East Asia, can manipulate their currencies and organize their economies under mercantilist lines.

The financial press and the economics profession has generally been approving of the heavy use of Keynesian and monetarist tools. How many times have you read that the European Central Bank (ECB) is finally doing the right thing by printing money and bailing out the debt problems of the otherwise deadbeat euro weaker states? The financial press, the majority of investors, the voting public—all expect Keynesian and monetarist principles will be followed in reaction to a downturn or a sovereign default.

Indeed, maybe the massive increase in public debt did avert a Great Depression. But it may have substituted a future Great Default. And all the global monetary easing may have set the stage down the road for a Great Inflation—a special type of default.

Government efforts to protect its voters from business downturn and risk don't end with demand management. In the nineteenth century, banking panics occurred with some frequency (although, as it has turned out, less frequency than today). In the panic of 1907, banker J. P. Morgan singlehandedly kept the United States from running out of gold and organized a banking rescue from his elegant Madison Avenue townhouse mansion in New York. Morgan locked his contemporary bankers in a room and sat waiting, smoking fine cigars until they came up with a solution. Morgan was a hero in some circles, but the ascendant Progressive movement didn't want the country dependent on presumably greedy bankers who operated in mansions in a secretive cloud of expensive cigar smoke.

Below is one description of J. P. Morgan during the Panic of 1907, from a website called "Cigar Aficionado." Historically, all evil capitalists have always been portrayed as having a cigar in their hands:

> One can imagine the 70-year-old Morgan sitting behind his desk, dressed in his standard dark gray suit, his intense stare . . . the stoic banker (listens) expressionless, his bushy mustache twitching from time to time beneath his bulbous nose. He (holds) an eight-inch-long maduro Havana cigar known as a Meridiana Kohinoor . . ."[13]

You have to wonder if Lloyd Blankfein, the unloved CEO of the now near-universally hated Goldman Sachs, would do well to take up cigars. "If you've got it, flaunt it," the saying goes. Nobody's going to like him anyway.

So the Federal Reserve was established in 1914. Its initial scope was limited. But with the outbreak of WWI and the major European countries withdrawing from the gold standard, the new Fed quickly morphed into a modern central bank with high-powered money creation and lender of last resort capabilities. Then came the Depression and deposit insurance. After that came the end of the Bretton Woods system in 1973, which got rid of the restraining influence of gold and set the world on the path of fiat money.

And downside risk in the banking system was socialized at the same time financial liberalization opened up more opportunities for risk taking. Then came too big to fail and one bailout after the other. *Moral hazard* became imbedded in the system. Subsequent chapters will deal with these issues.

The 2008 recession—sometimes called the Great Recession—is *sui generis* because of its severity, its legacy of debt, and its unfunded entitlement liabilities and unfavorable demographics that lie ahead. For starters, the high levels of debt that are its legacy make rapid economic growth more difficult. Rogoff and Reinhart estimate that a sovereign debt ratio over 90 percent debt/GDP ratio retards GDP growth by 1 percent.

Rapid economic growth in the past and favorable demographics offset the last major runup in sovereign debt that occurred during WWII. No such luck this time. The advanced countries have dug themselves into a hole from which they cannot escape. As Chapter 2 will show, the advanced countries are rapidly approaching or beyond the 90 percent threshold.

The Demographics Are Awful

Demographics are a key part of the coming default story. Birthrates have plunged while the politicians have been piling on the unfunded entitlement obligations. These obligations are pay-as-you-go, which means an ever-fewer number of workers will be available to pay for an ever-larger number of retirees.

This phenomenon arises from the same sense of fairness that underlies the concept of universal suffrage and is not some kind of exogenous variable or unrelated event. Universal suffrage democracies—and virtually all other modern governments as well—favor equal education for both men and women. Indeed, no one (except radical Islamists) would disagree with the proposition that greater knowledge and education is a desirable goal for both men and women.

But there is an unintended side effect. Demographers have noted that the plunge in birthrates is highly correlated with the education of women.[14] In traditional agricultural societies, birthrates and death rates were high, women's roles were circumscribed, women had little real control over what today would be called "reproductive rights," and women were not educated. A family's own children were its social security program. Having children who survived was a matter of one's own survival.

Today, very few people look to their own children as their primary old age support. Rather, today, private and public pension programs are paid for by someone else's children. Looked at from an economic viewpoint, children represent a huge financial cost imposed on their parents, with society reaping the benefits. The temptation to free ride and have few or no children is overwhelming when looked at from the cold viewpoint of economic self-interest. Dogs—the universal child substitute—don't contribute to taxes or funding entitlements. The linkage between the need to have children and survival has been broken in the minds of the average person.

But not in reality. Children are still necessary for the survival of nations and the funding of retirement programs. Government retirement and medical programs help create the illusion that children and families are not as necessary for economic survival as they were in the past. The fatal attraction of populism has created the programs. The programs have undermined the demographic base on which they depend. The birth dearth in advanced nations is not good news for the future funding of pay-as-you-go entitlement programs.

The reality is that the so-called investor class is older than the population as a whole. All senior and near senior citizens—rich or poor—are beneficiaries of the lavish social welfare systems that have been set up in the advanced Western countries. A dramatic means of testing these benefits would constitute a type of default for affluent retirees and those affluent citizens who will soon become retirees. *The affluent elders will be defaulted on by their own children or someone else's children.*

This default can come in ways that are almost invisible. For example, in the United States all senior citizens are eligible for Medicare. But the Affordable Care Act, informally called Obamacare, is cutting back on payments to doctors under Medicare. Doctors are dropping out of Medicare in some high-cost geographic areas, effectively leaving retirees on Medicare uninsured.

The Special Roles of the United States

The United States has two special roles in the global scheme of things. First, the dollar is the key currency in the international monetary system. This will be discussed at length in subsequent chapters, but suffice to say here that because of this key currency status, United States fiscal and monetary profligacy takes on an extra ominous dimension. And it also gives the United States more freedom in a number of spheres.

Second, there is the United States' self-appointed task of world policeman. Wars have always been major but temporary causes of spikes in government debt/GDP ratios. The winners in the post–WWII period grew their way out their war debt while the losers defaulted. But the US policeman function seems to be a chronic condition and adds to the US government debt/GDP ratio. Since the end of WWII, the country has been involved in what seems like a continuous series of expensive and not always small wars.

Admittedly, most of these wars were unpopular and did not come from populist pressures. And none of these wars arguably did anything for the United States, either financially or in terms of augmenting American territory. But its number one reserve currency status gives the United States a greater ability to fight these wars and to run both current account and budget deficits.

But these special roles just give the United States more rope by which to hang itself.

Universal Suffrage—The Holy Grail or the Villain?

A core belief underlying Western democratic thought is the desirability of universal suffrage. As mentioned, universal suffrage is based on an abiding sense of fairness that is intrinsic to human behavior. But universal suffrage has consequences that should be recognized. The historical movement to universal suffrage is a major underlying force tilting governments toward intervention and populism and indirectly contributing to a lower birthrate.

The desirability of universal suffrage is regarded as sacrosanct. Rarely do economists dare to even investigate the effect of the shift to universal suffrage on the economy. One exception is Barry Eichengreen, who has argued that the granting of universal suffrage by the major nations of the world during WWI (and the rise of unions) undermined the support for the classic gold standard.[15] After WWI, the expanded electorates would not allow their governments to leave monetary and macro policy to the workings of a market-directed supranational metal standard, no matter how efficient its operation. And so governments gradually assumed direct responsibility for the workings of the market economy and the business cycle and implicitly socialized risk.

The classical gold standard was abandoned and replaced by modern central banking, fiat money, and management of macro-economic policy. 1914—the year of the outbreak of WWI and the creation of the American Federal Reserve—was a major turning point. Later would come deposit insurance, various versions of social security and socialized medicine, Fannie Mae and Freddie Mac, too big to fail, stimulus programs, QE1, QE2, QE3, and more. This will be discussed further in Chapter 5.

Judging by the quote cited earlier, even James Madison himself was uncomfortable with the topic of universal suffrage. Eighteenth- and nineteenth-century United States was the world's leading laboratory for a new and developing model of governance. And so the United States went from being a republic to a universal suffrage democracy.

The Founding Fathers favored the concept of a *republic* versus that of a *democracy*—a republic with a propertied electorate. In a republic, ultimate power rests with the voters but it is their elected representatives who make the decisions in accordance with law. The Founding Fathers were aware that if only a few could vote, liberty was threatened. They feared that if everyone could vote, those "without property" would vote to take the property of those who had it. You can't find the word *democracy* mentioned even *once* in the American constitution. Today, the words *democracy* and *republic* are used interchangeably by most people who don't know or care about the difference. That would even include most members of the Republican Party.

President Woodrow Wilson, in asking Congress' permission to have the United States enter WWI, said he wanted to make the world "safe for democracy." It is doubtful that most of the US Founding Fathers would have been be enthused about such a goal. They might have advocated keeping the world "safe *from* democracy."

Madison and some of his fellow Founding Fathers would not be surprised by the overindebtedness that the Western democracies now find themselves burdened with. They would have simply said, "I told you so." Of course nobody likes "I told you so" people.

One early compromise on the republic versus democracy problem was the creation of a popularly elected House of Representatives and a countervailing Senate whose members were elected by state legislatures. This solution would later be discarded by the Seventeenth Amendment in 1913, which called for direct election of senators. The impetus in the United States for universal suffrage and democracy grew stronger over time. The republic that was inaugurated in 1789 has transmogrified into a democracy. Most people today would cheer this development.

But maybe not the government bond market. Of course, there might not be a government bond market were the country to have remained a republic with a limited propertied electorate. No borrowing, no bonds. No bonds, no bond market.

The history of the movement to universal suffrage varies by country, but the broad outline and result was usually the same: The franchise was initially restricted to propertied males but it later opened up to all adult and even near-adult citizens. Universal suffrage and the rise of the ultimately bankrupt populist interventionist state go together.

Universal Suffrage—The American Story

American history follows the broad outline of ever-expanding suffrage, although it is unique in the sense that it has a major racial/ethnic component. The issue of race and/or caste complicates the suffrage issue in a number of countries, as we shall see.

The dynamic of expanding suffrage allows no exceptions—all men, women, minority groups, affluent and less affluent, and near-adults (18 year olds).

Non-American readers may be unfamiliar with the American story. Here is a timeline of the American march to universal suffrage.[16] Numerous recent court decisions and laws not mentioned in the timeline have also continued the trend toward suffrage expansion.

1790 Only white male adult property owners had the right to vote (10 to 16 percent of the population).

1810 Last religious qualifications were removed.

1850 Property ownership and tax requirements were eliminated. Almost all white males could vote.

1855 Some states enact literacy requirements for voting, aimed at Irish Catholic immigrants.

1870 Fifteenth Amendment to the Constitution passed, giving former slaves the right to vote and protecting the right to vote of all male citizens of any race.

1880 Initiation of poll taxes and literacy tests in Southern states were designed to keep African Americans from voting. Ways were found to exclude poor whites from these requirements.

1913 Seventeenth Amendment to the Constitution passed, requiring members of the US Senate to be elected directly by the people instead of state legislatures.

1915 Supreme Court outlaws literacy tests for federal elections.

1920 Nineteenth Amendment to the Constitution guarantees women's suffrage.

1924 Indian Citizenship Act grants all Native Americans citizenship, including the right to vote.

1964 Twenty-fourth Amendment to the Constitution bans poll tax in federal elections.

1965 Voting Rights Act is passed, protecting rights of minority voters and eliminating literacy tests.

1971 Twenty-sixth Amendment to the Constitution sets minimum voting age of 18.

The big issue now in America is whether voters should be required to show some type of identification to register to vote. Minorities, notably African Americans and their representatives, have argued that this requirement discriminates against them. The Founding Fathers would be astounded by this discussion. We've come a long way, baby.

One friend has commented that I never talk about the *Founding Mothers*. I have no answer for this. But the question, meant in jest, embodies the modern view in some quarters that the American constitution is a relic produced by dead slave-owning white guys. Maybe so. But the Constitution enshrines property rights, a key requirement for investors. Investors of any color, male or female, should look fondly on its authors, dead white guys or not.

What the Founding White Guys did not view as "rights" were those that imposed an obligation on others. Thus, in the US Constitution there are no explicit rights to education, or health care. These rights are obligations that to be honored must compel the services (or the money) of others.

Rational Economic Man?

There are two alternative approaches to an economy that a democracy faces: Leave economic decisions to the markets or have them be guided and controlled by the government, generally with redistributionist and socialization of risk objectives. Note that control and guidance by the government does not require state ownership of the means of production. Looking at this from a broader perspective, the establishment of central banks, which manage interest rates and money supply growth, is logically seen as an instrument of the government to control and guide the economy. Similarly, Keynesian economics advocates massive monetary and fiscal stimulus to offset a decline in consumer spending. Money creation and government borrowing finance this. Monetarism offers a justification for massive high-powered money creation, even as the demand for conventionally defined money declines during a recession. As argued, whether you think it is good or bad, Keynesian and monetarist economics offers justification for government control and a mechanism for government demand management.

Similarly, citizens of representative democracies have perceived two options to improve their standard of living: (1) use of brains, hard work, self-improvement and maybe luck within the market system; or (2) voting for representatives that will allocate benefits (entitlements) to them and essentially overrule the market system.

Many theorists have implicitly assumed that in a democracy, some kind of "equilibrium" gets reached between the market and the government approaches. *Social democracy* is the term often used in Europe. A certain amount of redistribution and socialization of risk is necessary to curb the excesses of the market approach. Our view is that there is no equilibrium at all in the long term. Sovereign bankruptcy and default, if you like, is the end point. The government sector ever so gradually devours the private sector.

Since the end of the nineteenth century, populist urges have become more irresistible. Option 2 and government control, including redistribution of wealth and socialization of risk, has been the road increasingly taken by Western democracies (including Japan). Populist measures didn't get imposed all at once. They were imposed incrementally, over time. Their effects were cumulative but came with a lag. Their proponents could argue they did not have a deleterious effect on economic growth because initially, the effects were not always in evidence.

Economists of the free market bent have repeatedly argued that all citizens in the long run will come out ahead if the market rather than the state solution is followed. But—excepting the Reagan/Thatcher interlude—their voices have been ignored. Milton Friedman once argued that the most successful political party in the United States has been the now-defunct Socialist Party, which, according to Friedman, saw its entire 1928 platform enacted. In the United States, even the Republican Party, while it dutifully preaches the virtues of markets, has generally expanded the government, redistribution of wealth, and socialization of risk when in power. As officials facing reelection, Republicans could not ignore the deep-seated populist urges of their electorates, however conservative they pretended to be. I sometimes joke that the only difference between Democrats versus Republicans is that Republicans are more likely to wear a suit.

Economists in recent years have taken to exploring the fundamental behavioral tendencies of human beings and question whether humans are rational. According to Professor Bryan Caplan,[17] voters instinctively mistrust markets and are not rational on the subject of economics. Rational, by Caplan's (and my) way of looking at things, is to view the world through the lens of neoclassical economics. But voters, according to Caplan, are xenophobic and unduly pessimistic. Voters distrust foreigners, free trade, and globalization—the latter being essential ingredients in an efficient twenty-first century market economy. Caplan reports even his own students, to his frustration, proved impervious to his free market arguments for such ideas as free trade. They were generally opposed to free trade when they arrived in class, changed their attitude only moderately after he "enlightened" them, and reverted to their previous hostility once some time had elapsed after taking his course.

Take the subject of Medicare. Medicare is the US government program for health care for retirees. (Medicaid, in theory, is aimed at poor people not retired.) In 1966, President Lyndon Johnson launched the Medicare program in the United States as a medical insurance program for all seniors. How could the voters know then that over the next fifty to seventy-five years, birthrates would plunge and that the recipient/worker ratios would become so unfavorable as compared to 1966? How could they know that average lifespans would increase as much as they have? How could they know in 1966 that medical progress was going to become such an expensive proposition? How could they (with their anti-market bias) realize in 1966 that Medicare was going to become a grossly inefficient way to deliver health services? Why should they have worried, anyway? The government would pay.

Now that Medicare is firmly established in the American economic life, its recipients—even the more affluent ones—are reluctant to consider more efficient alternatives. Medicare has become a "right." And so will Obamacare.

Irrational Voters?

Economists—at least since behavioral economics has come along—have assumed that humans are rational. The economic man (or woman) makes choices between various goods and services and maximizes his or her *utility*. Utility is just another way of saying "well-being." Fundamentally, most economists believe (or hope) that in the long run if given a choice, the economic man will vote for things recommended by classical economic theory. That is what Caplan really means by economically rational.

But this is somewhat simplistic. What if most voters think taxing the affluent is in their interest and have no ability or desire to worry about the long run? Choices that may be suboptimal for society as a whole may still be perceived by the majority of voters as benefiting them.

Here's a good example. Economists have a pet theory called Ricardian equivalence, named after its author, David Ricardo. Ricardo is the same early-nineteenth-century economist who gave us the free trade theory of comparative advantage, which, according to Caplan, most voters, including his students, instinctively can neither understand nor accept. Ricardian equivalence is the notion that citizens increase their savings to offset government borrowing. Thus, spending on social programs using borrowed money won't increase GDP because citizens will increase savings to pay for today's borrowing later. Nice theory. But what happens if the people voting in favor of more benefits don't expect to be the ones paying off the debt incurred? You say they will worry their children will get stuck with the bill? What happens if the beneficiaries figure that the children of the rich will pay? What happens if the beneficiaries simply don't care at all about some obligation far off in the future?

Unfortunately, the future is now.

Is a Meritocracy Good for Everyone?

Economists traditionally have concluded that a free market will bring about the most efficient allocation of resources and maximize all citizens' wealth and societies' economic growth. A free market implies a meritocracy. Everyone is equal, there is no discrimination on account of race or religion, and people succeed or fail in the market depending on their talents.

Mainstream economists with some exceptions traditionally haven't worried about income inequality. Most economists would argue, if over a given period the top guys improved their incomes by twenty times and the bottom guys by only five times, everybody was better off. That was as good as it would or should get.

PhD economists in their studies have to learn something called Pareto efficiency, named after an Italian economist Vilfredo Paredo. In a Pareto-efficient economic equilibrium, no allocation of given goods can be made without making at least one individual worse off. Given an initial allocation of goods, a change to a different allocation that makes at least one individual better off without making another individual worse off is called a Pareto improvement. An allocation is defined as Pareto efficient or Pareto optimal when no further Pareto improvements can be made.

Pareto optimums have little to do with income distribution. If we can make the affluent better off without making the less affluent worse off, that is worth doing. Economists were taught that Pareto efficient was a good thing.

Pareto optimums have nothing directly to do with growth. But the assumption is that a static optimal distribution of resources would be optimum in the dynamic case of growth. Most free-market economists would favor the view that the top guys were the movers and shakers that drove the economy. Their outsized rewards were the incentive that they would keep creating new businesses, jobs, and economic growth.

But that theory that income equality doesn't matter if everybody is better off has some flaws. Recent economic work has demonstrated that income differences do matter to the average person. Jealousy is a basic human trait and sometimes merges with what people think is "fair." People have a concept of fairness that is sometimes at variance with Pareto efficiency and the behavior free-market economists might prescribe. *The politics of class envy is a viable political strategy in a democracy.* In recent years, the popular press has focused on income inequality as a bad thing and unfair, especially when it is occurring in period like the last few years when the market economy is not doing so well and the lower end of the population is not gaining much at all. The popular argument for "fairness" in income distribution and against income inequality does not seem to rest on the theory that the affluent have gained by cheating or exploiting the less affluent. Even if the affluent have earned their money honestly, somehow this is "unfair."

The investor class is the one that is likely to be the object of envy for the rest of the population. It is probable that in the coming age of sovereign defaults, the investor class will become an easy political target for desperate governments seeking to raise funds.

Do We Want a Meritocracy?

Let us start with the assumption that the ability to compete (however measured) in a meritocracy has a normal (Gaussian) distribution across a population. No one group has an advantage. It is plausible to conclude that all those with average or better ability to compete would be willing to take their chances in the market rather than short circuit the market through pressing the political process for entitlements. So at least 50 percent of the population has a logical basis to opt for meritocracy over government entitlements.

This assumption makes sense if the population is homogeneous. In other words, there are no differences among the population that would enable one subgroup to have a greater ability to compete.

Unfortunately, that is not the situation in all countries, including and especially the United States or, among developing countries, including Brazil, South Africa, or India. This is a sensitive area. But subgroups' ability to compete may differ by ethnicity, race, or caste. These differing abilities could be due to past or present discrimination, differing cultural values including attitudes toward education and business, differing access to basic food and shelter, genetic differences, and more. For this analysis, it doesn't really matter what the causes are, and we will not further speculate on them in this book.

Assume there are two subgroups in a population. Subgroup A, for whatever reason, has a greater ability to succeed in a meritocracy than Subgroup B. Assume that members of Subgroup B are aware of this and believe this situation will persist. Subgroup B then might rationally conclude that its members will always fail in a meritocracy situation and that pressing for governmental preferences and entitlements is the optimal strategy for them. If Subgroup B is numerically significant in the voting population, this will create a powerful incentive for politicians eager to appeal to Subgroup B to pass measures offering government entitlements and preferences benefiting Subgroup B, regardless of the budgetary consequences.

Needless to say, in my view in the long run Subgroup B, in choosing government over market, has made the wrong decision. Subgroup B is opting for long-term inferiority and has given up its freedom in exchange for government dependence. This is certainly the road to serfdom. But *long run* is a concept that is not popular in democratic politics.

Just imagine how much worse the situation would have been if the recent rioters in Greece who set fire to forty-five buildings were of a different *race* or *caste* from the average Greek. Imagine that members of that different race or caste harbored resentments for past mistreatment against the race or caste of the ruling group.

In this regard, an interesting example presents itself in Malaysia. In Malaysia the politically dominant Malay majority is explicitly favored by a widespread affirmative action policy called the *bumiputra* program. Malays are favored by law in education and in business. There is a more or less explicit recognition that Malays, in terms of educational achievement and economic success, cannot compete in a meritocracy with the Chinese and Indian minorities.

Public-Sector Unions—We Vote for You, You Reward Us

One of the consequences of universal suffrage was the increasing tolerance and encouragement for unionism. Despite this, for a variety of reasons, unions in the private sector in the United States and other countries have diminished in importance. But the public sector is another story. It took some time for public-sector unions to be accepted. There was an awareness that there is a big difference between public-sector and private-sector unionization, and that if unchecked, public-sector unions held great risks for fiscal probity.

In the private sector, the unions and management bargain. They each pursue their own objectives. Neither is obligated to the other. The unions don't appoint management, at least in most countries. The issue of contention is the share of profits of a company, to which the workers have certainly contributed.

Not so with the public sector. In the public sector, well-organized and well-financed unions contribute to and support the candidacies of politicians who, in turn, are effectively the very people they will be negotiating with. The negotiations are not about dividing up profits to which the workers have contributed but about dividing up taxes derived from the general public. *All this can be viewed as a giant conflict of interest.* Public-sector managements—ultimately, the elected politicians—in effect become dependent on the public-sector unions for their jobs. The result is overly generous payments to public-sector employees, both in wages and politically easier-to-disguise retirement and health benefits. There's also a natural tendency to overstaff the public sector.

Public-sector unions have become just one more powerful force toward public-sector bankruptcy. It is a force that is unfortunately rooted in the democratic process.

This situation becomes even worse when less-able-to-compete subgroups, as already described, are disproportionately represented in the public sector and in public-sector unions. American civil rights leaders, for example, have warned that cutting government workers unfairly targets African American workers, who have a high representation in certain government unions.

Historically, there had been substantial opposition to public-sector unionization. President Franklin D. Roosevelt, whose administration had certainly seen its share of pro-union legislation, was opposed. Roosevelt understood the risks involved. But in the late 1950s, New York City Mayor Robert Wagner issued an executive order allowing city workers to unionize. That opened the door. In 1962, President John F. Kennedy gave federal workers the right to bargain collectively.

In virtually all so-called advanced countries, public workers now have this right. As mentioned, the result particularly in Europe and the United States has been an alarming growth in the number and remuneration of public-sector workers. Universal suffrage and the temptation of politicians to appeal for union votes has made all this possible.

Unfortunately, at least in the United States as the state governments cut back, they preserve as much as they can the oversized retirement plans of state workers rather than provide services that they *should* be providing. For example, cutbacks have undermined the vaunted University of California system, thus closing what has been an avenue of upward mobility for minority groups. Similar cutbacks have been visited on law enforcement, infrastructure, and other necessary government activities. In a democratic, society pensions come before all.

Debt and Macroeconomics

Macroeconomists, with the major exception of iconoclast Hyman Minsky, whose theories we will discuss shortly, have not really thought much about debt. Stephen G. Cecchetti, M. S. Mohanty, and Fabrizio Zampolli, have argued in a very important recent Bank for International Settlements paper, that as modern macroeconomics developed over the last half-century, most people either ignored or finessed the issue of debt. With few exceptions, the focus was on a real economic system.[18] Every debt incurred has an offsetting asset. The rational man of classical economic theory will not take on more debt than is prudent. Case closed. Why worry about debt? Debt will take care of itself.

This view, I have concluded, is totally wrong. This ignoring of debt is a glaring omission for which macroeconomics—and investors—are now paying the price. Debt, it turns out, is not something that just takes care of itself.

What is really interesting about the Cecchetti, Mohanty, and Zampolli paper is their finding that since 1980, not just sovereign debt has been rising. Rather, all debt—household, corporate, and government—has been marching upward. All kinds of theories can be advanced—a weakening of moral values, a fundamental inability of humans to reject the temptation of borrowings, the "human condition," and so on.

One possibility is that there is a subconscious assumption in the private sector that if things turn out badly, the government will assume responsibility for private-sector liabilities. Democratic populism at work again! Indeed, this has happened in the United States since 2008 with the banking, auto, and housing sectors. It will likely happen with student loans. In Europe, it has happened in the cases of Irish and Spanish banks. As it turns out, debt flows uphill!

The core theme of this book is that government debt has been driven by the dynamic of universal suffrage combined with the tendency of politicians to reward their electorates with benefits that are unaffordable in the long run. It is my view, which will be developed in Chapters 4 and 5, that democratically elected governments in the twentieth century have discarded the discipline of commodity-based money for that of undisciplined fiat paper money. The gold standard stands in the way of populism, as William Jennings Bryan with his "Cross of Gold" speech understood so well in the 1890s. This is all part of the same process.

Unfortunately, the creation of unlimited amounts of paper money has unleashed not just government but also private borrowing.

This book will stick to worrying about government debt, recognizing that private-sector borrowing may ultimately become government obligations—and that the tendency toward greater government borrowings may be part of a broader human tendency, encouraged by universal suffrage in democracies.

The question has to be answered why this upward swing in all debt has occurred. Cecchetti, Mohanty, and Zampolli offer four reasons:

1. *Financial liberalization and innovation.* Hyman Minsky would certainly agree with that. Financial liberalization of one sort or another has preceded all major debt-driven asset bubbles globally in the post–WWII period. I am certainly not arguing against financial liberalization, but the fact is, it has enabled households and corporates to take on massive debt and associated risks. Banks, too, have amassed great debt. Clearly, the calls for bank reform must take into account both the need for a financially *unrepressed* system and the historically demonstrable tendency of economic agents everywhere to assume more and more debt and risk.

2. *Comfort in borrowing money.* Cecchetti, Mohanty, and Zampolli's view is that since the mid-1980s until the start of the recent crisis, the world had become more stable and therefore borrowers felt more comfortable in borrowing more. Humph. I take issue with that one. What about first Latin debt crisis of 1980, the Japan bubble of 1990, the Mexican crisis of 1995, the Asian Crisis of 1997, the Russian crisis of 1998, and the dot-com bubble of 2000? It will be argued in Chapter 5 that

the global fiat money system is ultimately part of the populist problem and has been at the root of one debt-driven bubble after another, including that of 2008.

3. *Ease of carrying debt.* Since the 1990s, the substantial decline in real interest rates has supposedly made it easier to support ever-higher levels of debt. There's some logic to this, although Cecchetti, Mohanty, and Zampolli admit this is hard to quantify.
4. *Favorable tax policies.* The tax treatment of interest in many countries favors debt over equity financing. No question about that.

Hyman Minsky: Another View of Debt and Macroeconomics

Now to Hyman Minsky.[19] Minsky was an oddball in the economic profession. His views really didn't fit into the prevailing monetarist/efficient market and Keynesian schools of thinking. Minsky generally wasn't mentioned in graduate courses in monetary theory and was someone graduate students had to discover on their own. Minsky is the originator of what he called the financial instability hypothesis, or FIH. Under the FIH, the financial system would be dominated by debt-financed asset bubbles, including real estate, which would eventually crash and bring about the insolvency of both the banking system that financed them and the borrowers themselves. Minsky therefore believed the financial system was inherently unstable and that humans had an incurable desire to incur debt and speculate.

The FIH is not totally incompatible with monetarist and behavioral finance theories. An increase in the money supply, for example, can set off a debt-financed asset bubble. But Minsky would argue that a debt-financed bubble could occur without a jump in the money supply. More recent behavioral finance theories, of which Minsky may not have been aware but which hold that humans are not rational at all times in their investment choices, are certainly compatible with the FIH.

Minsky's FIH is definitely at variance with the efficient market hypothesis (EMH), which has been the prevailing orthodoxy in economics in the postwar period. The EMH, with its assumptions of rational man and perfect markets, does not treat the issue of debt as being important. Financial liberalization is a desirable thing and governments can take a very hands-off approach to regulation. Alan Greenspan as Fed chairman was a major believer in the EMH. Derivatives, complicated asset-backed securities, the rise of debt—for Greenspan, no problem. The efficient market would take care of all.

Unfortunately, as will be discussed in Chapter 5, one hundred years of ever-larger moral hazard, thanks to the socialization of risk, had been built into the global financial system. The founding of the Federal Reserve in 1914, the addition of deposit insurance, too big to fail, and so on—all encouraged risk taking and debt since there would be little or no penalty for failure. In response to universal suffrage and the corresponding need of the government to shield its citizen voters from all economic pain, losses had been socialized and risk taking had been incentivized. The EMH never had a chance.

Minsky's FIH helps explain the majority of debt-financed bubbles and busts of the postwar period, including the Japanese bubble of 1990 and the recent calamity of 2008. The associated busts with these episodes have given rise to major increases in government debt for both Japan and the United States. Big increases in government debt come almost automatically after a bank crisis and asset bust, as Rogoff and Reinhart have documented. Minsky's ideas have been given their proper place in the work of late financial historian Charles Kindleberger,[20] who incorporated it into his influential *Manias, Panics, and Crashes.*

If all those financial practitioners with their expensive MBAs had just read Kindleberger and thrown out their EMH-dominated finance textbooks, they would have been so much better prepared for the storms that came in 2000 and 2008.

From my perspective, however, Minsky has one major failing. His FIH has nothing to say about government debt. Investors who buy government debt aren't speculating on assets. Governments usually aren't borrowing to finance assets. Minsky has taught us that debt is important in itself and that individuals will take on more debt than the EMH man would. And in many cases, like that of Ireland, private-sector insolvencies caused by debt-financed asset bubbles ultimately result in the private-sector debt being transferred to governments. Modern governments with their populist slant often ultimately take on responsibility for private debt.

But still, allowing for that, we must look elsewhere for explanations and forecasts for the coming sovereign debt age of defaults that lies in front of us. Advanced-nation governments carry huge debt burdens as the result of the crash of 2008, but going forward, they face slow growth with exhausted Keynesian/Monetarist stimulus remedies, unfavorable demographics, and huge unfunded entitlement liabilities.

2008 was a Minsky moment. Ireland with its real estate and banking problems was a Minsky moment. Spain, with its overbuilt real estate sector financed by private borrowings, is having a Minsky moment.

But the coming government defaults will be something new.

Culture Counts

Different countries have differing cultural values, which make some more prone to populist tendencies and large governmental interventions to promote the socialization of risk and the redistribution of income. As mentioned, the response of the Korean populace in 1997 in the face of the Asian crisis contrasts with that of the Greek populace in 2012.

The Puritan ethic, which preached the value of hard work and self-reliance, was embodied in the US Constitution. It was the prevailing cultural ethos in nineteenth-century America, characterized by an aversion to big government, and a strong sense of property rights. But this gradually changed with the advent of President Theodore Roosevelt's Progressive movement at the turn of the century, which was then followed by the creation of the Federal Reserve in 1914 and Franklin Roosevelt's New Deal in the 1930s. The government and dependency on the government has become the "new normal" in the United States, contrasted with the Puritan ethic and self-reliance which was embodied in the Constitution and was the prevailing cultural ethos in the nineteenth century. One illustration of this was the legalization of the income tax via the Sixteenth Amendment to the Constitution, passed in 1913. The Constitution, as interpreted by the Supreme Court in the nineteenth and early twentieth century, did not allow a tax on incomes. The socialist movement in the late nineteenth century United States strongly advocated an income tax. But the Constitution itself had to be changed, as the Supreme Court on this issue refused to roll over. Most Americans today view the income tax as a perfectly normal institution and are unaware that it was once illegal.

Today in Asia there has been much talk the revival of so-called Confucian values, which—particularly in regard to work habits—are similar to the values espoused in the Puritan ethic. Of course, the definition of Confucian values is an area of controversy. Chairman Mao tried to get rid of Confucian thought in Chinese society.

Obedience to authority permeates Confucian values, along with hard work. Obedience to authority was not a prevailing part of nineteenth century US cultural ideology. But an electorate's tendency toward obedience to authority does give the authorities a little more ability to say no to populist demands.

Countries such as Singapore, which have Confucian values as part of their cultural DNA, so far have been better able to resist populist ideology. But longer term, the battle between Confucian values and democratic populism will go on. It does not help that learned Western advisers and journalists are constantly lecturing Confucian societies such as China that they must have greater social safety nets. These advisers seem totally oblivious to the fact that their own countries are going bankrupt precisely because of their out-of-control safety nets.

One Note of Optimism

In the last five centuries as human progress and economic growth has accelerated, sometimes insurmountable problems have been solved by inventions and innovation. An example today is the sudden emergence of horizontal drilling and fracking, which is in the process of altering the world's energy picture.

The area of medical entitlements cries out for innovation that would cut costs. So far it hasn't happened, and all the new medical technologies have added to the cost of medical entitlements. But that has not been the history of the last five hundred years. For example, apparently there are breakthroughs in the pipeline in early cancer diagnosis. Cancer is so much more treatable if discovered early. There are estimates that new diagnostic technologies could save as much as $100 billion annually.

If you are in need of a dose of optimism, one book worth reading is Ray Kurzweil's *The Age of Spiritual Machines*.[21] Kurzweil has some interesting ideas about artificial intelligence, which you don't have to agree with. But the main theme of his book is what he calls the *Law of Accelerating Returns*. Under this law, the growth of technology is accelerating exponentially. Technology itself is the next step in human evolution.

Pie in the sky? We certainly are not putting this into any of our estimates. But we can hope. Other than default, this may be the only way out. If you read Kurzweil's book you realize that over the long term you don't want to be short stocks. Progress will accelerate, despite the stupidity of governments.

Notes

1. Citibank has had more than one famous CEO who has made a notable foot-in-mouth statement. Wriston made his infamous statement right after Mexico defaulted in 1982 and Citi was to have a near death experience as the result of the Latin debt crisis. Chuck Prince, Citibank's CEO in 2007, said in response to a question about Citi's aggressive posture in the leveraged buyout market, "As long as the music is playing, you've got to get up and dance. We're still dancing." Thanks in no small measure to Prince's leadership, Citi danced its way to another near death experience and a government bailout in 2009.
2. Carmen M. Reinhart and Kenneth Rogoff, *This Time Is Different: Eight Centuries of Financial Folly* (Princeton, NJ: Princeton University Press, 2009).
3. Ibid., 34.
4. It also may have turned out that some moneylenders actually evolved to become smarter. See "Medieval Evolution, How the Ashkenazi Jews Got Their Smarts," in Gregory Cochran and Henry Harpending, *The Ten Thousand Year Explosion, How Civilization Accelerated Human Evolution* (New York: Basic Books, 2009).
5. Actually, serfdom would have been a step up for some of then slave state Mississippi's children at that time.
6. George W. Edwards, *The Evolution of Finance Capitalism* (New York: Longmans Green & Company, 1938), 149.
7. David Graeber, *Debt: The First 5,000 Years* (New York: Melville House Publishing, 2011).
8. Ibid., p. 389
9. Michael Hudson, "The New Economic Archaeology of Debt," *Michael Hudson* (April 23, 2002). http://michael-hudson.com/2002/04/the-new-economic-archaeology-of-debt/
10. Francis Fukuyama, *The End of History and the Last Man* (New York: Avon Books, Inc., 2006).
11. *Property: James Madison, Note to His Speech on the Right of Suffrage* (Chicago: The University of Chicago Press, 2000). http://press-pubs.uchicago.edu/founders/documents/v1ch16s26.html

12. Monetarists may take exception to this. But Fed Chairman Ben Bernanke himself apologized to Milton Friedman for the Fed's failure to support the economy in 1929–1933. Bernanke went on to launch QE I and QE II and Operation Twist II, implicitly under the monetarist banner. Friedman in his *Monetary History of the United States* and in other writings always referred to money as M1 or M2 and not the monetary base, which Bernanke has expanded at a dramatic pace. The growth of the M1 and M2 has been slow as the so-called monetary base money multiplier has declined. It is unclear what Friedman, the high priest of monetarism, would have said about Bernanke's actions but it seems pretty clear that Bernanke thinks he is acting in accordance with monetarist principles and Friedman's approval.

13. Thomas J. Gillen, "Zeus of Wall Street," *Cigar Aficionado Online* (March/April 2000). http://www.cigaraficionado.com/webfeatures/show/id/6151. Accessed September 2012.

14. David Goldman, *How Civilizations Die: (And Why Islam Is Dying, Too)* (Kindle Locations 657–659). Perseus Books Group. Kindle Edition.

15. Barry Eichengreen, *Golden Fetters: The Gold Standard and the Great Depression, 1919–1939* (New York: Oxford University Press, Inc., 1992).

16. "US Voting Rights." Infoplease.© 2000–2007 Pearson Education, publishing as Infoplease (August 29, 2012), http://www.infoplease.com/timelines/voting.html

17. Bryan Caplan, *The Myth of the Rational Voter: Why Democracies Choose Bad Policies, New Edition* (The United Kingdom: Princeton University Press, 2007).

18. Stephen G. Cecchetti, M. S. Mohanty, and Fabrizio Zampolli, "The Real Effects of Debt," *BIS Papers* (September 2011).

19. Hyman Minsky, *Stabilizing an Unstable Economy* (New Haven: Yale University Press, 1986).

20. Charles Kindleberger and Robert Aliber, *Manics, Panics and Crashes, 5th ed.* (Hoboken, NJ: John Wiley and Sons, 2005).

21. Ray Kurzweil, *The Age of Spiritual Machines, When Computers Exceed Human Intelligence* (New York: Penguin Books, 2000).

2

The Sorry Fiscal State of the Advanced Countries

Call it socialism or whatever you like. It is the same to me.
— German Chancellor Otto von Bismark, who introduced the first social security program in 1881

When national debts have been accumulated to a certain degree, there is scarce, I believe, single incidence of their having been fairly and completely paid.
— Adam Smith, *The Wealth of Nations*, 1776

Predicting when a nation will default and when the bond markets will deny a country access on reasonable terms is neither easy nor is it a science. There is no one indicator that unequivocally signals that a nation must default. In fact, when comparing one country against the other, and the interest rates on their respective debt issues, it is sometimes hard to figure out why the markets seem to prefer one country over another. For example, consider France versus the United Kingdom. In late 2011, officials in France somewhat ungraciously complained that their country's debt deserved a lower interest rate than that of the United Kingdom. You could easily make a case that the French were right. But the markets thought otherwise. French bonds, denominated in euros, carried substantially higher interest rates than comparable British bonds denominated in pounds. And for now, the United States, despite its soaring debt levels and current account deficit, is regarded as a place of refuge for global money. When Standard & Poor's downgraded the United States last year, US bond prices *rose*.

But the entire complex of relevant indicators, when derived for the advanced Western countries including Japan, shows a very dire fiscal picture. In the final analysis, of course, economic statistics are only suggestive of a problem. The real problem for governments is when the bond vigilantes, as they are called, decide they don't want any more of a government's sovereign debt. The bond vigilantes seem to be like lions hunting wildebeest. They go for the weakest of the herd first. Hence, Ireland, Iceland, Greece, Italy, and Spain were attacked first.

Our view is that sooner or later, the vigilantes will come for the whole lot of advanced overindebted countries, including the United States. Economists might not fully understand the selection process. Nevertheless, the overall outlook for the advanced countries can be considered dismal.

The obligations of advanced country sovereign states can be divided into two categories: sovereign debt and unfunded entitlement liabilities. Statistics for the former are easy to obtain, while statistics for the latter are not and are subject to wide errors of estimation. Unfortunately, while it is the sovereign debt statistics that are grabbing the headlines now, the huge and in many cases difficult-to-estimate unfunded entitlement liabilities are the icebergs that will sink the sovereign Titanics.

Sovereign Debt/GDP

The following is an expanded list of major indicators that economists, the rating agencies, and the markets look at:

1. Sovereign debt/GDP
2. Debt maturity schedule
3. Percentage of debt held by foreigners
4. Budget surplus (deficit)/GD
5. Current account/GDP
6. Rate of GDP growth
7. Interest rate being paid on debt
8. Unfunded entitlement liabilities
9. The demographic future

The list could be made longer. But if there is one statistic that the financial media and the rating agencies focus on, it is government borrowings as a percentage of gross domestic product (GDP). Before getting into individual countries, it might be a good idea to examine this ratio in some detail. It seems like a simple concept, but naturally like everything else, economists differ as to its definition.

Right now, we know the average reader is entering the land of yawns. Accounting definitions are sleep inducing. But the devil is in the accounting details! For example, it makes a big difference which definition of government borrowings you use for the United States or Japan. If you use gross debt/GDP, the United States is in bad shape but the results for Japan are frightening. Net debt/GDP, on the other hand, gives a still grave but less somber picture for these two countries.

There are numerous sources where you can find sovereign debt/GDP statistics, including the International Monetary Fund (IMF) and Reinhart and Rogoff (discussed in Chapter 1). Eurostat is another source, and it follows the definition provided under the Maastricht Treaty, which created the European Union and its currency, the euro. The Organisation for Economic Co-Operation and Development (OECD) provides a host of statistics at its website, www.oecd.org. Or if you want, you can go to the websites of each of the countries and calculate your own ratios.

Unfortunately, none of them give exactly the same numbers. Anyone reading the financial media will notice no two articles ever seem to quote exactly the same number for the same country.

This book will use the IMF definitions for general government net debt/GDP when available. For some countries, only gross numbers are published by the IMF, and these countries require special analysis. The IMF net statistics are probably the best numbers, combined with the rollover schedules and expected budget deficits, for measuring potential market pressure on a country's sovereign bonds. But the gross numbers have their uses, too, particularly in assessing a country's overall budget situation.

The following is derived from a paper by the Center on Budget and Policy Priorities, which lays out the major definitional issues involved:

1. *Is the debt central or general?* Most IMF and OECD statistics focus on general or total public government debt—that is, debt owed by all levels of government in a country. In the US context, *general government* means *federal, state, and local.*

More narrowly, what the IMF and OECD call *central* government means (in the US context) *federal*.

2. *Debt versus liabilities?* Often, what the IMF and OECD call *debt* actually represents a broader category of *financial liabilities*. Such figures include credit-market instruments (like US Treasury securities) issued to raise cash, which is the conventional definition of "debt," plus various other financial liabilities of government.

3. *Gross versus net debt?* Governments incur financial liabilities, but they also own financial assets: gold, foreign exchange, currency and checkable deposits, student loans and other loans, accounts receivable, and other assets. Net debt (or more accurately, net liabilities) consists of gross debt (or liabilities) minus those assets (based on the assets' actual worth).[1]

Reinhart and Rogoff have concluded that beyond a 90 percent sovereign debt/GDP ratio economic growth is penalized. This has now become received wisdom among economists who study this issue. But even 90 percent isn't a hard and fast rule. It is unclear, for example, if a high debt ratio is the cause of slow economic growth or just the result. And of course all the authoritative sources carry different numbers for debt.

The IMF net, as opposed to gross definition, is the better one for the purpose of measuring a country's immediate vulnerability to attacks from the bond vigilantes. There's no need to exaggerate the problem. The facts are bad enough. Government debt owed to itself either has already been monetized or is just an accounting gimmick or represents a totally inaccurate estimate of future entitlements.

Clearly, the net debt/GDP ratio isn't enough. We must examine a whole complex of indicators to get a complete picture. We will do that in the country analysis in Table 2.1.

A casual review of Table 2.1 reveals an interesting phenomenon. Although Greece would be an exception, the countries with the best (i.e., the lowest) General government net debt/GDP ratios tend to be small and relatively homogeneous. This suggests (to me, anyway) that citizens of small countries, even when they have a tradition of socialism like the Scandinavian countries, are more capable of understanding the implications of profligate government spending and borrowing. Is it that citizens of large and heterogeneous countries view government spending and borrowing as somebody else's problem?

Table 2.1   General Government Net Debt/GDP Advanced
Countries 2011

Countries	General Government Net Debt/GDP (Percent)
Australia	8.163
Austria	52.098
Belgium	81.394
Canada	33.101
Denmark	.234
France	78.779
Germany	55.326
Greece	165.412
Ireland	74.697
Italy	94.90
Japan	126.412
Netherlands	31.702
New Zealand	8.347
Norway	−168.151
Portugal	97.327
Spain	57.485
Sweden	−18.175
Switzerland	25.908
United Kingdom	76.559
United States	80.284

Source: International Monetary Fund

Outlook for the United States

We believe the United States is hurdling toward fiscal disaster. But we also think America has time to avert this disaster. Unfortunately, in my view, the American election of 2012 was not a step in the right direction.

At first, the United States doesn't look so bad. As Table 2.1 shows, the United States had a general government net debt/GDP ratio of 80.275. Not great and getting worse in recent years, but not Japan, Greece, or the bulk of the non-Scandinavian European countries.

Appearances can deceive. In many ways, the United States is actually worse off than Europe.

For starters, the United States federal government ran a cash basis budget deficit of $1.3 trillion for fiscal year (FY) ending September 30, 2011, which is approximately 9 percent of GDP. A similar deficit was run in FY 2010. Projections for FY 2012 budget deficit are now starting to come together, and it is looking like FY 2012 will equal or exceed the previous year's deficit.

The conventional forecast is—or maybe I should say *was*— that as the United States recovers from the 2008 recession, the US budget deficit/GDP ratio will decline in the next few years before unfunded entitlements really become a problem. But the US economic recovery, so far, is so anemic as to render that forecast optimistic. The recent elections may have been the most important in American history. The Obama administration has a statist view of what America should be. Now that Obama and the Democrats have won (except for the House), the emphasis will be on more taxes and no serious cuts in spending. I believe the tax increases, thus enacted, won't achieve the desired revenue projections. The staggering deficits will remain and economic growth will be stunted. From an investor's point of view, this is the worst-case scenario. Especially if, assuming all of Obama's tax proposals are enacted, investors will have to contend with dramatically higher capital gains and dividend taxes.

US federal spending historically has averaged about 20 percent of GDP. However, since 2008 under the Obama administration it has soared to 25 percent. This number will rise dramatically in the coming years unless changes are made.

Forecasting the federal budget is an art, not a science, and it becomes more difficult and error prone the further you go out. Underlying any budget deficit forecast are assumptions about economic growth, interest rates, inflation, and demographics. A little tweak here, a little tweak there, gives you a completely different number. For example, were interest rates to move back up to something more akin to historical norms, the budget deficit would soar. Much also depends on what Congress does regarding various programs and what political compromises are arrived at. Forecasting the budget deficit is like reading the book of Leviticus: The reader sees what he wants and makes assumption on what suits him.

I see no reason to believe anything that comes out of official Washington. We are inclined to believe more pessimistic numbers, given the record of deficit acceleration in recent years. Plus, as the work of Reinhart and Rogoff shows, economic growth after a major banking crisis cum recession tends to be slow. *Unlike the post–WWII period where the sovereign debt/GDP ratio had risen to high levels, the United States will not grow its way out of debt.*

Various forecasts have US debt exploding as we move out in years. Entitlements consume the budget. If interest rates rise to reflect the budgetary disaster, the situation becomes that much worse. We refer to work done by the Heritage Foundation, a respected Washington think tank.[2] According to the Heritage forecasts, publicly held US government debt begins to skyrocket after 2010 and reaches about 195 percent by 2036. (*Note*: Heritage's calculation of public debt is not the same as the IMF's. But the numbers are close enough and it's the trend that counts.)

Clearly, this explosion in debt isn't going to happen in the real world. If reforms aren't undertaken, some type of default will occur long before then. The bond vigilantes will spoil the entitlement party.

Dismal Demographics

Longer term, the American budget deficits and federal spending will explode upwards thanks to *unfunded entitlement liabilities.* The big four of the entitlement programs are Social Security, Medicare, Medicaid, and Obamacare. These unfunded entitlements will devour the federal budget in the coming years. These are funded on a pay-as-you-go basis. The public, via its elected representatives, have awarded themselves a cornucopia of benefits that will take up an ever-larger portion of GDP. James Madison, were he alive today, might be saddened—but he wouldn't be surprised. The morphing of the limited suffrage American Republic into the universal suffrage American democracy for America's Founding Fathers would have made this outcome inevitable.

In theory, unfunded entitlement liabilities could be paid for by huge increases in taxes. The Heritage Foundation estimates are that if current spending trends continue, federal government spending on Medicare, Medicaid, Social Security, and Obamacare subsidies will hit 19 percent of GDP by 2049 versus 10.3 percent in 2010.[3]

But in practice, the huge increase in taxes would be resisted by the affluent and, to the extent they were enacted, would kill economic growth and might not produce the projected tax revenues.

As discussed, there is debate as to what point an increase in taxes significantly discourages work and innovation. But whatever that point is, barring a dramatic reduction in unfunded entitlement liabilities, America (and the rest of the advanced countries) is bound to reach that point in the coming years. Yes, Virginia, there is a Laffer curve, even if nobody is sure at what point along the curve tax revenue is maximized as tax rates increase. (The Laffer curve, named after its originator, economist Arthur Laffer, projects that increases in tax rates will only produce higher tax revenues up to a certain level of rates after which government tax revenues will decline as taxpayers cease working or attempt to reduce their taxes.)

Moreover, as the years go on, the demographics become more and more unfavorable. Longer life spans for retirees and fewer workers thanks to lower birthrates will be a significant negative. For example, in 1960 the ratio of worker to recipient was 5.1 for the Social Security program. In 2010, it was 2.9. Barring major changes in the retirement ages, this ratio will only undergo serious decline in the years to come.

In 1935, when Social Security was instituted, the average American lifespan was only 61.7 years. In 2007, it was 77.9 years.[4] When President Franklin D. Roosevelt picked 65 as the retirement age, he clearly had envisioned the Social Security program as one of old-age support. It wasn't supposed to be a retirement program for healthy adults. Ironically, by living longer and retiring, the average citizen only adds to his or her nation's budget deficit. Truly patriotic Americans would drop dead the day they retire, thus relieving their country of lengthy retirement and heavy late life medical expenses!

What is most likely here is a combination of some kind of partial default (in the broad sense as I have defined it) on these obligations and an increase in taxes. Not good news for anyone.

A 46,000 Percent Return for Ida May Fuller!

In a Ponzi scheme, it pays to be the first out. The Old Age, Survivors, and Disability Insurance (OASDI), better known as Social Security, was enacted in 1935. In 1940, the first benefit check, for $22.54, was paid to one Ida May Fuller. She ended up collecting $22,889 in benefits after paying only $49.50 in taxes into the system.

That made for a 46,000 percent return. We can assume Ms. Fuller was pleased. Such large returns compared to payments have, up until now, cemented support for the program among beneficiaries.

Ms. Fuller—known as "Aunt Ida" to friends and family—received her first Social Security check in 1940. She lived to be 100 years old, somewhat beyond the 61.7 average American lifespan in the 1930s. Very unpatriotic.

At the time of Aunt Ida, there were forty-two workers paying into the system for each retiree drawing funds out of it. Today there are just more than three. With fewer workers to pay the taxes to support Social Security benefits, future retirees face dwindling returns. Social Security is a Ponzi scheme of sorts, despite the façade of a trust fund. It's a pay-as-you go system whose future payments are underfunded by the dwindling number of workers who will pay for it.

The Social Security trust funds and the payroll tax to fund them were pure politics. As Franklin Roosevelt famously said to his disapproving advisor Luther Gulik, "I guess you're right on the economics. They are politics all the way through. We put those payroll contributions there so as to give the contributors a legal, moral, and political right to collect their pensions and their unemployment benefits. With those taxes in there, no damn politician can ever scrap my social security program. Those taxes aren't a matter of economics, they're straight politics."

Hey, who remembers Luther Gulik?

Source: http://www.ssa.gov/history/Gulick.html

Race and Ethnicity—An American Complication

The United States is sometimes compared favorably with Europe and Japan where the demographic picture is much worse. Current birthrates are much lower than in the United States, and worker/recipient ratios will become more unfavorable than those of the United States. Japanese and some European populations will actually decline in the next fifty years. But the United States may not be as well off as simple worker/recipient ratio projections suggest. US population growth will be driven by growth in the Hispanic and African American populations, whose percentage share of the population has been continuously rising thanks to immigration and higher birthrates. Both of these groups have historically been underperformers with regard to education and per capita income and have been more needy in terms of government entitlements.

Hopefully, the performance of these groups will improve. This is a social question far beyond the perspective of this book and a very sensitive subject. But for the purpose of forecasting in this financial book, there is no justification to indulge in wishful thinking and assume that the performance of these groups will improve.

Moreover, under the extremely progressive US tax structure, almost 50 percent of Americans don't pay any income taxes at all. Presumably, African American and (non-Cuban-American) Hispanic minorities are heavily represented in this group since they have lower family incomes as compared to whites and Asians.[5]

These underperforming groups may—quite rationally—conclude that intransigent opposition to the cutting of government benefits may be the most intelligent and beneficial strategy for them since other different ethnic groups (i.e., whites, Cuban-American Hispanics and Asians), will be paying for the government benefits. This statement, of course, is somewhat broadbrush as no doubt there will be plenty of African American and Hispanic Americans who will be stuck with paying for the entitlements.

That said, unlike in some other countries, default or reneging on government entitlements is likely to take on an additional ugly and racially divisive overtone in the United States. In Greece, at least your typical brick throwing protesters look the same as the storied Greek multimillionaire shipping magnates lounging on their yachts in the Mediterranean.

Unfunded Entitlements and Dismal Accounting

Forecasting the present value of unfunded entitlements is an inexact a process as forecasting budget deficits. But the estimates out there are staggering and range from $100 trillion to $200 trillion.[6] The "big four" in unfunded entitlements are Social Security, Medicare, Medicaid and—although it's a little early to make an accurate forecast of a program that nobody fully understands and that might significantly change before it is fully implemented—Obamacare. But there are lots more unfunded entitlements for smaller programs, as will be mentioned later in this chapter.

Longer term, as mentioned, is the unfunded entitlements that are driving US government debt upward. The unfunded liabilities become due, taxes don't cover them, and the result is a huge increase in borrowings. When will the markets start to care?

The US government reports its deficit on a cash basis. Were it to report on an accrual basis, as do all private-sector corporations under generally accepted accounting principles (GAAP), the reported deficit would be much larger because the future unfunded entitlements would be taken into consideration. The *2010 Financial Report of the United States Government*, put out by the US Department of the Treasury, has one estimate of this accrual basis deficit. For FY 2010, this report estimated a GAAP-based 2010 deficit of $2.080 trillion, which widened from $1.254 trillion in FY 2009.[7] But more conservative (realistic?) GAAP-based estimates go as high as $5 trillion.[8] Five trillion could be high, but I am inclined to distrust Treasury numbers.

I referred to the *big four* of the US federal entitlement programs—Social Security, Medicare, Medicaid, and Obamacare. But there is a whole slew of "minor" entitlement programs plus a variety of accounting gimmicks. Among the minor entitlements are federal military pensions, veterans' benefits compensating for death or disability resulting from active service, liabilities for federal civil service retirees, liabilities connected to the Federal Deposit Insurance Corporation (FDIC), Federal Housing Authority (FHA) mortgage guarantees, and federal student loan guarantees.

Then there are Fannie Mae and Freddie Mac, both with negative net worths and now effectively part of the federal government. The government sold off Fannie Mae in 1968 since at the time, with Lyndon Johnson's "guns and butter" budgets, the federal government didn't want Fannie adding to the budget deficit. But when Fannie and Freddie went back into the government in a conservatorship program in 2008, unlike in 1968, they were not reintegrated into the federal budget.

The states' pension plans are an egregious example of the excess of the universal suffrage model taken yet to a higher (lower?) level. Since state public-sector unions were allowed in the 1960s, the following paradigm has obtained: The public-sector unions select candidates (usually Democrats) and contribute to their election with the votes and money of their members. The elected representatives then make sure the unions get what they want in the way of remuneration. Remuneration is typically augmented in things like future pension benefits, which the public does not understand. Now that states like California have reached budgetary impasses, cuts are made in spending in areas the state needs, such as education and infrastructure. The pension benefits are retained, at least for existing workers. As mentioned, California, the vaunted state higher education system is being gutted at the very time when the less skilled and rapidly growing Latino population could most benefit.

Fannie and Freddie: From Little Acorns to Corrupt Crony Capitalists

This author (Peter Treadway) served as chief economist at Fannie Mae from 1978 to 1981 and as an equity analyst at Smith Barney following, along with savings and loans, Fannie Mae and Freddie Mac's stocks from 1985–1997. During the time I followed these stocks, the companies were growing and profitable. I generally kept a "BUY" rating on them. "It's not too late to get a little Fannie," became my mantra in those more innocent, less politically correct times. The stocks performed well, I got my bonuses, and I made the All Star team published by *Institutional Investor* magazine.

Deep in my free-market heart, I believed that political pressures would eventually undermine Fannie and Freddie's mortgage underwriting standards and that once they had gobbled up the entire mortgage market, these companies would blow up. Moreover, I couldn't see the logic of having specialized mortgage companies, spectacularly undiversified as to assets. These companies had a firmly held view of their indispensability vis-à-vis the American mortgage market, a view I didn't share.

But I generally never mentioned these things to clients. Why? Because I had no idea when that sad day of Fannie and Freddie's demise would come, other than it would be far off in the future. As it turned out, that day came in 2008. If with perfect foresight I had told my institutional clients in, say, 1990 that Fannie and Freddie were going to crash and burn in 2008, they would not have been able to restrain their incredulity or laughter. They wanted to know how Fannie Mae and Freddie Mac would do in the next *quarter*. And in those days, Fannie and Freddie would do very well in the next quarter.

That's the whole trouble with issuing jeremiads against the evils of populism. The world is never perfect and humanity soldiers on. Things fall apart so slowly. Prophets grow old before they are proved right. It's like watching the grass grow. But the populist excesses do eventually have to be paid for. I consoled myself that Fannie and Freddie were doing a social good, putting people into houses. The fact that they were undiversified lenders dependent on government goodwill to retain their funding advantages was just something the future would have to worry about. My free-market philosophy was offended, but the real world is never perfect. And the purpose of Wall Street research, as a former boss once told me, is not to search for truth but to find stocks that would go up.

I had the opportunity to watch Fannie Mae, and later Freddie Mac, morph from little acorns in the mortgage market to monsters that dominated the whole market. Fannie Mae was "privatized" in 1968 and listed on the New York Stock Exchange (NYSE) in 1970.

Freddie Mac, basically a Fannie Mae clone, was formed in 1970 and listed on the NYSE in 1989. Freddie Mac was formed at the insistence of the savings and loan industry, which believed mortgage bankers had an advantage over them since Fannie Mae in its early days did deal mostly with mortgage bankers. It always seemed absurd that savings and loans actually would lobby for the creation of a favored government-sponsored enterprise that would compete with them. After all, funding mortgages and making the spread, along with originating mortgages, were savings and loans' two main functions. Freddie Mac by buying or securitizing these mortgages was going to take one of these functions away from the savings and loans (thrifts, as they were called.) And yet, they lobbied for exactly that! But that's another story. (John Kenneth Galbraith, in one of his many memorable statements, once said that banking is one occupation where good grooming counted for more than intelligence. I always felt that it was the same in the savings and loan business—except they didn't care how you dressed.)

Fannie Mae's origin was Franklin Roosevelt's New Deal Federal National Mortgage Association, founded in 1938. The publicly traded Fannie Mae was carved out of this. The name *Fannie Mae* started out as Wall Street slang but the company eventually started to use it to refer to itself. It was a similar story with Freddie Mac, originally the Federal Home Loan Mortgage Association. The names "Fannie" and "Freddie" were a little undignified for the more old-fogy-type early managements of these companies. The management of Freddie Mac took particular umbrage. But they came around, and Fannie and Freddie became globally recognized names. Of course how were they to know that one day there would be companies with totally un–buttoned-down names like Yahoo! or Google. But that's another story.

The new publicly traded Fannie Mae, according to its charter, was supposed to provide "supplemental liquidity to the secondary mortgage market." (This somewhat restrictive though fuzzy language was quietly removed from the charter much later.) Ten directors were elected by the shareholders and five were appointed by the President of the United States. Fannie and later Freddie were not supposed to originate mortgages but rather, buy them from the originators. The privatization took Fannie Mae off the government budget, an important consideration for the Johnson administration with its "guns and butter" policy. Those days seem like lost innocence now. No such scruples seem to bother the Obama administration, as Fannie and Freddie are in the government again, but not back on budget. Nobody seems to care.

(continued)

(Continued)

The early CEOs of the new Fannie Mae saw the company has having a somewhat limited role, as envisioned by the congressional authors of the privatization legislation. There were occasional quixotic comparisons with NYSE specialists. Fannie Mae was supposed to be a buyer of mortgages when times were tight, and a seller when they were easy. Fannie Mae wasn't supposed to keep expanding come rain or shine. Regulation Q limited the interest banks and thrifts could pay on savings accounts. Bouts of disintermediation would hit the mortgage market when Fed tightening pushed rates above the Reg Q caps and the mortgage market would be starved for funds. Thus, you could say that the government created publicly traded Fannie Mae to offset the damage done to the mortgage market by the government. Fannie borrowed short, lent long, and when interest rates rose under Paul Volker in the late 1970s, Fannie almost went broke.

At that point, Fannie got itself a new CEO named David Maxwell, whose mind was unencumbered by the original fuzzy though limited congressional intent for Fannie Mae and who understood the real power and value of the Fannie Mae franchise. All the specialist comparisons were forgotten, if Maxwell had ever known (or cared) about them at all. Fannie Mae as a government-sponsored enterprise had what was termed *agency status* in the debt markets, which gave it an important funding advantage over other participants in the mortgage market. Fannie and Freddie paid interest rates just above those paid by the risk-free government. And compared to other financial organizations, they had to maintain very little capital. After all, the government was their capital. Maxwell reorganized Fannie Mae, took full advantage of its agency status, jumped into the burgeoning mortgage-backed securities market, and righted Fannie's asset liability duration mismatch.

Wall Street was very enthused about this, and Fannie's stock soared. Peter Lynch, the great stock guru and portfolio manager at Fidelity, was a big fan. People started comparing Fannie Mae with other great major corporations. Except there was one major difference. Companies such as Apple, IBM, Microsoft, or Coca-Cola have great franchises/brands/monopolies—whatever you want to call it—that *they* have created. Their brands and technology aren't dependent on governments. For them, government is a hindrance, not the source of their profitability. Their brands or franchises are major examples of value added by the private sector. But Fannie Mae and Freddie Mac could make no such claim. Their funding advantage franchise was dependent on the largess and goodwill of the US government. Agency status wasn't something the brilliant financial engineers at Fannie or Freddie invented. It was something the government gave Fannie and Freddie. So the threat, as Don Corleone might have put it, was that one day in return, the government might come and ask for a special favor. As it turned out, the government would come to ask for a lot of favors.

Actually, the demand for favors started even before Maxwell got there. When Jimmy Carter took over as President in 1977, his administration demanded that the entire board of Fannie Mae resign and that the company embark on a program of low-income lending. Low-income lending was supposed to be the province of that part of the old Federal National Mortgage Association that had stayed in the government. But the temptation to appropriate the new Fannie Mae's riches for their low-income constituents was too much for Carter's liberal populists to resist. Fannie Mae's CEO at that time was Oakley Hunter, an affable former Republican congressman. Hunter and Fannie Mae eventually prevailed over the Carter people, but at a cost. Fannie Mae's management did not have to resign and the company retained its independence. But Fannie Mae had to agree to embark on program of purchasing low-income loans. Fannie Mae at that time quietly let Wall Street know that these requirements were no big deal, that they would meet them with very little change in Fannie's operations. Wink, wink.

But they were a big deal. They opened an intellectual door—a door whose opening would become wider and wider as time went on, until the crash of 2008. The winds of populism, defined in a unique US way with racial minority groups being targeted for favorable treatment, were blowing in the American housing sector. In 1977, Congress passed something called the Community Reinvestment Act (CRA). The CRA, while it did not apply to Fannie and Freddie, required depository institutions to make credit available to low- and moderate-income communities. In the United States, low and moderate income is code for the African American and Hispanic communities—traditional Democratic constituencies. (If Fannie Mae had been in India, no doubt all of its loans would have had to go to Dalits, Muslims, and Other Scheduled Tribes.)

The CRA set a tone. In 1992, as part of the savings and loan bailout, Congress required Fannie and Freddie to set "affordable housing goals" and do a certain amount of business with people of modest incomes. The two GSE mortgage twins were required to meet "affordable housing goals" set annually by the Department of Housing and Urban Development (HUD). The initial annual goal for low-income and moderate-income mortgage purchases for each GSE was 30 percent of the total number of dwelling units financed by mortgage purchases and increased to 55 percent by 2007.

The degrading of Fannie and Freddie's credit quality standards had begun in earnest. In 1999, Fannie and Freddie came under further pressure from the Clinton administration to expand their lending into areas defined as distressed under the CRA legislation. Again, all of this was driven by America's unique racial situation. Words like *redlining* came into lenders' lexicons where they were accused of withholding credit in African American and Hispanic neighborhoods. The process of credit degradation would continue right up

(continued)

(Continued)

until the crisis of 2008. All was happiness and Fannie and Freddie raked in the bucks buying and securitizing more and more subprime loans, which implicitly had no credit risk since house prices would rise forever. Except they didn't. Of course, when the bubble burst, members of minority groups who had gotten mortgages they would not have qualified for under more stringent, sounder criteria found themselves in financial distress.

Congressional oversight took the form of encouraging Fannie and Freddie to make riskier loans. Representative Barney Frank and Senator Chris Dodd, both Democrats, led the defense of Fannie and Freddie's franchises against the Bush administration's attempt to curtail them and tighten government supervision of these institutions. Both were responsible for significantly undermining Fannie Mae and Freddie Mac's credit standards.

In 2003–2004, Fannie and Freddie got in trouble for accounting issues. Both companies' CEOs had to resign. The *Wall Street Journal* and other critics of Fannie and Freddie circled for the kill. But thanks to Representative Frank, Senator Dodd, and other Democrat friends of Fannie and Freddie, the companies survived and went on to fund the great mortgage bubble. In retrospect, attacking Fannie and Freddie for accounting peccadillos seemed like arresting Al Capone for spitting on the sidewalk. The economic damage done by both was immeasurable. That was the real crime.

The American housing bubble can be explained using the Minsky financial instability hypothesis, introduced in Chapter 1. But not entirely. Yes, people behaved as the model predicted and overborrowed from financial institutions, which would fail later when asset values collapsed. And Wall Street, like hungry wolves being fed a delicious live lamb, feasted. But three more factors made things much worse than even Minsky would have imagined:

1. *The politicians poured on the pressure on Fannie Mae and Freddie Mac to make unsound loans.* And their managements, humbled by the accounting scandal and staffed at the upper levels with individuals with ties to the Democratic Party (which controlled the House over most of this period), acquiesced with enthusiasm. Subprime used to be defined as mortgage loans Fannie and Freddie wouldn't buy. Until in the years prior to the bubble's peak they started buying them. Critics of the private sector will argue that Fannie and Freddie were not responsible for all the bad loans that were made. But Fannie and Freddie set the standards, and when their standards dropped, the private-sector's standards dropped even more.

2. *Alan Greenspan's Fed held short-term interest rates near zero.* Greenspan's Fed stoked the flames of an asset bubble. Central bankers can do so much damage but, since the "average Joe" in the electorate doesn't have a clue as to what they do, they escape criticism.

3. *We cannot forget the malfunctioning international monetary system.* China and others were busy buying dollars to hold down the value of their currencies. The dollars got invested in the United States, pushing down US interest rates and feeding the housing bubble.

Minsky couldn't have imagined these three phenomena. The first two egregious political acts, essentially populist in nature, poured kerosene on a fire that would have been bad enough without them. Economic historian Charles Kindleberger rightly pointed out that swindles always happen at the peaks of bubbles. Nobody should have been surprised, when Fannie/Freddie, the Fed, and the Chinese teamed up to create one of the largest bubbles in history, that the crooks and promoters from Wall Street and the public as a whole would rise to the occasion and even outdo Fannie and Freddie. The public sector set the meat out for the private-sector wolves, and they feasted.

Fannie and Freddie were always a bad idea, and now Americans and the world are paying for it. Fannie and Freddie over the years morphed into organizations that were truly corrupt. They came to represent a form of corrupt crony capitalism in its most reprehensible form. Both—especially Fannie Mae—understood the politically derived nature of their franchises. Top management at these companies was recruited based on their political connections, especially with the Democratic Party. Major lobbying efforts by these companies were set up to stroke Congress and make sure that these franchises were left undisturbed. Huge amounts of money were funneled to Democrat-affiliated activists in the housing area, including a notorious activist group called ACORN. ACORN's primary mission seemed to be to increase the flow of credit to members of minority groups who were not qualified to be mortgage borrowers. And all the while Fannie and Freddie donated huge amounts of money to friendly politicians, including Barney Frank, Chris Dodd, and then Senator Barack Obama.

The frustration of it all is that it's possible that none of the individuals involved, from Fannie and Freddie executives to Barney Frank, ever did anything that was technically illegal. Well—if they have done something illegal, they have been protected. Corrupt actors without political ties, such as Bernie Madoff, are relatively easy to catch and incarcerate. And the voters appreciate this when it happens. Nothing like a good hanging, especially when it's an evil financial guy. But corrupt crony capitalist systems can't be incarcerated and are harder to understand, much less catch. *Corrupt systems are far more harmful than corrupt individuals.* Bernie Madoff didn't cause the housing bubble of 2004–2008. But Fannie and Freddie and their congressional supporters must share a great deal of the blame, along with Alan Greenspan and the People's Republic of China.

(continued)

(Continued)

Some "Delightful" Quotes Regarding Fannie and Freddie and the 2004–2008 Mortgage Crisis

These two entities—Fannie Mae and Freddie Mac—are not facing any kind of financial crisis. The more people exaggerate these problems, the more pressure there is on these companies, the less we will see in terms of affordable housing.

I think we see entities that are fundamentally sound financially and withstand some of the disastrous scenarios. And even if there were a problem, the federal government doesn't bail them out.
        —Representative Barney Frank, then Ranking Democratic Member of the
House Financial Services Committee, 2003

I think that the responsibility that the Democrats had may rest more in resisting any efforts by Republicans in the Congress, or by me when I was President, to put some standards and tighten up a little on Fannie Mae and Freddie Mac.
        —President Bill Clinton, 2008

And my worry is that we're using the recent safety and soundness concerns, particularly with Freddie, and with a poor regulator, as a straw man to curtail Fannie and Freddie's mission.
        —Democratic Senator Charles Schumer, 2003

There is no reason for the kind of reaction we are getting. The fundamentals are sound—these institutions are sound, they have adequate capital, they have access to that capital, and this is a reason for people to have confidence in these GSEs, in Fannie and Freddie.
        —Democratic Senator Christopher Dodd, 2008

And Then There Are the American States

The American states and municipalities currently have some $1.1 and $1.7 trillion outstanding in debt and, again depending on whom you read and what assumptions are made, at least $3 trillion in unfunded pension liabilities. We'll see how this gets handled.[9] As mentioned, states have defaulted on their obligations several times in US history. The United States isn't the Eurozone, where the rich Germans pay for the fiscal sins of the lazy Club Med countries.

The pension liabilities of the states illustrate how governments operate, in contrast to the private sector. Most private pension plans in America today are *defined contribution* plans. The beneficiaries contribute a defined amount and their payoff is a function, among other things, of how well the invested money did. Public-sector pension plans, on the other hand, are *defined benefit* plans, whereby the recipients receive a defined amount regardless of how well the investments did or whether enough was invested. Most public-sector state pension plans today assume an unrealistic average of an 8 percent return, according to a report by the Joint Economic Committee.[10]

The Ownership of US Government Securities

According to US Treasury Bulletins, as of June 2012, total US federal public debt including agencies totaled $15.9 trillion. Of this, US government accounts held $4.8 trillion, leaving $11.1 trillion held by the public and the Federal Reserve. Of the $11.1 trillion, the Federal Reserve held $1.8 trillion and foreigners held $5.1 trillion (March, latest data). This means that US private institutions and individuals held $4.2 trillion of government debt.[11] Foreigners presumably are mostly foreign central banks and sovereign wealth funds. It is possible that the Treasury statistics understate debt held by foreigners. In any case, using the official statistics, foreigners are the number-one owners of US government debt. The Federal Reserve's purchase of mortgage-backed securities under the QE3 program are not included in these numbers as, although they are guaranteed by the Federal government, the bulk of the mortgage-backed securities are not classified as US government debt.

It can be seen that the US government is very dependent on foreigners for its financing, especially when compared to Japan or even Italy, where the bulk of public debt is held domestically. It's hard to see this getting better as long as the US is running a major budget deficit. The potential vulnerability here is considerable.

Of course, there is always a bright side. In the first of the 2012 presidential debates, former Governor of Massachusetts Mitt Romney stated he wasn't going to have the US government borrow from China to fund "Big Bird." What he didn't say was even better. The US can't borrow from China to finance a war with China. *Imagine no more Big Bird, imagine no more war, it's easy if you can.*

Actually, I have nothing against Big Bird.

If Something Cannot Go on Forever, Then It Will Stop

The above title is a quote from the late American economist Herb Stein. The dire forecasts for debt and unfunded liability explosions as presented here are not going to materialize. I see massive defaults coming in the broad sense I have defined default. It's not a pretty picture.

From investors' point of view, will these defaults come in a benign rational manner, or does the future hold the likelihood of financial repression, major hikes in taxes, and spikes upward in US government bond yields and hyperinflation. We'd like to be optimistic and hold out hope that a clean sweep by fiscal conservatives in the 2012 elections will see a voluntary cutback in unaffordable entitlements. But obviously this hasn't happened. Politically, it will be the rich investors versus the poor recipients, although as we have mentioned on occasion they will not belong to the same ethnic subgroups. We think investors should be prepared for the worst.

Europe—The Default Process Has Already Begun

The default process in Europe has already begun. Greece has already defaulted in a legal sense. As we use the term, Portugal, Italy, Spain, Cyprus, and Ireland have also defaulted. In an economic sense, if you need a bailout, that's a default. The only way legal defaults have been avoided so far in these latter countries is by massive money printing by the European Central Bank (ECB) and occasional bailouts. Each country in Europe is its own story, with its own idiosyncrasies.

I would add at the outset that the situation in Europe is so fluid that anything written about Europe becomes obsolete as soon as the ink is dry.

Let us begin with some generalizations that apply to all or most of the countries. None of these generalizations necessarily apply to the Scandinavian countries, which are in relatively strong fiscal shape, partly thanks to past crises.

The situation in Europe is complicated by the need to preserve the euro. Had there been no euro, there most likely would have been no bailouts by northern European countries and no money printing by an ECB. Of course, Greece and the other euro countries would not have been able to borrow so much had they not been allowed into the euro. Taken by itself, the concept of a common currency for Europe is a positive development and example of a financial value added. But the euro has a fatal flaw. It is fiat money of which the ECB can print all it wants. It should be remembered that under the gold standard from roughly 1879–1914,

Europe (and the world) *had* a common currency—gold. In that sense, the euro is not really new. All major currencies were exchangeable into gold at a fixed price that was not expected to change. The ECB has succumbed to the populist universal suffrage demand that governments must socialize risk and protect their citizens from economic pain. The gold standard never permitted that.

In nineteenth-century America, as mentioned, states defaulted on their obligations in the 1840s and again after the American Civil War in 1865 without any collapse of the American monetary system. Despite pressures to the contrary, the federal government did not bail out the states. Nor was there a central bank to print money. That was the kind of market solution the Europeans don't trust or like. No matter that it worked. That nineteenth-century American solution was never under serious consideration in Europe.

The European demographic situation is significantly negative, with Germany—the paragon of economic virtue by European standards—having one of the worst outlooks. Birthrates have plunged to well below the 2.1 children per woman necessary for the reproduction of society, and lifespans continue to increase. Worker/retiree ratios have nowhere to go but down. Most state pension systems are pay-as-you-go. The decline of worker/retiree ratios will be a slow process but it will continue inexorably. Immigration has partly alleviated this, but while the United Kingdom and Ireland may have benefited from more culturally compatible immigration from Eastern European countries, post–WWII immigrants in continental Europe are predominantly from the Middle East, which brings its own set of problems. The media, for example, over recent years has reported considerable unrest by the children of immigrants and considerable resentment of immigrants by native Europeans. Islamic extremism is a problem in countries like France. Europe may be moving to a situation similar to that in the United States, where underperforming subgroups bring a sense of grievance and make disproportionate demands on society. At the same time, despite immigration (unlike in the United States), populations will be declining.

Long-term forecasts depend greatly on assumptions. A 2009 study prepared for the European Parliament estimated using what it euphemistically called "less optimistic assumptions" that public pension expenditures would go from 10.2 percent of GDP in 2007 to 18.9 percent in 2060.[12]

The sovereign debt situation of the various European countries is well documented by the IMF and other international sources.

Europe—especially continental Western Europe—has been enamored with what can be called the social democratic model of development. Europe has a socialist intellectual tradition, in contrast to the United States. The social democratic model embraces significant government intervention, an elaborate welfare system and governmental socialization of risk. Governments have a greater share of the economy than in the United States or Japan. Government expenditure in France, for example, accounts for 56 percent of GDP. Markets are mistrusted. In addition, public-sector unions play a significant and in our view negative role in most continental European countries. The social democratic model, in our opinion, is a product of universal suffrage and a socialist intellectual tradition and is doomed in the long run.

The responses to default thus far in Greece and Italy in particular are not encouraging. Europe needs a drastic simplification and reform of its tax system and a dismantling of its welfare state and burdensome regulatory apparatus. Supply-side reforms, in other words. But instead, what seems to be coming are higher taxes and police-state methodologies to collect those taxes. *Anti–supply-side economics!* Why should affluent citizens want to pay higher taxes to support a massive and unproductive welfare state overstaffed with overpaid public-union workers?

Although some of the published estimates suggest otherwise, given the more socialist traditions of Europe and given the relatively poorer demographic picture for Europe versus that of the United States, one might guess that Europe would be in worse shape regarding unfunded entitlement liabilities than is the United States.

Anti–Supply-Side Economics: Italy to Launch Skynet Tax Collection System after 197% YoY Borrowing Increase

Here is an Internet blog that has gone viral. As blogger Simon Black writes, it is something out of an Orwellian science fiction movie.

From Black's blog post on March 21, 2012:

> The Italian tax authorities are now field testing a new system called 'reddito-metro', a database that automatically collects and analyzes taxpayers' tax data versus spending data based on automated collection of credit card and banking information.[13]

Source: http://www.sovereignman.com/expat/italy-to-launch-skynet-tax-collection-system-after-197-yoy-borrowing-increase-6205/

The Euro—What Should Have Been

I think more of the little kids from a school in a little village in Niger who get teaching two hours a day, sharing one chair for three of them, and who are very keen to get an education. I have them in my mind all the time. Because I think they need even more help than the people in Athens . . . So, you know what? As far as Athens is concerned, I also think about all those people who are trying to escape tax all the time.

—Christine Lagarde, IMF Managing Director

Concerned about the Wrong Thing

IMF Managing Director Christine Lagarde recently came out with some controversial statements, which are quoted above. Her theme that rich countries of Europe don't really have problems when compared to the poor of Africa is well taken. But her comment about Greeks and taxes shows how she is part of the problem. Her comments embody the thinking that pervades Western official institutions. The problem, as they see it, is how to pay for the ever-larger role of government in the economy.

It doesn't occur to Ms. Lagarde that she is advocating a wealth destruction regime. Why should any Greek want to pay any taxes to a bloated and malevolent welfare state that is devouring the private sector and destroying the productive ability of the country? I'll talk more about this later. I would advocate broadly defined supply-side reforms.

But here is an ultimate irony. In many cases, individuals as voters vote for a greater role of government while in their market activities they try to avoid paying for that government. The same voters who vote for politicians who expand their benefits do their best to avoid paying for them.

I Told You So

The "I told you so" people are having a field day right now regarding the euro. They said it would never work. They said you can't have a common currency without a fiscal and political union. Well, results are what count, and right now it looks like the "I told you so" people were right. The euro may or may not survive—the odds are, it will survive—but either way, it's looking more like a disaster. Only the cost of dissolution seems to be holding back the euro's demise. The so-called peripheral and core countries stay in the euro like a long-married couple who now hate one another but can't afford to get a divorce.

At this moment the only way for the euro to survive is for the European Central Bank (ECB) to print more money and for Europe to sucker the Germans and maybe the IMF and other international softies (the Americans?) into supporting more bailouts. Except, as the quote from the ostensibly hard-hearted Christine Lagarde suggests, the softies aren't quite soft enough. So German Chancellor Angela Merkel throws an occasional Teutonic tantrum about fiscal responsibility, but in the end, ECB President Mario Draghi prints.

This is a very disappointing outcome. It didn't have to be this way. The euro is a magnificent example of real value added in the financial sphere. The advantages of the euro seem overwhelming. First, a single financial zone was created to parallel and facilitate the free trade area called the European Common Market. No more francs, lira, pesetas, deutschmarks, or guilders to confuse and complicate the lives of tourists and businessmen alike. Second, a new international reserve currency was created to give some needed competition to the almighty dollar. Third, nations, whose principal means of social intercourse in the prior century was waging war on one another, suddenly were peacefully bound together in a common currency.

As previously mentioned, a common currency, by the way, was really nothing new for Europe. From 1880–1914, Europe had a common currency that worked very well—gold. All the major currencies of Europe were convertible into gold at a fixed price, and there were no capital controls. This period was one of unparalleled human progress and low inflation. It was a period of a common currency and no fiscal union.

Do you ever see the euro discussed this way in its historical context? Do the media ever acknowledge that there was a highly successful common currency called gold? The system worked extremely well until 1914 when it was dismembered and Europeans gave in to their historical preference for killing one another.

What Europe Should Have Done Differently

The current unhappy state of the euro was *not* inevitable. The concept of a single currency without fiscal and political union was not necessarily doomed. But the Europeans have persisted in following practices and making faulty decisions that have grievously undermined their common currency. One must look at the underlying fundamentals and decisions.

The Europeans have snatched defeat from the jaws of victory.

First, the Europeans didn't trust markets. And they have paid the price. Mistrust of markets is a core theme in the Eurozone. Take one of the key concepts in the Maastricht Treaty, upon which the euro is based. All the countries were supposed to maintain a deficit/GDP ratio no greater than 3 percent. Big mistake. No such meaningless and unenforceable requirement should have been placed on member countries. This ratio is not completely under governments' control for starters, and as it turned out, many countries violated this rule with impunity. Big economic slowdowns cause this ratio to explode. There should have been no requirement in this regard. The requirement created both the illusion of fiscal soundness and a lack of respect for the official rules. Fiscal discipline for the individual countries should have been left to the markets. Countries running excessively loose fiscal policies should have been disciplined by higher borrowing costs and ultimately denial of market access. *The acceptability of a member state default should have been the primary Maastricht weapon to ensure fiscal probity.* Member countries, banks, and the markets should have been left with the *caveat emptor* message that the member countries were on their own when it came to fiscal policy. Yes, the Maastricht Treaty contains language barring bailouts. But the markets and the politicians quite correctly (unfortunately) did not take this language seriously.

Instead, European operating policy was designed to suppress the market signal, which should have been early-on higher interest rates for fiscally irresponsible countries. And the markets unfortunately accepted this suppression until it was too late. After joining the euro, the Greeks suddenly could borrow at the same rates as Germans. And so could condo buyers in Spain. Greek sovereign debt, as was the sovereign debt of all the member states, was considered a risk-free asset for the purposes of bank regulation and bank capital. The markets were encouraged to assume that the risks of the two were the same. And when the markets finally woke up and decided Greece and Germany did not carry the same risk, Greece was way over its head in debt. And until far into the crisis, Greece was still not allowed to default. And now, much Greek debt is held by official Vestal Virgins (like the ECB and the IMF), which are allowed to not sully themselves by being defaulted on. With Greece, Europe made a joke out of the credit default swap (CDS) which, for all its bad press, serves a useful economic market driven function. Needless to say, this same explanation fits just as well for Ireland, Spain, Portugal, and Italy.

As mentioned, US states defaulted in the 1840s without permanent damage to the American union. Between 1841 and 1843, eight US states and one territory (Florida was not then a state) defaulted. Pressure was exerted for a federal government bailout. But there was none. It was the responsibility of the states to take care of their own obligations. And guess what—the United States and its currency union survived. Those were days when the United States was still more of a republic than a democracy, and populist urges for the government to fix all problems were not so strong. And it had no central bank to print money.

But instead, one bailout after another has been enacted or will likely be enacted for the weaker Eurozone countries, and the European Central Bank has been cranking up the printing press. High-powered money is being created left and right, and new acronyms are sprouting up to dignify what is a very undignified situation. Take as an example so-called LTRO (Long-Term Refinancing Operation). LTRO is a complete economic disaster. Under LTRO, the ECB prints money and lends it to potentially insolvent national banks so they can buy the bonds of their potentially insolvent governments.

The bailouts themselves brought with them one giant tax-raising exercise under the euphemism "austerity," which only made things worse.

Second, the euro is getting blamed for the sins of socialism. I find it hard to tell the difference in practice between populism and Euro socialism. European countries have operated on the social democratic model by which governments assumed an ever-greater role in the economy with higher taxes, higher spending, and more regulation. The fatal attraction of populism has been quite evident in the European political process, which has promised more and more ultimately unaffordable benefits. The governments in Europe for quite some time have been gradually devouring their economies. The bulk of the countries in Europe are headed for bankruptcy anyway, and the euro is taking the blame.

Table 2.2 illustrates just how great a role the governments play in the European economies. Contrast the Government

Table 2.2   Government Expenditure/GDP

Country	Government Expenditure/GDP (in percent)
China	22.5
France	56.7
Germany	47.8
Greece	49.6
Hong Kong	18.0
India	28.0
Ireland	65.6
Italy	50.5
Japan	39.0
Korea	21.0
Portugal	51.4
Singapore	16.9
Spain	45.4
United Kingdom	45.7
United States	42.1

Source: IMF: Data as of 2011

expenditure/GDP ratios of Europe versus emerging Asia or even the semi-social democratic United States.

Third, the Europeans managed to saddle themselves with a bank clearing mechanism that effectively allowed weaker states to pile up with impunity more debt obligations to the strong states. This, of course, has provided the peripheral weaker countries with another ATM machine not subject to market discipline. The European bank clearing mechanism is called TARGET 2. TARGET stands for Trans-European Automated Real-time Gross Settlement Express Transfer System. TARGET 2 is a complicated arcane subject, whose significance has only recently become appreciated by the markets. One aspect of this system is that with the creation of the ECB, the domestic central banks like the German Bundesbank never really went away but still play an important secondary role in the new system. Cutting through the arcania, under TARGET 2, a citizen of, say, Greece can withdraw euros from Greek banks and redeposit the euros in German banks. Under TARGET 2, the ECB, and by implication the Bundesbank, winds up financing this transfer of funds. So the Germans are effectively financing the current bank run on Greek banks. At the end of April 2012, the Bundesbank reportedly had a TARGET 2 positive balance with the ECB of reportedly some 650 billion euros. This implies an offsetting negative balance of the same amount, presumably from peripheral countries like Greece, Italy, Portugal, and Ireland. These negative balances are *not* included in the usual Debt/GDP ratios computed by the IMF and other sources. Bottom line: If Greece or the other peripherals wind up leaving the euro, Germany and the ECB are left holding the TARGET 2 bag.

Fourth, the banking systems of Europe were not allowed to become integrated. Each country has its own set of national banks that have their own sets of regulators and that tend to be undiversified in terms of deposits and lending. The banks are captives of the national governments for whom financial repression a routine practice. The situation differs from countries like the United States or Canada, which have national banks that cover the entire country. Nobody would be tempted to remove cash from Citibank New York and move it to Citibank Florida.

This is a complicated subject. But it seems that instead of pushing for fiscal union, the push should have been for Eurozone banking integration. This would have required a Eurozone bank regulator. The regulator might have been the ECB, which is the lender of last resort for the Eurozone anyway. The Europeans seem now to be finally considering this option.

The Third German Attempt to Take Over Europe Will Fail, as Did the Last Two

As this is being written, the signs are that the Germans want to force a fiscal union on the rest of Europe. Of course, they would be the ones in charge. Of course when I say "Germans," I mean Angela Merkel. Her voters don't want any part of this grand European experiment, which, in their opinion, means they will wind up paying for the sins of the weaker countries. All this has little to do with the populist thesis espoused in this book. But the euro is an additional complication for a group of countries on their way to default.

Merkel's attempt to force a fiscal union on the rest of Europe is unnecessary from an economic perspective and foolish from a political one. As previously argued, if the rules had been set out that each country used the common currency but was on its own as far as fiscal policy went, the euro would not be in crisis today. It is becoming more and more obvious that the euro was designed with the hidden agenda that one day a crisis would force a fiscal union, despite the wishes of the European populaces. This was a mistake. The euro should have been designed assuming that a fiscal union would *never* occur. I know this flies in the face of all conventional wisdom. But to design something based on an impossible assumption dooms it to failure. This type of behavior, of course, is characteristic of socialist planners who always assume people will behave the way they want them to rather than the way they actually behave.

But the political side is truly ill-advised. This represents the third attempt in the last hundred years by the Germans to assume leadership of Europe. It will never happen. Memories of the last attempt have not sufficiently faded. The excesses of the occupying WWII German *Wehrmacht* and the horrors of both World Wars are too great to be forgotten so quickly. How could they be? An estimated 70 million people died in WWII, the overwhelming majority in Europe. The Germans may be richer and work harder than everyone else but the various nation states of Europe aren't going to give up their sovereignty. Europeans can't even hold a soccer game without fans from the opposing countries beating one another up. Yes, the bureaucrats in Brussels have acquired substantial power over the years, mostly by stealth. But this overt German attempt at a fiscal union is overreach in the extreme. A free trade area and a common currency were magnificent achievements. Why did they have to go and spoil everything?

The last person to successfully politically integrate Europe was Charlemagne (circa 800 AD). Napoleon failed (circa 1795–1815). The euro-dreamers want to create a United States of Europe. Their model is the United States of America. Wrong model. Despite counterculture efforts to malign the American model, America has been a melting pot with a common language, common market, a common currency and a common culture. Greeks, Germans, Brits, Irish, Jews—they didn't come to America to fight one another as they did in Europe but rather, they wound up living peacefully together and often marrying one another.

A more relevant model for the euro-dreamers to look to is India. The Indian Union is a collection of heterogeneous peoples and states that differ as to language, religion, and race. But an outside force—a *deus ex machina* if you will—in the form of the British came along to pull together the disparate Indian cultures and states and impose a common language and government. The British in a sense created modern India. Unfortunately, there's no *deus ex machine* in sight for Europe. The Germans as insiders are not qualified and are failing for the third time in that role. The United States at the end of WWII could have assumed that role but it did not.

The euro-dreamers need a different model. Common trading market, common currency and that's enough. Individual countries, if they can't keep their spending under control, should go broke. No bailouts, no LTROs.

The situation in Europe is careening out of control. "Don't throw good money after bad" is an old Wall Street adage. But that is exactly what Europe has done to preserve the march by stealth to full fiscal union. It is unfortunately what Europe is likely to keep doing. And ultimately, there will be no fiscal union.

Europe has many great companies. It has an intelligent, well-educated population with high levels of technical skills. Europe is the last place that should be having economic problems. Unfortunately, the addiction to socialism offsets all these assets. In 1998, Asia was rocked by crisis. Assets, including equities in countries like Indonesia, Thailand, and Korea, became once-in-a-lifetime cheap. But these countries learned from their crises and went on to structural reforms.

Is Europe at that point where Asia was in 1998? Has Europe learned any lessons from this? Not yet. The bulk of the fiscal "reforms" introduced thus far have been tax increases. Who wants to pay even more taxes to support already swollen and intrusive governments? Will higher taxes promote economic growth? Will the Europeans abandon their fondness for socialism? Will they adopt a more realistic model for European integration.

Eventually they will have to. But not yet.

The United Kingdom—Not a Euro Country

"The wogs begin at Calais," the British are fond of saying. This little aphorism refers, of course, to the general British aloofness from the rest of Europe and its troubles. Most Brits would happily say that their generally provincial attitude toward Europe has kept them out of the euro disaster.

There are intellectual and practical differences between the United Kingdom and continental Europe. The United Kingdom is not in the euro. Its unfunded pension obligations are not as relatively high as southern Europe. The United Kingdom, after all, did have Margaret Thatcher as prime minister. Margaret Thatcher was a genuine and effective free-market proponent, unlike most of the so-called "conservative" politicians on the continent of Europe. And the United Kingdom is the home of Adam Smith, David Hume, and a whole host of neoclassical economists. But it is also the home of Marxist Harold Laski and the socialist 1930s London School of Economics. With the election of a Labour government in 1945, the United Kingdom turned statist and socialist. Its current prime minister is aware of the fiscal crisis his country will be facing and has introduced some reforms. But the Bank of England, once the paragon of banking prudence in an era now in the distant past, has embraced aggressive quantitative easing.

Looking at net sovereign debt/GDP or general government expenditure/GDP, the United Kingdom looks a little better than, say, France. But the United Kingdom in the opinion of many observers, gets its more favorable rating because it has its own independent central bank. It's hard to argue with that although the totally disastrous nature of the euro and ECB makes for an easy comparison.

I have to say, I'm rooting for David Cameron and his reforms to succeed. But it's much too early to put the United Kingdom in a different category than the rest of Europe.

Japan—The Enigma

As Table 2.1 shows, as measured by General government net debt/GDP, Japan is right up there with Greece. Moreover, Japan is running a Budget deficit/ GDP ratio of over 8 percent. It also has the most rapidly aging population of the advanced countries with its current population of about 128 million projected to decline to 95 million by 2050. Its retiree-to-worker ratio today is the most unfavorable in the Western world and as the years progress, it will become even more unfavorable. Its rate of real GDP growth in the last ten years has averaged around zero. Its growth prospects are poor.

Traveling around Asia, one constantly hears comments from hotel people and shop owners like, "We don't see the Japanese like we used to." Japanese students studying abroad, particularly in the United States, have dropped off in numbers and have been replaced by Chinese and Indians. One would think Japan by now would have been denied access to the bond market.

So far, the opposite is the case. Japanese government bonds carry the lowest interest rates in the world. There is a joke among money managers that you are not a seasoned manager until you have lost money shorting Japanese government bonds. Not only that, but the Japanese currency continues to be a strong performer against the major world currencies.

Various explanations have been given for this. The explanations usually start with Japan's high savings rates and current account surpluses, plus its accumulated foreign reserves of some $3.3 trillion. The Japanese themselves hold the overwhelming percentage of Japanese government bonds. It does not seem to bother the Japanese that their own government bonds yield so little as compared with foreign alternatives.

Why is this? First, as Japan has experienced actual deflation in the last decade, Japanese bondholders actually received a positive *real* return. Second, with the yen potentially strong, Japanese investors may simply have wanted to avoid exchange risk. Third, given Japan's renowned insular culture, *home bias*—the tendency of people to invest in their own country regardless of diversification opportunities abroad—may be an especially strong motivating factor. Fourth most buyers of Japanese bonds are financial institutions, not individuals. They have no major choices and may be subject to political pressure.

Still the ever-mounting budget deficit and debt situation cannot go on perpetually in Japan. Many observers have pointed out that as a percentage of GDP, Japan's taxes are relatively low compared to Western countries. These observers believe Japan's situation is not so serious since it could simply raise taxes to eliminate its budget deficit. Its tax take would then simply be raised to that of other mature economies.

Increasing taxes will have a negative impact on economic growth, and projected increases in tax revenues will not be attained by tax rate increases. The Hashimoto government increased taxes in 1997. This sent the Japanese economy into a tailspin, and there is no reason to believe this will not happen again. But not only that. The Japanese savings rate and current account surplus will falter as an increasingly elderly populace dips into its past savings to finance its final years. The domestic savings will not be there to finance an ever-larger deficit. The situation will actually deteriorate as the country's foreign exchange reserves are repatriated into yen, the currency temporarily appreciates, and exports and the current account suffers further. The appreciation of the yen will hurt Japan's current account. And of course, Japan is not immigrant friendly. Immigrants might otherwise ameliorate Japan's demographic decline.

I am in the camp of those who tend to this pessimistic explanation. But we are also of the view that Japan's current situation can persist somewhat longer before its government debt crisis begins. This crisis could be further off than that of the United States, which faced the most important election of its history in 2012.

One positive for Japan is the country's vaunted homogeneity. There will not be identifiable subgroups to fight one another for government spoils. As we see it, in Japan it will be the old versus the young. Since there will be more old than young, the young will lose.

Other than its dismal demographics, Japan's real problem is *supply side* in nature. Japan has its own version of the hierarchical East Asian economic model, which is highly protectionist, has a high tax structure that needs reform, is unable to write off past mistakes in its banking system, is heavily government directed, and is filled with restrictions and restraints on trade.

Notes

1. James R. Horney, Kathy A. Ruffing, and Paul N. Van de Water, "Fiscal Commission Should Not Focus on Gross Debt, Policymakers Should Aim to Stabilize Debt Held by the Public as a Share of GDP," Center on Budget and Policy Priorities (July 21, 2010).
2. The Heritage Foundation, "Debt and Budget Deficits under President Obama Charts." http://www.heritage.org/federalbudget/national-debt-skyrocket
3. http://blog.heritage.org/2012/04/26/federal-budget-in-pictures-shows-medicares -path-to-cr
4. Pearson Education, Inc. "Life Expectancy at Birth by Race and Sex,1930–2010." www.infoplease.com/ipa/A0005148.html
5. US Census Bureau, "People in Poverty by Selected Characteristics." http://www.census.gov/hhes/www/poverty/data/incpovhlth/2011/

tables.html. Accessed September 20, 2012. See also: http://taxfounda
tion.org/article/number-americans-outside-income-tax-system-contin
ues-grow

6. Peter Ferrara, *America's Ticking Bankruptcy Bomb* (New York: Broadside Books, 2011).

7. The US Department of the Treasury. *2010 Financial Report of the United States Government.* fms.treas.gov/fr/index.html

8. John Williams, "Special Commentary No. 340, 2010 Financial Report of the United States Government," Shadow Government Statistics, American Business Analytics & Research, LLC (December 22, 2010). www.shadowstats.com/article/no-340–2010-financial-statements-of-the-usgovernment

9. See, for example, Joshua D. Rauh, and Robert Novy-Marx, "Public Pension Promises: How Big Are They and What Are They Worth," *Social Science Research Network* (October 8, 2010), papers.ssrn.com/sol3/papers.cfm?abstract_id=1352608

10. Joint Economic Committee Republicans, "States of Bankruptcy" (December 8, 2011). http://jec.senate.gov/republicans/public/?a= Files.Serve&File_id=1fcd61a8-d8c9–43ab-bcfb-ecdca93c3d01

11. See US Treasury bulletins.

12. *Pension Systems in the EU—Contingent Liabilities in the Public and Private Sector,* http://www.europarl.europa.eu/document/activities/cont/201111/20111121ATT32055/20111121ATT32055EN.pdf

13. Simon Black, "Italy to Launch Skynet Tax Collection System After 197% YoY Borrowing Increase," *Sovereign Man* (March 21, 2012). http://www.sovereignman.com/expat/italy-to-launch-skynet-tax-collection-system-after-197-yoy-borrowing-increase

CHAPTER

3

A Diversion to India and China

If you see a Brahmin and a snake, kill the Brahmin first.
                                        —Indian proverb

One generation plants the trees, and another gets the shade.
                                        —Chinese proverb

This book is mainly concerned about the so-called advanced democratic countries, which are verging on sovereign default but really should not be.

But this chapter will deal with India and China, both of which now are so important for the world economy and present some interesting contrasts and similarities with the advanced countries.

India—The Democratic Surprise

Although as a group they have made amazing progress in achieving fiscal discipline in recent years, historically emerging-market countries have had to contend with poorly developed institutions and sometimes violent "birth histories" due to revolutions leading to their creation, which left debt and destruction in their wake. Default on sovereign debt and currencies that deteriorated to worthlessness have been common events with emerging-market countries. In historical analyses of the gold standard, economists have tended to classify emerging countries as "periphery" countries, unable to adhere to gold standard discipline. The implicit assumption more or less has been that emerging-market countries, because of their institutional weaknesses, violent histories, and low levels of per capita incomes, cannot be expected to act responsibly in matters of fiscal and monetary policy.

But India requires some discussion. Indian democracy has proved to be a very resilient institution that has been magnificent in many ways. The modern Republic of India has a birth history that was exceedingly violent and disruptive. In 1947, the departing British partitioned what was the Imperial "Raj India" into what are now three countries: India, Pakistan, and Bangladesh. The partition saw the loss of millions of lives and was quite arbitrary as to the division of lands. For example, what is now Pakistan was a core part of the British Raj India and the Moghul dynasties, which preceded the British.

With such an unhappy beginning, it is amazing that democracy has survived in India. But it's not all good news. *Unfortunately, Indian democracy has proved to be very susceptible to what I have termed the fatal attraction of populism. India is living proof that a country doesn't have to be rich to be populist.*

Chapter 1 spoke of how differences in abilities of various groups can create a major problem for democracies. The low-performing groups, if they have a sense of a separate identity and a history of grievances, will vote for government interventions that are perceived to benefit them rather than subject themselves to the competition of a free-market meritocracy where they believe they will be at a disadvantage. These low-performing groups prefer to try to advance themselves via the government and their elected representatives, rather than depending on the market. This situation constitutes a powerful force for populism particularly if the low-performing groups form a significant part of the population.

Whereas in homogeneous Japan this is a non-problem, in India this is a huge problem—perhaps a bigger one than that encountered in the United States. In India, the big problem is caste and to some extent religion. Although many Indian leaders have sought its abolition and in the cities and modern sectors it is becoming less important, the Indian caste system has been a fundamental part of the Hindu religion and culture. The caste system as it is practiced in India is quite complicated, with significant regional differences. The caste system goes back in millennia. Until recently anyway, it

Table 3.1   Indian Caste and Religious Breakdown

Caste or Group	Percent of Population
Brahmin (historically priestly and top caste)	4–5%
Other upper (higher) castes (warrior and merchant)	20–22%
Others (Christians, Buddhists)	9–10%
Muslims	10–12%
Scheduled castes (Dalits and others) and scheduled tribes	24.4%
Other "backward" classes	28%

Source: Census of India 2001, *Wall Street Journal* (December 29, 2007)

was endogamous (i.e., people did not intermarry out of their own caste). So a sense of caste separateness is a major fact in Indian sociological history.

Table 3.1 presents a simplified breakdown of India by caste and religion. Note that these are estimates and the exact numbers are a matter of controversy in India.

As can be seen, the Brahmins and other upper castes make up a minority of Indians. Current emigration, effective discrimination in government against upper castes, and demographic trends will further reduce their percentages. Under the British, these upper or "higher" castes predominated in the Indian civil service. The Indian independence movement was led by then Brahmin-dominated Congress Party. Jawaharlal Nehru, India's first prime minister, was a Brahmin whose family had its origins in Kashmir. Mahatma Gandhi, the preeminent leader of the Indian independence movement, was of the higher Gujarati merchant class.

Since independence, the world of caste has changed in India. While it is true in urban and modern industrial sectors that caste has been breaking down, it is a very powerful force in the political sphere. Indian democracy has made possible the political ascendancy of the lower-caste groups, including Dalits (formerly known as Untouchables), at the expense of higher-caste groups, particularly Brahmins. Notably in south India, Brahmins have been on the receiving end of reverse discrimination and in many cases have had to emigrate. Extensive quotas have been put in place favoring lower-caste groups in universities and for government jobs. Needless to say, everyone in India who is not in the higher castes wants preferential treatment. This would include India's roughly 150 million Muslims.

What exists today in India is a government, both at the union (national) and state levels, that is increasingly run at least in the ostensible interests of lower castes and other disadvantaged groups. The private sector, on the other hand, has managements dominated by upper caste groups. Then there are the complications of regional politics and coalition national governments.

This is not a healthy situation. Strong populist pressures show themselves in the Indian budget. In India, the problem is not unfunded entitlements for old-age medical and retirement benefits, as in advanced countries. It is subsidies for basic necessities. Forget about retiring and Bismarkian old-age pensions. In still-poor India, it is the unfunded "here and now" and day-to-day survival that counts for a substantial portion of the overwhelmingly lower caste groups. The government, with an eye to the next national election, has introduced a plethora of subsidy programs estimated at some 2.4 percent of GDP and aimed largely (though not exclusively) at lower caste groups. Such terms as "right to work" and "right to food" have been incorporated into the Indian political lexicon. These subsidy programs come at the expense of infrastructure, education, and the private sector in general.

There is an old expression found in many cultures, "Better to teach a man to fish, rather than giving a man a fish." The Indian government, contrary to this homespun advice, is giving away a lot of fish. In India, the inefficiencies and waste resulting from the democratic process are sometimes called the *democracy tax*. The tax is quite high.

A second point unrelated to caste. The American constitution contains strong protections for property rights. The American Declaration of Independence and the US Constitution were written in 1776 and 1787, respectively. Adam Smith's *Wealth of Nations* was published in 1776. The same concepts of natural law and private property percolated on the American side of the Atlantic as in Britain. Of course, American property rights have been eroded over time by constitutional amendments and Supreme Court decisions, all derived from the populist pressures of democracy. But the starting concept of property rights still remains embedded in the American political psyche as a bulwark against populism.

But India's constitution and political psyche is heavily influenced by Nehruvian socialism and the leftish 1930s London School

Table 3.2   A Quick Summary of Statistics for the Republic of India

General Government Gross Debt/GDP	67.0%
Investment/GDP	35.0%
Current account/GDP	−3.435%
GDP per capita (US dollars)	$1513
Consumer price inflation	8.858%
Unemployment rate	N/A
Official reserve assets	$290 million
Population	1.206 billion

Source: IMF, data for 2011

of Economics, not Adam Smith. Regarding property rights, India has flip-flopped on this, with property rights by constitutional amendment being downgraded to legal versus fundamental.

India today is running a union budget deficit it estimates will come in at 5.9 percent of GDP. Throw in the states' deficits and a much higher number emerges. India's sovereign debt/GDP ratio (general government gross debt/GDP) is just below 70 percent (Table 3.2). But keep in mind that in this respect, India has one "advantage." The bond markets due to India's history aren't going to finance a massive run-up in India's debt. Unlike the United States and even as Greece was as a privileged member of the Eurozone, public-sector India is on a very short leash in the international markets. Unfortunately, the offset here is that India indulges in a great deal of financial repression. India's banks, the bulk of which are government owned, are forced to overinvest in Indian government bonds. Similar policies exist in the insurance industry. A second offset, equally unfortunate in our opinion, is that India has been a favorite recipient of soft loans from the World Bank and other donors.

Investors who visit India can be easily fooled. India's larger companies are among the best run in the world. The information technology and pharmaceutical sectors are cases in point. Corporate governance standards are high, managements are world class, technologically savvy, and English is the working language, not just an ornament trotted out for foreigners. But these companies have to compete with a malevolent government.

The Indian rupee has seen a major decline in 2012. Somewhere in the next one to three years, India will have its own crisis. As this book went to press, the Indian government under Prime Minister Manmohan Singh had initiated a number of reforms which have certainly gotten the markets excited. If these reforms actually happen, perhaps I am being too pessimistic. We'll see.

Excluding debt from the international associates like the World Bank, the bulk of Indian foreign debt is private rather than governmental. Despite a relatively comfortable foreign reserve position at the moment, if the crisis of 1991 is any guide, if another crisis happens India will simply run out of foreign reserves and the rupee will stay on its downward slope. Hopefully, then genuine big reforms will be enacted and some rollback of recently introduced welfare programs will occur.

China—Not a Democracy, Populism Less of a Problem

It's very simple. China is not a democracy in the sense the word is usually used. China does not have elections or rival political parties. The underlying populist urges in Chinese society—which certainly exist as in any other society—do not have the usual democratic channels to manifest themselves. Overall, we would conclude that China has not been put at risk of default by the excesses of populism.

Now hold it right there! Just because China's lack of democracy has helped contain its excess populist urges doesn't mean I am advocating an extreme authoritarian government. China has its own set of excesses, the result of what has been called the East Asian Model of economic development.

Investors, however, are going to have to understand China even if it is opaque, not a democracy. The Chinese economy, by some measures, is now the world's second largest. Hard landing, soft landing, civil unrest, dominant economic superpower—the forecasts flow freely regarding China. The fact that good data is hard to come by regarding China does not seem to inhibit many outside observers. But you have to have a view.

My view is that China is not on the default sick list. But its torrid GDP growth rate of the recent past cannot continue, even if the rest of the world does well, which is unlikely. It's not just the law of big numbers making last year's numbers harder and harder to beat. The official target for real GDP growth in 2012 was 8 percent.

Assuming the reported numbers are reasonably correct—and that's a big assumption as will be discussed—8 percent is no longer regarded as feasible by most observers. The recent weaknesses in global nonagricultural commodity prices in part reflects a Chinese slowdown that is already underway.

There are two negatives hanging over China's GDP growth. First is the flawed Chinese economic model. Following the state-directed, protectionist, export-driven East Asian model pioneered by Japan and influenced by China's one-party state, China has been misallocating capital for years. Growth will slow down in future years and not go back to the faster earlier levels unless there are major economic reforms. China's marginal productivity of capital has to decline. Capital cannot be wasted on the scale China has been so doing without the marginal productivity of capital declining. This slowdown due to declining productivity will be noticeable and per-manent. This conclusion is reached based on the defects in China's economic model and not on conditions in the rest of the world.

Second, export-oriented China has to contend with a Europe in deep recession, a United States close to recession, a Japan in stagna-tion and India near crisis. The Chinese model depends on exports and the 2012 global environment is not a friendly one for exports. Chinese economic results in 2012 will be a disappointment.

China's core problem is its following the mercantilist East Asian model of both overemphasis on capital investment at the expense of consumption and overemphasis on exports via subsidies, an undervalued exchange rate, and significant protectionism. China's banking system is a tool of the state, and at the direction of the state overlends to capital and real estate projects that are not com-mercially viable. China's banks periodically require bailing out by the government. Parenthetically, it's hard to see how investing in Chinese banks makes any sense at all.

The following should be kept in mind:

- The Minsky (Kindleberger) bubble model is not generally applicable to China. Outside observers visit China and see empty cities and excesses in capital, infrastructure and real estate investments. They think they see Western style, mar-ket bubbles. The Minsky model with its financial instability hypothesis describes an environment where *private* investors become overenthused about a particular asset and become overleveraged. The ensuing bubble followed by collapse brings about distress and panic for indebted investors and the financial system, which has extended them credit. This model describes what happened in the United States and other Western countries very well. But it does not describe what is happening in China where the public rather than the private sector is doing the borrowing. You do not hear stories of private mortgagors overborrowing to buy houses, as happened in the United States. It is a forgone conclusion in China that the government will eventually pick up the tab for bad loans made to local public-sector entities and bail out the banks if necessary. The Chinese economy is state (or more precisely Communist Party) directed, not market directed. Minsky-style bubbles and collapses are characteristics of Western market economies, not state directed ones where overleveraged private investors are not playing a major role in the process. As long as the state has the financial resources to cover these losses, a bubble-type collapse can be avoided. At this point in time, the Chinese state has those resources.

- China has benefited from a massive shift of labor from the countryside to the city. People moved from low- to zero-productivity activities in the rural areas to higher productivity activities. But this is a one-time event. If it has not come to an end yet, it will soon. China is rapidly becoming an urban country.

- China as a latecomer has benefited from being able to import Western technology. Examples abound in this area. Internet search, telecommunications, airlines, medicine—the list goes on. Many have argued that stealing Western technology has been a core part of the Chinese development strategy. I believe these charges have a great deal of truth. But some scholars, in China's defense, have argued that the United States did exactly the same thing by "stealing" British technology in the nineteenth century. Information wants to be free, Stewart Brand famously said. Be that as it may, this phenomenon is also a one-time event although it probably has a longer "shelf life" than the urban migration phenomenon.

- China's one-child policy and current trends will produce an unfavorable demographic situation in the long run. The Chinese worker/retired beneficiary ratio is projected to decline steadily from here on. Actually, attributing this entirely to the government directed one-child policy may not be entirely correct. All the Asian Confucian societies—Hong Kong, Singapore, Japan, Korea, and Taiwan—now exhibit birthrates at close to half the replacement rate of 2.1 children per woman. All face an unfavorable demographic future. Several of these countries—notably Singapore—have tried to encourage its citizens to have more children but to no avail.

- China as currently structured is not suited to the needs of a knowledge economy. Restraining the flow of information is a major characteristic of the current regime. A knowledge society requires complete freedom of information and political freedom in general. One can argue that at lower levels of income and development, democracy is often an obstacle. India and its problems are cited as an example. But at higher levels of income and development, where knowledge plays an important role, the opposite is true. Moreover, Confucian culture with its emphasis on obedience is not necessarily compatible with a knowledge society. One may ask how a Steve Jobs—college dropout, drug user, and one-time hippie—would have fared growing up in China or even Singapore or Japan. Of course he would have been squashed. And not necessarily by any laws, but, rather, by the culture itself. Apple would still be a fruit, not a company. One might ask why Sony could not maintain a culture of innovation. Is it a basic reverence for authority and stability built into Japan's cultural DNA? Is Apple today a better bet to maintain its culture of innovation than Sony was?

- China is a Confucian society, despite all efforts of Chairman Mao to get rid of Confucian thinking. Confucian societies emphasize obedience to authority. The unelected Chinese authorities, while they certainly have to take populist urges into account, are better able to command obedience from a population historically conditioned to obey government authority. Nobel prize–winning author Amartya Sen has written a book titled *The Argumentative Indian*.[1] Nobody's ever written such a book about the Chinese.

- The work ethic and the obsession with material improvement of the Chinese people are big investment pluses for China. Of course, the current economic system in China is a major improvement over the Mao era. But it is still a highly defective protectionist state-dominated system that misallocates resources. The work ethic, relatively high level of education, and obsession with material improvement of the Chinese people have helped make China a success in spite of the current economic structure.

- China is homogeneous. Ninety percent of China's people consider themselves Han and nowadays read and speak the same language. There are no major religious divisions. The minority groups, notably Tibetans, Uighurs, and Hui (Chinese Muslims), are not united and overall are not a special treatment problem. (Rather in the case of the Uighurs and Tibetans, they are advocating self-determination.) They certainly are not a voting bloc that has to be placated.

But the Dynasty Will Survive

Now here's an optimistic thought. The idea that China is about to disintegrate or be afflicted by serious public disorders is at variance with Chinese history. Yes, there are thousands of local protests each year. Yes, China has its share of dissidents. But take a look at Chinese history. Chinese history has a 2,500-year pattern of disorder, ascending dynasty (increasing order), dynastic peak, declining dynasty (increasing disorder), disorder. I would argue that China is in the Ascending Dynasty phase at the moment. I would argue, for example, that the Bo Xilai incident is basically noise—not much different in significance than John Edwards's problem with his mistress.

Some might argue that the current Communist regime is not a dynasty in its pure feudal sense. But I would argue that the differences between the current Communist "dynasty" and prior dynasties are basically superficial. For example, the country remains centrally controlled, thought is tightly managed, and the thousand-year-old Imperial Examinations have simply been replaced by the Gao Kao college entrance exams.

Yes, succession is no longer hereditary—Hu Jintao's son is not becoming the new emperor and, alas, the Communist emperor is not permitted at least in public a bevy of concubines. But even in the case of succession, the leaders are chosen from a select group where having the right parents counts. (The Qing emperors' sartorial choice of resplendent yellow robes puts the current Communist emperors' choice of attire to shame!)

The Chinese population has experienced more than two hundred years of war and turmoil that effectively only ended under Deng Xiaoping. This period of turmoil began with the White Lotus Rebellion in the 1790s, which resulted in millions of deaths and weakened the ruling Qing Dynasty. The White Lotus Rebellion was followed by the Taiping Rebellion (1850), disastrous wars with the British (1840,1860), and the Japanese (1894), fall of the Qing Dynasty (1911), invasion by the Japanese (1937–1945) and then the Chinese Civil War. Disorder only ended with the demise of the highly disruptive Cultural Revolution and the death of Mao in the 1970s.

Like the Germans, who still fear inflation because of the post–WWI experience with hyperinflation under the Weimar Republic, the Chinese people are tired of turmoil. Historically, China has alternated between periods of ascent and strong dynasties and periods of weakened dynasties and disintegration. China is in an ascent phase at this time. I regard books predicting the imminent collapse or disintegration of China as nonsense. The Chinese people do not want revolution and will put up with a lack of welfare benefits, as have been granted by the bankrupt advanced countries. The Chinese people want Louis Vuitton, Chanel, and the good life as they imagine it is lived in the West. (Come to think of it, in the sagging West a lot of people want the good life as the Chinese imagine it in the West.)

For the benefit of those unfamiliar with this, Table 3.3 is a simplified version of Chinese dynastic history. Note that the Qin and Sui Dynasties were short lived but were immediately replaced by another Chinese dynasty, not a period of disorder. The relatively shorter-lived Yuan Dynasty was one imposed on China by a foreign conqueror who did not fully "Sinicize" and was ultimately kicked out and replaced by the Chinese Ming Dynasty.

Note the long life of most of the dynasties. Four of them lasted longer than the entire lifespan of the American Republic, which began operations under its Constitution in 1789. The current Communist Dynasty is a relative youngster, having been in power for only 63 years. Certainly, China's political system will evolve, but anyone predicting its early demise or disintegration is going against the record of Chinese history. To repeat: China is in the ascending period of a dynasty in which order increases.

Chinese data are, in many cases, totally unreliable. Let's start with general government gross debt/GDP. The IMF data in Table 3.4 only presents a ratio on a gross basis for China. It is unclear why

Table 3.3   Timeline of Chinese Dynasties

Dynasty/Period	Dates	Number of Years
Qin Dynasty	221 BC–206 BC	15
Han Dynasty	206 BC–220 AD	427
Six Dynasty Period (Disorder)	220–589	369
Sui Dynasty	581–618	38
Tang Dynasty	618–906	288
Five Dynasty Period (Disorder)	907–960	53
Song Dynasty	960–1279	319
Yuan Dynasty	1279–1368	89
Ming Dynasty	1368–1644	276
Qing Dynasty	1644–1911	267
Republic Period (Disorder)	1911–1949	38
People's Republic	1949–present	63

Table 3.4   A Quick Summary of Statistics for the People's Republic of China

General Government Gross Debt/GDP	25.8%
General Gov't Expenditure/GDP	22.6%
Investment/GDP	48.3%
Current account/GDP	2.8%
GDP per capita (US dollars)	$5,413
Consumer price inflation	5.4%
Unemployment rate	4.1%
Foreign reserves (approx.)	$3.3 trillion
Population	1.348 billion

Sources: IMF, data for 2011, Reserves from newspaper accounts

a net number is not given. As can be seen, the general government gross debt/GDP as reported by the IMF (Table 3.4) is very low at 25.8 percent. But another respected source, Eurostat, reports this ratio at 43 percent. There are so many unknowns with the Chinese sovereign debt ratio. One is the amount of borrowing by local government related entities, which are heavily indebted to the banks.

Then there is the fact that China has some $3.3 trillion in foreign exchange reserves. Part of these are offset by borrowing by the central bank (PBOC) from commercial banks, which resulted from sterilization operations. China's strong reserve position is largely the result of the huge trade surplus of prior years and the attempts to hold down the value of the currency by buying dollars. Chinese government debt has risen, not from populist entitlement programs, as in the West, but from borrowing to finance infrastructure and real estate. Most of this debt is owed domestically, not internationally. There are prophets of doom sounding the alarm that the Chinese sovereign debt situation is as bad as that of the West. I'm not one of these, but at the end of the day nobody can be completely sure. Still, with its huge foreign reserve position, China cannot, as some have done, be compared with Greece or Italy.

Let's take a second number, GDP growth. Thanks to Wikileaks, it has become known that Chinese officials themselves have questioned the reliability of China's GDP numbers. Provincial estimates of growth don't add up to the national numbers. The national numbers are released quickly after each quarter ends and, unlike in the United States, are never revised. Even without political bias, the national numbers would seem to be highly inaccurate and unbelievable. Analysts will be watching statistics such as electricity consumption and cement output as well as global commodity prices.

Note

1. Amartya Sen, *The Argumentative Indian: Writing on Indian History, Culture and Identity* (New York: Farrar, Straus and Giroux, 2005).

4

The International Monetary System— In Desperate Need of Repair

The gentleman from Wisconsin has said he fears a Robespierre. My friend, in this land of the free you need fear no tyrant who will spring up from among the people. What we need is an Andrew Jackson to stand as Jackson stood, against the encroachments of aggregated wealth.

If they dare to come out in the open field and defend the gold standard as a good thing . . . we shall answer their demands for a gold standard by saying to them, you shall not press down upon the brow of labor this crown of thorns. You shall not crucify mankind upon a cross of gold.

—William Jennings Bryan

In 1896, at the Democratic National Convention in Chicago, William Jennings Bryan launched his famous jeremiad against the gold standard, the final portion of which is quoted above. The gold standard was in its heyday when Bryan uttered these words, and with the benefit of hindsight was the most successful international and domestic monetary system the world has yet seen. That didn't seem to bother Bryan. To be fair, Bryan was arguing in favor of bimetallism (i.e., currency backed by gold and silver and not a flat-out fiat paper money system). But in fact, he was really one of the great populists arguing for cheaper money. Unfortunately, he has ultimately got his way.

The populists could never abide by a financial system essentially run by an anonymous metal. Bryan's reference to the "encroachments of aggregate wealth" resonates today. But is a Robespierre ultimately going to be needed to keep the triumph of the populists in place and enforce the financial repression and ultimately defaults that are coming?

Let's Start with History and Economics

We are currently in a period of debt deflation and recession. But how we got here and how the measures being taken to ameliorate this situation could bring tremendous inflationary harm in the future must be understood. The role of the international monetary system and how it helped get us into our current predicament requires understanding of both economics and history.

The international monetary system, since 1973, and the final demise of the Bretton Woods system, has become a global fiat money creation system. The Fed, the ECB, the Bank of England, the Bank of Japan, the Swiss National Bank—all the central banks of the world—have become nothing more than ATM machines with the ability to print an endless supply of high-powered money (bank reserves plus currency, i.e., the monetary base). This high-powered money is backed by nothing except the trust of its users. The system totally lacks discipline, and it has served as financier of fiscal profligacy and excess borrowing for governments around the world. Moreover, because the US dollar is the core reserve currency and the United States has usually taken a passive, noninterventionist approach to its own currency's valuation, other countries, notably in East Asia, have promoted protectionist policies and have been able to manipulate their own currencies towards undervaluation, thus following a mercantilist strategy favoring their own manufacturing industries and hurting those of the United States.

Prior to 1914 and the outbreak of WWI, the gold standard served as a major check against the tendencies of democratically elected representatives to vote for "goodies" for their electorates that ultimately were unaffordable. Governments couldn't print money to finance their spending under the gold standard. But the gold standard simply was too restrictive for modern twentieth-century democracies with universal suffrage. Volumes have been written on the technical aspects of various international monetary systems, including the various gold standards. The gold standard had its faults. But the bottom line is not technical. It is simple. The

Golden Fetter, to use economic historian Barry Eichengreen's term for the gold standard, was just too much discipline for universal suffrage democracies.[1]

The fact that the gold standard was usually suspended when a war began is proof that the gold standard always stood in the way of fiscal laxity. Governments in the past resorted to the printing press to finance wars, which was impossible to do under the gold standard. By the late twentieth century, democracies' need for ever more unfunded entitlements and the socialization of risk had become an even more powerful motive than war. And wars, unfortunately, haven't gone away. Gold, following the botched attempt at restoration during the post–WWI period, has been conveniently consigned to the intellectual dustbin as, to use Keynes' famous phrase, a "barbarous relic." It has been rejected by the bulk of the economics profession who have been indoctrinated with the primacy of Keynesian and monetarist demand management, supervised, of course, by armies of PhD economists. The gold standard in its pure form would eliminate demand management and a lot of economists' jobs.

Under the current post–Bretton Woods fiat money system, governments can print all they want and manipulate their currencies as well. As mentioned, Eichengreen in his seminal work *Golden Fetters*,[2] lists the expansion of suffrage during WWI and the rise of unions as factors working against the restoration of the gold standard. Universal suffrage made possible the rise of unions. Governments were now held fully responsible for their economies by their electorates and were unwilling to allow their monetary policies to be dictated by an anonymous metal that was not under their control.

One of the oddities of today's system is that central banks basically are not banks at all. They are government Departments of Fiat Money Creation. It doesn't matter what a central bank's leverage ratio is or what its balance sheet looks like. It can print high-powered money. As long as people accept this money, that's all that matters. You read Wall Street research from time to time worrying about the capital position of the Fed or the ECB. Stupid in my opinion. Even people on Wall Street don't understand what fiat money is and how they have been hoodwinked by the government. Fiat money is convertible into nothing. It is backed up by nothing. It can be created by central banks arbitrarily. Central banks don't need capital. They only require the backing of their (bankrupt) governments and the willingness of the public to use the money they have created.

Reform of the international monetary system will be a necessary part of a successful emergence from the coming age of sovereign defaults. For most citizens, the intricacies of the international monetary system are beyond their intellectual capacity or interest. The typical person might argue that the intricacies of international finance are best left to technocrats. But the design of the system depends ultimately on political will.

Nevertheless, since gold is an obvious investment choice in the age of sovereign defaults, I will spend some time reviewing the history and theory of the gold standard.

Note that, although it might seem like it, this is not a book whose primary purpose is to argue for the restoration of the gold standard. Perhaps the gold standard wouldn't work today. But by looking at the theory and by examining the past, some light may be shed on designing a new international monetary system. The current one needs replacing.

The Gold Standard in Theory—The Price-Specie Flow Mechanism

Perhaps it would be a good idea to begin by reviewing just how a gold standard was supposed to work. In practice, there have been various versions of the gold standard and the real world never fully corresponded to the theoretical. The various versions start with what we might call a "pure" gold standard and then move on to introduce various restrictions, complications, and compromises. It is important, therefore, to first understand the basic theoretical model underlying the pure gold standard.

The model universally cited for this is David Hume's price-specie flow mechanism. Hume was a Scottish philosopher, historian, economist, and essayist. A towering intellectual figure of his day and contemporary of fellow Scot Adam Smith, he actually died in 1776, the year of publication of Adam Smith's *Wealth of Nations* as well as the American Declaration of Independence. A propitious year for the exit of a towering intellectual of his day!

Hume's price-specie flow mechanism is as relevant today as it was in 1776. The price-specie flow mechanism is an argument set forth against the then-prevailing mercantilist notion that a nation should strive for a positive balance of trade. Smith's *Wealth of Nations,* of course, is itself probably the most important intellectual assault against mercantilism that has been written. (But not everyone is impressed. The mercantilist notion that a nation must run a positive balance of trade unfortunately has found a permanent place today in the economic strategies of Japan, China, Korea, and other nations in Asia.)

Under the price-specie flow mechanism, gold is the official means of international and domestic payments and each nation's currency is in the form of gold itself or paper currency fully convertible into gold at a preestablished price that cannot be changed. On the international front, when any country on a gold standard has a positive balance of trade, gold will flow into that country in the amount that the value of exports exceeded the value of imports. Conversely, when a country has a negative balance of trade, gold will flow out of the country in the amount that the value of imports exceeds the value of exports. The money supply will rise in a country with a positive balance of trade and fall in a country with a negative balance of trade. Money in today's terminology would be high-powered money or the monetary base (bank reserves plus currency) as Hume's model did not allow for fractional reserve banking. Relying on the quantity theory of money, Hume argued that in countries where the quantity of money increases, inflation will set in and the prices of goods and services will tend to rise. In countries where the money supply decreases, deflation will occur as the prices of goods and services fall. The higher prices will, in the countries with a positive balance of trade, cause exports to decrease and imports to increase. This will alter the balance of trade toward a neutral balance. Conversely, in countries with a negative balance of trade, the lower prices will cause exports to increase and imports to decrease, again producing a neutral balance.

Hume's model did not allow for capital flows or the existence of modern central banks. His model can be easily modified to allow for both. Under what later would come under the "rules of the game," a central bank if it existed was supposed to raise interest rates when its country had a current account deficit and lower interest rates when its country had a balance of payments surplus. This would encourage stabilizing, symmetric capital flows in accordance with the spirit of the Hume model.

Regarding a modern central bank's creation of high-powered money, if all holders of a given currency can exchange their currency or checks for gold at a predetermined fixed price, then it is the public rather than any central bank that would have the final say on the supply of high-powered money. The price-specie flow system will therefore continue to work. The fatal flaw here is when the public cannot convert its currency and checks for gold. Then central banks have the power to create high-powered money out of thin air. Under this system where the public cannot exchange its currency and checks for gold at a pre-established rate, central banks can and have perverted the workings of the gold standard in practice.

Nevertheless, with adjustments for capital flows and more modern commercial banks than those prevailing in Hume's day, the model describes reasonably well the way the world worked during the heyday of the gold standard from 1879–1914. Of course, the real world is always messier than an economic model and Eichengreen, Kindleberger, and others have documented where there were deviations in practice over this period.[3]

Countries did not always play by the "rules." One area of dispute is what role central banks, notably the Bank of England, played in the successful working of this system. Was the system as autonomous as the Hume model suggested, or did it require strong intervention and cooperation among central banks under the leadership of the Bank of England? Note that during this period some countries (e.g., the United States) did not have a central bank.

Deviations and all, the following conclusions can be reached about the gold standard, whether one is talking about Hume's model or to a large extent actual practice during the gold standard heyday of 1879–1914:

1. No country could print money out of thin air to finance budget deficits.
2. Globally, the high-powered global money supply grew only when new gold came into the system. New gold could come into the system only through mining and conversion from jewelry and commercial uses.
3. No central bank would be allowed or able to offset the inflows or outflows of capital by printing high-powered money.
4. No country could manipulate its currency downward to encourage its own exports.

5. Overall balance of payment equilibrium would always obtain. No country, as the United States and China have done in recent years, could run up giant current account deficits or surpluses year after year.
6. Paper money and checking accounts could be freely converted to gold at the established rate.

Historically, gold was just one of several metals, along with silver and copper, that were used in commodity-backed financial systems. But gold's greater scarcity, indestructability, fungibility, and desirability enabled it to eventually win out.

The Sad Evolution of the International Monetary System

One of the things about economic trends is that they sometimes happen so slowly that nobody notices and people become used to changes and consider them normal. They don't realize that what is normal today was not the practice in the past. And sometimes they don't realize how much things have changed. For example, you can still run into people who think the dollar bill in their wallet can be turned in for gold or silver. The international monetary system, without the general public noticing or caring, over the last 150-plus years has morphed from an engine of financial probity and discipline to one that actively facilitated and promoted financial indiscipline. So the study of economic history is really a requirement for anyone who wants to understand what has really happened.

Below is a thumbnail review of the history of international monetary systems since the beginning of the nineteenth century.

Bimetallic/Silver Standards Pre-1879

At the turn of the nineteenth century, intellectually the concept of a commodity backing for all currencies was unchallenged. Paper money was a new innovation and was rapidly replacing coins in most countries. But all major paper moneys were commodity money in that they were backed by either gold or silver, or often both. Having used coins for centuries, the public required a commodity backing for the new invention of paper.

For the first part of the century, countries were on bimetallic gold/silver standards of one sort or another or on a silver standard. Until the later part of the eighteenth century, the global markets groped for a decision as to whether gold exclusively, silver and gold, or silver exclusively would back currencies. But there was no intellectual acceptance of fiat paper money although many of the newer countries, like the new South American republics, were deficient in institutional development and could not maintain commodity money standards.

Britain was early with regard to the gold standard. Britain had actually de facto adopted the gold standard in 1717 when Sir Isaac Newton, then Master of the Mint and now regarded as a towering genius in the world of physics, apparently unintentionally set the relationship between gold and silver in favor of gold. Faced with financing the long Napoleonic Wars, Britain went off gold in 1797 but formally returned in 1821 after the end of the Napoleonic Wars in 1815. The Napoleonic Wars had brought inflation but after the war, Britain in pre-universal suffrage, pre–trade union nineteenth century, was able to come back onto gold at the prior parity. Other countries, notably Russia and Austria, had more difficult experiences restoring metallic standards after the Napoleonic Wars.

The Classical Gold Standard (1879–1914)

Under the classic gold standard, gold really was the international currency. All the major currencies were convertible into gold at fixed parities and market participants assumed these parities except in war would not be changed. There were no restrictions on capital flows.

The choice of 1879 as the beginning of the Classical Gold Standard is somewhat arbitrary. The choice of 1914 as the end of the classical period is not. WWI shattered what was a hugely successful system. The United States went on to the gold standard in 1879 after an inflationary paper money standard called the greenback period during the American Civil War (1860–1865). As mentioned, Britain had been on gold since restoration, after the Napoleonic wars in 1821. Canada, Australia, and Portugal had done so before 1879. Newly emergent Germany adopted the gold standard in 1871 after the Franco-Prussian War. France joined later in the 1870s, as did Belgium, Switzerland, the Netherlands, Denmark, Norway, Sweden, and Finland. Other major countries joined as the years went on, with the exception of China, which stayed on the silver standard.

Central banks were not expected to create high-powered money to offset every hiccup in the economy. The United States, Canada, and Australia did not have central banks during this period. As mentioned, Peter Bernholz has found no major trends in inflation or deflation during the period. During this time the world economy made enormous strides in terms of industrialization and economic growth. Government budget deficits on the scale of what has occurred today just didn't happen. Financial panics did occur from time to time but were short as compared with the twentieth-century variety. The United States in 1890 brought the markets down on themselves with the passage of the Sherman Silver Purchase Act, which ignited fears the United States would slip off the gold standard in favor a more inflationary system using silver.

Keynes would have been regarded as a dangerous quack in this world.

One objection to the gold standard in this period was that it seemed to work better for "core" countries like the United Kingdom, or Germany but not so well for "periphery" countries like Brazil, which had difficulty maintaining their parity with gold. Ironically, today it is some of these periphery countries which have more solid fiscal situations as compared with the traditional core countries.

The WWI Fiat Money Period

Commencing in 1914 with the outbreak of WWI, most of the major countries, including Britain, Germany, and France, withdrew from the gold standard and commenced printing money to help finance the war. Nobody—well, at least nobody in power—in 1914 thought the war would be as long or as expensive as it was. The Germans, in particular, thought the war would be short, that the French and the Russians would lose, and that Germany as victor would be reimbursed by the losers for the cost of the war. That had been the case with the German victory in the Franco-Prussian War of 1871. Unfortunately for all nations involved, the war was incredibly long and costly. Unfortunately for the Germans, they lost, and it was Germany who was made to pay for the war. The United States stayed on the gold standard but the newly created Federal Reserve created high-powered money out of thin air as if there were no gold standard. Inflation jumped in all countries.

During the war, the world changed in many ways. Universal suffrage came in and unions became more powerful. Before the war in 1911, a man named Norman Angel wrote a book called *The Grand Illusion,* whose principal theme was that a war would be unthinkable because its results would be so catastrophic and so expensive.[4] He was right. War would be catastrophic and expensive but the unthinkable happened anyway. From the viewpoint of the international monetary system, the "shackles" of international monetary discipline had been broken and the world had begun the slide down the long, slippery slope to where we are today.

Gold Exchange Standard (1921–1936)

After WWI, once again the countries of the world tried to restore the gold standard. Unfortunately, after WWI the world was such a mess that successful restoration of the gold standard proved impossible. Opponents of the gold standard will argue that it was a deflationary yoke in the post-WWI period.[5] In a narrow sense, they are probably right. But there were extenuating circumstances. My view is that the world economy was in severe disrepair after WWI and this made the restoration of a smoothly functioning international monetary system an almost impossible task. The list of difficulties was a long one. German reparations payments, German (and Hungarian and Austrian hyperinflation), the introduction of Communism in Russia and the default on Russian bonds, the breakup of the Austrian-Hungarian and Ottoman empires, the unrealistic decision of the British in 1925 to go back on gold at the prewar rate, and the refusal of the United States to play a leadership role commensurate with its new economic importance, made it impossible to put the gold standard Humpty Dumpty back together. No standard would have worked in that period. Plus there was the enlargement of suffrage during the war. The new electorates weren't as tolerant as before of gold standard discipline.

Nevertheless, after WWI intellectually nobody questioned the requirement to restore gold backing for money. Besides, people always want to bring back the "good old days." For example, after the fall of Rome in the fifth century AD, the people of Europe held in their memories of the ideal of a Roman empire. In the ninth century, Charlemagne made an effort to restore that empire and founded the less-than-successful Holy Roman Empire.

So it was with the gold standard after WWI. Monetary authorities tried to revive the old empire but the effort ultimately failed. The monetary regime prevailing after the war until the mid-1930s and the Great Depression was called the gold exchange standard. This is a controversial area, but the gold exchange standard is usually defined as a regime where international reserves are held as gold bullion or securities of a key country that are convertible into gold bullion.

One of those key currencies was the British pound. Unfortunately, in 1925 the British under then Chancellor of the Exchequer Winston Churchill made the fateful decision to return to the gold standard at its prewar parity. As mentioned, Britain had successfully returned to gold at the prewar parity in 1821 after the Napoleonic Wars but post-WWI 1925 was a different story. The decision to rejoin at the old parity in 1925 turned out to be excessively deflationary and beyond Britain's capabilities. It kept Britain in recession more or less continuously until it left the gold standard in 1931. At the same time, the United States sterilized the inflow of gold during the 1920s by reducing those bank reserves that had been created out of thin air during the war. This was another deflationary event that would not have happened under the classical gold standard where central banks, if they existed at all, would not have had the ability to create or destroy high-powered money. As long as central banks have the power to create high-powered money out of thin air, the gold standard isn't going to work very well. In my opinion, the Federal Reserve's decision to sterilize gold inflows in the 1920s undermined the gold standard.

Overall, with the exception of the hyperinflation in Germany, Hungary, Austria and the other defeated Central Powers after WWI, the decade of the 1920s was a period tending toward deflation, not inflation. The gold standard was blamed for this and was discredited intellectually as deflation became an overwhelming force in the 1930s. Intellectually, the world was set up to receive doctrines of demand management, notably Keynesianism and later monetarism. Under Keynes's banner, starting in the 1980s politicians would find intellectual cover to run gargantuan budget deficits and satisfy their constituents' demand for an ever-greater unpaid-for cornucopia of entitlements. Under the banner of monetarism, central banks under quantitative easing programs would be allowed to print unlimited amounts of high-powered money so to push up growth rates in conventionally defined measures of money such as M2. Central banks would be empowered to bail out bankrupt financial institutions. Risk would be socialized to prevent economic pain from being visited on angry voters.

The gold exchange standard didn't end at any one date. Germany went off the gold standard in 1931, to be followed a few months later by the British. France finally left the gold standard in 1936. Revolutionary Russia in 1917 not only went off gold but confiscated gold in all forms. In 1933, the new administration of Franklin Roosevelt criminalized the private ownership of gold and authorized a default on government and private bonds that were payable in gold.

A quote from Nazi economist Werner Datz might be illustrative. Datz declared that "in future, gold will play no role as a basis for European currencies, because a currency does not depend on what it is covered by, but rather it is dependent on which it is given by the state, or in this case by the economic order which is controlled by the state."[6] Datz was right on the money. Fiat paper money depends on the state. Indeed, it not only does not depend on what it is covered by, but is covered by nothing but the willingness of citizens to use it.

The Bretton Woods System (1945–1971)

At the end of WWII, the United States assumed the leadership role it had shunned after WWI. It pushed though the adoption of what came to be called the Bretton Woods system. Under Bretton Woods, the rest of the world maintained a fixed parity with the US dollar while the United States alone pledged to redeem to other nations' excess dollars for gold. The Bretton Woods system was the "Gold Standard Lite." Only central banks could exchange dollars for gold, not ordinary citizens. It required the United States to maintain monetary and fiscal discipline, which ultimately it did not. Lyndon Johnson, president from 1963 to 1969, pushed through a number of programs including the Medicare program. Medicare is probably the United States' most underfunded and out of control entitlement today, and its cost exceeds the projections at the time of its founding by multiples. Johnson also embarked on the war in Vietnam—"guns and butter," it was called at the time. The United States, partly because of the unique position of the dollar, has been able to launch massive social programs and wage war at the same time. This cannot go on forever.

By the time Richard Nixon assumed the presidency in 1969, things were going from bad to worse. Requests for conversion of dollars into gold were coming in fast, notably from the French. Nixon in 1971 abrogated the US obligation to sell gold for dollars to foreign central banks. By 1973, all the world's currencies floated against one another and were no longer backed by gold or any other commodity. A brave new world of global fiat money creation had arrived.

The Current Dollar-Centric Fiat Money System (1973–Present)

With the breakdown of the Bretton Woods system, all ties with gold were cut. Henceforth all currencies would be fiat money currencies, backed only by the trust of their holders. Monetarists in particular were happy since they thought currencies would then float against one another and values would be determined by the market. If country A wanted to pursue an inflationist policy with excess money growth, so be it. Country A's exchange rate would simply decline against other currencies. Under the new system, the United States was to act in a very passive way, not intervening to affect the value of the dollar, which would remain as the world's primary reserve currency. It was assumed that other countries—at least other large countries—would take a similar hands-off approach.

The supporters of this system didn't realize what an inflation-prone, bubble-creating monster had been created. Or maybe they didn't care. First, without the discipline of gold, there was no restraint on central banks printing money. Monetarist admonitions about controlled growth of the money supply were ignored at important junctures around the world. Second, the countries of Asia, first Japan and then Korea, Taiwan, and China, had a mercantilist rather than free market model in mind. Call it the East Asian economic model. In order to promote exports, they have maintained highly protectionist policies on imports and intervened in the markets to reduce the value of their currencies. Ultimately, these interventions added unprecedented liquidity to the world economy, generated significant bubbles around the world, damaged American exports and manufacturing, and helped finance a consumer/mortgage boom in the United States.

The mechanism for this was as follows. Facing a glut of dollars from its country's current account surplus and surplus of exports over imports, East Asian central banks bought the dollars to hold down their own currencies value. Those dollars got invested in American assets, largely US government and agency securities. These investments showed up as increased reserves for the Asian country and in a sense can be viewed as vendor financing for East Asian exports. American interest rates were lowered as dollars were reinvested in the United States and credit was supplied to the United States. And exports to the United States soared. At the same time, the Asian central banks created high-powered money in their own currency as they purchased the dollars. What has resulted is an explosion of global liquidity.

The New World of Quantitative Easing (2001–?)

Technically, the structure of the global monetary system hasn't changed since the collapse of the Bretton Woods system in 1971–1973. But in fact, the major central banks have entered into a new world of money printing and debasement beginning with the Bank of Japan's quantitative easing program in 2001. My view is that this new world will eventually end in inflationary chaos and the dawning of a new global financial system.

In the last few years, central banks have come to the realization that there is no limit to the amount of high-powered money printing that they may engage in to prevent financial collapse and deflation. Central banks are printing money all over the world. New names have been given to what is really an age-old phenomenon. Desperate governments have traditionally debased their currencies when they have no other way of financing their deficits. Quantitative easing, LTRO, Fed/ECB swaps, whatever. A new technocratic lexicon has been invented to cover what is really a time-honored expedient of debasement and paper money printing.

This is qualitatively different from the excess money printing and debasement that went on in the past. In the past, monetary authorities printed money and debased their currencies to finance *wars*. But this time it's not wars but the prevailing orthodoxy that Keynesian and monetarist demand management policies must be used to micromanage economies; and to finance democracies' underlying tendency to inexorably move to fiscal excess and bankruptcy.

As I have been arguing, *citizens vote to obtain through the political process what they cannot obtain in the market.* Modern democratic governments are expected to socialize risk and redistribute income from the smarter affluent minority. The welfare state grows and grows, its costs disguised in the complexity of the budget process and ignored by the public anyway.

And nobody has to bother lifting the fetters of a commodity money conversion requirement that was so important in the age of the classical gold standard before WWI. Richard Nixon cut the last of those golden fetters in 1971 when the United States ceased to honor its commitment under the Bretton Woods Agreement to sell gold for dollars at a fixed rate to other central banks. Since the demise of Bretton Woods, every central bank in the world can be its own ATM machine. And indeed they have.

So far, the world's central banks have been "lucky." Thanks to the prior global bubble ending in 2008 and the realization that the so-called advanced countries are reaching the end of their borrowing capacity, the world is in a massive deleveraging mode, which tends to be deflationary. For the moment, the central banks can get away with printing all the money they want without massive increases in consumer price indexes. Especially when the price indexes may have been "calibrated" just a little to present a rosier picture. The public doesn't connect increases in prices of commodities like gold or oil with the current bout of money printing. But if history is any guide, this money printing will matter and the age of deflation and deleveraging will be followed by an age of inflation. Deleveraging or no, entitlements already promised will grow inexorably larger. Inflation, of course, is one way governments can effect major defaults on sovereign debt and unaffordable entitlements.

The International Monetary System Must Change—But to What?

The following section discusses some alternatives to the current ruleless international monetary system.

Keep the Current System But Set Up Rules

The current system, at least on the international level, could still work. What if all major countries would start to use that time honored nineteenth-century phrase, playing by "the rules of the game"? The rules in this case would require an end to East Asian mercantilist policies of strong protectionism and concerted efforts (already described) to hold their currencies down against the US dollar. That means no mercantilist interventions to hold currency values down and no "vendor financing" and buildup of excess reserves. And eventual financial discipline imposed on the United States. The major buildup of their dollar reserves by China, Japan, and other Asian countries is proof of mercantilist manipulation. Without this vendor financing and higher interest rates, the United States might have been incentivized to be more responsible in its fiscal policy.

As mentioned, some monetarists in 1971–1973, when the Bretton Woods system was finally put to rest, jumped for joy. The new system would allow each country to pursue its own monetary and fiscal policies. If country X was profligate, well, its currency would just crash to offset the internal depreciation via inflation. If country Y had a major trade surplus, fine. Its currency would just appreciate to offset the surplus and make country Y's exports more expensive. Voila! A system that forced automatic adjustment on an international level, just like David Hume and Adam Smith would have wanted. And at the same time, countries could pursue their own internal demand management and borrowing programs as they saw fit. The best of both worlds. It didn't occur to the monetarists in their naiveté that nations would be able to subvert this system so easily.

The continuance of the current post–Bretton Woods system would require some rules to be established that East Asian and all other countries including the United States would have to follow. Sounds simple, but don't hold your breath. Countries only make major changes in the face of a crisis.

So until that day when rules are agreed upon, we continue down the road to eventual market crisis. The dollar and, secondarily, the euro are the two major reserve currencies. Unbalanced as it is, the current international monetary system will persist until market confidence in both these currencies disappears. That is only likely to happen when the United States and the strong countries in the European Union in particular have trouble funding their debt. Europe's and the euro's current problems will be deferred to the future by the ECB's money-printing LTRO program and other ways the ECB finds to print money. The market will force the adaptation of a new global monetary system only when funding becomes impossible for the major Western countries.

Before predicting what that system will look like, perhaps it would be a good idea to list the essential characteristics of a successful international monetary system:

- Central banks have no ability to print high-powered money without restraint.
- An automatic mechanism restores balance of payment equilibrium between deficit and surplus countries.
- Central banks or countries have no ability to pursue mercantilist policies by undervaluing their currencies.
- Sufficient liquidity is provided to facilitate international trade and global economic growth.
- There are no restraints on international capital flows.
- The core currencies involved hold their value.

A New Gold Standard?

Many argue for a restoration of the classic gold standard. But virtually all governments and most economists are opposed. Various technical objections are given. The gold standard in standard economic textbooks has been portrayed as a contributing factor in the Great Depression of the 1930s, and many economists have a bias against it as a result. But the real objection is the fundamental belief that governments should not give up control of Keynesian and monetarist demand management tools. Essentially, their electorates expect them to socialize risks and soften the blows of the economic cycles and to continue to expand the welfare state. Governments will not give up these goals unless forced to do so by the market.

Still it might be useful to review some of the technical objections to the restoration of the gold standard. The first is that there is not enough gold in the world to back up outstanding bank checking money and currency and that a gold standard would be excessively deflationary. Answering that is easy. The price of gold will have to go up until there is enough gold. Of course, barring punitive taxes, speculators who own gold would be rewarded. But so were speculators who bought discounted state obligations after the American Revolutionary War Alexander Hamilton's consolidation plan, in fact, rewarded these speculators, but in return the new United States had a sound monetary system that served it well until the American Civil War in 1860. The second objection is that the price of gold is too volatile to allow it to be the centerpiece of the global monetary system. Answering that is also easy. Once a realistic price for gold would be established, its value would be fixed against all the world's currencies. Economies would adjust to the price of gold. The third is that gold is not equally distributed in the world today. Countries with little gold would suffer a major deflation while countries (like the United States) would suffer a major inflation. I admit that's a tough one to answer, but solutions could be found. Were gold to be revalued by some multiple upward to support the current world money supplies now outstanding, the United States as the largest holder of gold today would benefit. But with the United States' huge current account deficit, gold would immediately flow out of the United States. The last objection is a philosophical one. It is argued that gold other than jewelry and some industrial uses serves no useful function and produces no real wealth. Digging gold up out of the ground is a waste of resources. The answer to this is, what more useful monetary function could there be than providing a needed store of wealth? Fiat paper money has deteriorated in value significantly everywhere and to zero in many instances. Fiat paper money can be depreciated to zero by over issuance by government authorities, while the gold supply can only increase by some 1 to 2 percent a year through mining.

Central banks in Asia and Russia today are reportedly adding gold to their reserves. Clearly, this reflects a renewed confidence in gold as a store of value—one of the main functions of money. It also reflects a desire for an alternative to the dollar and the euro. But it is only a first step. So long as central banks have unrestrained powers to create high-powered money, they can buy all the gold they want but that will not address the points for a successful international monetary system. So long as the public cannot convert its currency and checking accounts into gold, the central banks will have a monopoly on unrestrained money issuance. So long as there is no automatic mechanism to correct imbalances in payment accounts among nations, the system will be vulnerable to mercantilist policies.

It has been suggested that countries like China that are accumulating gold and are unhappy with the dollar and the euro might want to back their own currencies with gold. No doubt this would immediately elevate the renminbi into reserve currency status. But it would also put massive upward pressure on the renminbi as demand for the currency would soar. It is doubtful that China, with its current mercantilist protectionist policies, would be interested in seeing this happen.

Governments have a monopoly on creating money at the present time. They will not give up this monopoly easily. If there is a flight from the dollar and the euro into gold, it would not be surprising if governments tried to prohibit the ownership of gold by their citizens. This has to be a big worry for gold investors.

If gold turns into a major rival for the dollar, there certainly is a risk that the US government would either restrict, prohibit, or otherwise punish holders of gold. Already, the Internal Revenue Service (IRS) classifies gold as a "collectible," thereby making profits taken in gold ineligible for more favorable long-term capital gains treatment. And history can be our guide. In 1933, the ownership of gold was made illegal in the United States. Gold clauses, which required payment in gold at the lender's request, were abrogated by the Roosevelt administration under Executive Order 6102. When challenged in the Supreme Court, the Court rolled over and allowed the Roosevelt administration's abrogation.

In the past and today, many nations have placed various restrictions on their citizens owning gold. During the German hyperinflation of 1921–1923, laws were passed making the holding of gold difficult. Desperate governments do desperate things. Today, for example, Vietnam has placed restrictions on the mining of gold as its citizens have lost confidence in their own currency.

Alternative Private Moneys

Austrian school economist Frederick von Hayek proposed that various types of privately sponsored money should be allowed to circulate. Central bank–issued money would be allowed to compete with the private money. One type of private money might be gold backed. But there could be others. How practical such a system would be remains to be seen. Hayek's ideas and the emergence of the Internet and computer technology have generated a cult of techno enthusiasts dedicated to creating new types of money. They may succeed on a technical level. But technical issues aside, let's not lose sight of the fundamental underlying problem.

Governments will not voluntarily give up their monopoly for creating money. In all cases, we can expect alternatives to government-issued fiat money to be met with resistance by governments around the world. In fact, this has already happened. Governments have the power of law and coercion behind them. They can enlist the same Internet technologies to undermine Internet-based moneys. And don't confuse digitally created fiat government money with alternative moneys.

Keynes's Bancor

At the Bretton Woods conference in 1944, John Maynard Keynes proposed a sort of global central bank be established that would issue a type of money called *bancor*. The United States was opposed and the idea was basically shot down. Recently, Chinese central

---

Do You Think I Am Paranoid? Then Read This: By Executive Order of the President of the United States, March 9, 1933:

By virtue of the authority vested in me by Section 5 (b) of the Act of October 6, 1917, as amended by Section 2 of the Act of March 9, 1933, in which Congress declared that a serious emergency exists, I as President, do declare that the national emergency still exists; that the continued private hoarding of gold and silver by subjects of the United States poses a grave threat to the peace, equal justice, and well-being of the United States; and that appropriate measures must be taken immediately to protect the interests of our people.

Therefore, pursuant to the above authority, I hereby proclaim that such gold and silver holdings are prohibited, and that all such coin, bullion or other possessions of gold and silver be tendered within fourteen days to agents of the Government of the United States for compensation at the official price, in the legal tender of the Government.

All safe deposit boxes in banks or financial institutions have been sealed, pending action in the due course of the law. All sales or purchases or movements of such gold and silver within the borders of the United States and its territories and all foreign exchange transactions or movements of such metals across the border are hereby prohibited.

Your possession of these proscribed metals and/or your maintenance of a safe deposit box to store them is known by the government from bank and insurance records. Therefore, be advised that your vault box must remain sealed, and may only be opened in the presence of an agent of the Internal Revenue Service.

By lawful order given this day, the President of the United States.

—*Franklin Roosevelt, March 9, 1933*

bank president Zhou Xiaochuan proposed that the IMF assume a role that resembled Keynes's proposal. Good luck. As the world's largest creditor nation, China wants some ideal replacement for the US dollar that suffers from zero inflation and no credit risk. More likely, any new global central bank that could create money out of thin air would be an engine of inflation. Does the world need more central banks?

Notes

1. Barry Eichengreen, *Golden Fetters: The Gold Standard and the Great Depression, 1919–1939 (NBER Series on Long-Term Factors in Economic Development.)* (New York: Oxford University Press, Inc., 1992).
2. Ibid.
3. One useful source is Michael Bordo and Ronald MacDonald, *Violation of the "Rules of the Game" and the Credibility of the Classical Gold Standard, 1880–1914.* NBER Working Paper 6115, http://www.nber.org/papers/w6115
4. Norman Angel, *The Great Illusion—A Study of the Relation of Military Power to National Advantage* (Obscure Press, 2006). Kindle edition.
5. Eichengreen. Op. cit.
6. Detlev S. Schlichter, *Paper Money Collapse: The Folly of Elastic Money and the Coming Monetary Breakdown* (New York: John Wiley & Sons, 2000), 169.

CHAPTER 5

The Road to Worthless Paper Money

The American Republic will endure until the day Congress discovers that it can bribe the public with the public's money.

—Alexis de Tocqueville

Chapter 4 reviewed money from the perspective of democracy with universal suffrage and the international monetary system. This chapter will try to bring the reader/investor to the realization, if he or she hasn't come to this already, that domestic or international, the history of fiat paper money is one of a descent into worthlessness. This descent into worthlessness precedes the twentieth century phenomenon of universal suffrage and democracy itself. Even without universal suffrage and democracies, governments have succumbed to the temptation to debase their currencies.

Prior to twentieth-century financing, war was the main threat to paper currencies. Ignorance and corruption have also played a role. Serious scholars and economic historians over and over have documented the sad history of paper money. The mainstream of public and economists ignores this history. We will repeat this history in this chapter. Skip it at your peril.

Mankind has used money in one form or another for at least the last 4,500 years. Sumerian clay tablets as far back as 2,400 BC reveal standards for silver used as money. References to silver as money can be found in the Old Testament. Coins were the major form of money up until the nineteenth century. Paper money made its appearance about a thousand years ago. Paper money, in so many ways, adds financial value, as compared to carrying around some commodity that serves as money. But paper money has such a sad history. Prior to 1914, the usual sequence of events has been the introduction of paper money with at least partial commodity backing (i.e., gold, silver, or in earlier times, copper or iron). But the need to finance wars and the resultant pressures on government budgets, along with general government incompetence and corruption, led time and time again to the gradual reduction of the commodity backing, the transition to fiat money, and frequently the end result of worthlessness.

Perhaps the future will be different. But, in a little-known book that should be required reading for anyone interested in the history of money, Ralph T. Foster, in his *Fiat Paper Money, the History and Evolution of Our Currency,* has compiled a list of some 440 paper notes that descended to worthlessness each decade over 1900–2010.[1] A great deal of what follows on Chinese paper money is based on Foster's work.

Most of the countries on Foster's list are indeed periphery countries that were newly emerged from revolutions and wars and had poorly developed institutions. But now it is the turn of so-called advanced countries, whose well-developed democratic institutions may have a fatal populist flaw, and whose currencies have not become worthless but, since 1971, have suffered serious deterioration in value. And that was before quantitative easing.

China—The Birthplace of (Worthless) Paper Money

Since so many people think China will become the world's number one economic power, perhaps it would be interesting to look at Chinese history and see what happened with paper money in that country. Most people are aware of the hyperinflation that afflicted China during WWII and the subsequent Chinese Civil War. But China's unhappy experience with paper money goes way back. Long before Guttenberg, paper (105 AD), fluid ink (400 AD), and block printing (600 AD) were invented by the Chinese. So it is only fitting that paper money was invented in China as well.

Paper money itself was first introduced in the province of Sichuan in 1024 during the Song Dynasty. According to Foster,[2] upon its introduction, the paper money was backed 29 percent by copper coins. No question, the paper money had practical advantages over the relatively clumsy strings of copper coins that were in use. This paper money experiment was successful for a while, but then military pressures from northern Jin (Jurchen) invaders (1115–1234) brought the need to print money without any copper backing. The paper money thus created eventually became worthless.

This would prove to be the first of many examples of how financing a war would lead to a *debasing* by printing paper notes without any commodity backing. Wars are never popular once the citizens realize the cost and governments cannot finance the wars completely by taxes.

The Chinese experiment with paper money was repeated with various dynasties in the centuries that followed, always with the same unhappy ending. Gold and silver were used to back later issues. The pressure of northern invaders is a recurring theme in Chinese history, but the corrupting effects of the need to print money to finance wars to fight off the invaders usually isn't mentioned. The need to finance defense, along with ignorance of monetary theory and corruption, inevitably produced an end result of paper money worthlessness. That was the story during the Song (918–1279), Jin (1115–1234), Yuan (1179–1368), and Ming (1368–1644) Dynasties. As a result of this experience, after one brief experiment the Qing Dynasty (1644–1911)—China's last imperial dynasty, as it turned out—refused to issue any paper money.

One presumes that the current People's Bank of China (PBOC) is aware of this ancient history.

There are numerous interesting facts associated with these early issues of paper money. One Jin issue carried the warning, "Counterfeiters will be decapitated," suggesting that counterfeiting of paper money also has its own long history. (Actually, similar warnings could be found on some American banknotes in the nineteenth century.) Some notes issued in the later (Southern) Song Dynasty were made of silk and perfumed. Notes were given high-sounding names like "Heavy Treasure of the Yuan-Kuang Era" or "Precious Currency of the Hsing-Ting Era." Fancy names or sweet scents notwithstanding, as the paper moneys became worthless, merchants refused to use them in spite of imperial decrees requiring that they do so. Governments don't give up easily but individuals do not willingly commit economic suicide.

Those interested in the early Chinese experience should read Foster's book.

A Persian Diversion

Prior to the introduction of fiat money, the Chinese had a long experience with rudimentary financial institutions such as pawn shops, credit loan societies, and so-called money shops where money and commodities were bought, sold, exchanged, or deposited. According to Foster, paper vouchers and promissory notes laid the groundwork for later Chinese fiat paper money systems.[3]

Countries that did not have this background did not accept the introduction of fiat paper money so easily. In the late 1200s, as they had done in China as the Yuan Dynasty, the Mongolians conquered Persia. A man named Ezuddeen Musuffer convinced the Mongolian ruler of Persia to introduce a system of fiat paper money, as had been done in China.

The Persians had been using precious metals as money for centuries but reacted violently against this introduction of paper money. Muzuffer reportedly was torn apart by a mob and thrown to the dogs.[4]

This is a story with which officials at the Fed, the Bank of England, the ECB, the Bank of Japan, and all other central banks engaged in quantitative easing might care to acquaint themselves.

The American Story—"Honest Abe" Prints Some Money

The American experience with paper money in the eighteenth and nineteenth century fits the historical pattern (i.e., fiat paper money gets issued to finance a war and then rapidly loses value). British mercantalist laws prohibiting the formation of banks in the American colonies and the coining of money had left the rebelling American states with a primitive financial system and a shortage of specie. Various coins, including those of Spanish and British origin, were used, along with various bartering systems and fiat paper money issued by the states, which always depreciated in value.

The American War of Independence, therefore, had to be financed by the issue of paper currency known as the Continental. The Continental was pure fiat money, with no pretense of convertibility into any commodity. As the war progressed, more Continentals were issued with the predictable result. By the end of the war in 1783, the Continentals had deteriorated in value to the point of worthlessness. The expression "not worth a Continental" became part of the general lexicon.

When the Founding Fathers sat down to write the US Constitution in 1787, they had this unhappy colonial and revolutionary war experience with fiat money in mind. An explicit prohibition was placed in the Constitution against the states making anything but gold and silver legal tender. State-issued paper money was banned. Congress was granted the power to coin money. But nothing was mentioned in the Constitution regarding a national paper money.

But the presumption was that the Congress of the new government would not have this power and that to issue such paper money would be unconstitutional. The American Civil War changed all that. The federal government and President Lincoln—Honest Abe, as he was known—needed money to finance the war. Lots of money. Lincoln had to choose between the survival of the United States and sound money. He chose the former and ignored the presumption that this was unconstitutional. To finance the war, Lincoln had the federal government issue fiat paper money, popularly known as greenbacks. These, of course, went to a discount against the gold dollar.

In the past, if you were going to accept the fiat money of a country at war, it was certainly better for you if the issuing country *won* that war. Winning the war is a necessary though hardly sufficient condition for some future restoration of convertibility, as the hapless holders of Continentals found out. But the Union government and Lincoln did win that war and things turned out better for greenback holders. After the war, under the administration of President Ulysses S Grant, convertibility of the greenback to gold was introduced and was finally accomplished in 1879 when the United States *de facto* joined the global gold standard. After the war ended in 1865, the Supreme Court first ruled that Lincoln's actions were indeed unconstitutional. But a later ruling just a few years later reached the opposite conclusion. One hundred years had passed since the writing of the Constitution and the American Revolution. Times change, people forget or want to forget.

This is consistent with the view that investors cannot rely on constitutions and laws to protect their wealth when governments are threatened. Constitutions are not mathematical formulas. They can always be reinterpreted to conform with prevailing needs of government and popular ideological winds.

Massive issues of fiat paper currency were also emitted by the losing Confederate side. Needless to say, Confederate currency did become worthless and there was no introduction of convertibility to gold after the war. Fiat paper moneys issued by losers of major wars are themselves sure losers.

You might ask how history would have turned out if, as the American Civil War started, President Lincoln had to deal with a federal budget that included massive unfunded entitlement liabilities and a huge federal debt. Good question.

German Hyperinflation—Is This the Prototype?

Investors today might be vaguely aware of the German hyperinflation of 1921–1923. The better informed might have seen the parabolic graph showing German prices going to levels best expressed in exponential terms at the end of the period. They perhaps heard stories of people carrying huge amounts of currency in wheelbarrows just to buy routine items. They are aware that German holders of fixed-income securities were wiped out by this incredible hyperinflation, as their investments became effectively worthless:

> On the afternoon of July 31st, 1914, the Reichsbank, on its own initiative, suspended the conversion of notes, which in the previous days had come, in great quantities, to its branches to be exchanged for gold. On August 4th the conversion of notes was suspended by law, with effect as from July 31st . . . in the two weeks from July 24th to August 7th the quantity of Reichsbank notes in circulation increased by more than two milliard marks. Thus was initiated a monetary inflation that was without precedent in history.[5]

What isn't also appreciated is that all the losers—Austria, Greece, Hungary, Poland, Romania, Russia, the Balkan nations, and Turkey—suffered hyperinflation after the war. The history of their inflations are similar to that of Germany, although as in the case of Russia, their solutions were different in each case.

The German story is a simple one. As mentioned in the previous chapter, Germany expected the war to be short, and the losers would compensate Germany. Wrong on both counts. Germany financed the war by issuing bonds to a trusting public that had dealt with a rock-solid German mark that had been convertible into gold from the 1870s until 1914. And it printed money—lots and lots of fiat paper money.

After the war, German found itself the loser with a substantial portion of its territory lost, horrendous human losses of some two million men, a massive reparations bill owed to the victorious allies, and in 1923 with its key Ruhr territory occupied by France. The massive debt and money supply buildup during the war caught up with the Germans after the war. During and immediately after the war, inflation had been a problem, but after 1921, inflation turned into hyperinflation.

The suffering and misery of the German people during this period has been well documented.[6] But what is interesting for our purposes is how investors survived during this period. The short answer—it wasn't easy.[7]

The following were investor experiences with various investment classes:

1. Holders of cash—Wiped out by inflation.
2. Holders of bonds, mortgages and other fixed rate instruments—Wiped out by the inflation. In fact, by 1921—before the worst of the hyperinflation—most German fixed-income holders who had patriotically and cluelessly bought government bonds, mortgages, and so on during the war—were *already* wiped out largely by the high inflation that cranked up in 1914 and accelerated into the hyperinflationary period beginning in 1921.
3. Holders of gold and foreign currencies such as the dollar—Maintained their wealth. But restrictions on buying these assets were a problem as the inflation intensified.
4. Holders of real estate—Mixed. Mortgages on real estate became worthless, which benefited borrowers. But various types of rent controls and price controls instituted during the inflation reduced the real value of real estate.
5. Holders of common stocks—Mixed. The German stock market exhibited extreme volatility during this period in real terms. It mattered a great deal when an investor entered the market and what he or she bought. But large corporations were, in many cases, able to obtain favorable funding from government programs and banks. Moreover, when the hyperinflation ended in 1923, the German stock market recovered and rose to new highs up until 1928. So stocks would appear to have been an imperfect second best alternative to gold and foreign currencies.

One problem that German investors had was information, or, to be specific, lack of it. The German stock exchange was closed in 1914 and did not reopen until December 1917. In fact, most of the world's major stock exchanges closed when the war started in the summer of 1914. New York and Paris reopened in December 1914, London in January 1915. Unlike investors who were citizens of their opponents, German investors thus were basically ignorant as to the value of their equity holdings for most of the war. Even when the exchange reopened, in the following years German investors had a hard time evaluating their shares or any other investment in real terms because of the inflation. Good statistics were not available. Many an investor thought he or she had made money in paper marks when in fact, in real terms they were suffering substantial losses in real terms.

A few numbers from Bresciani-Turroni might be helpful. He had several choices in measuring the inflation (i.e., domestic price data, gold as the reference point or the dollar/market exchange rate). He used all three. The different measures did not always move in exact lockstep in the short run, but in the long run they paint the same picture of accelerating inflation and economic ruin. All numbers quoted here are as Bresciani-Turroni presented them and are not always totally consistent from period to period but are indicative nonetheless.

Indexing 1913 to 100, by October 1918 Prices of Goods Produced in Germany and Prices of Goods Imported (using Bresciani-Turroni's headings) went to 239 and 214, respectively. Thus, a fixed-income buyer in 1914 would have seen the real value of his or her investment cut in half in real terms as the war came to an end. The Quantity of Money In Circulation hit an index value of 440 by October 1918, suggesting that a future acceleration of inflation could have been expected as money during the war grew over twice as fast as inflation. And accelerate it did. Reindexing October 1918 to 100, by February 1920 Internal Prices and Prices of Imported Goods exploded to 506.3 and 1898, respectively.[8] All the while the dollar/mark exchange rate was collapsing as well. Repressed inflation from price controls during wartime no doubt surfaced in 1919. After a period of relative stability in 1920–1921, helped no doubt by the short but deep Depression of 1921 experienced in the United States, the hyperinflation began. By June 1923 and setting July 1922 to 100, Internal Prices and Prices of Imported Goods hit 18194 and

22496, respectively. The numbers just got worse until the currency reform at the end of 1923.

Modern Inflation

The values of the currencies of the major advanced countries haven't gone to zero. But they have substantially deteriorated in purchasing power (when adjusted for inflation) since 1971, the year Richard Nixon chose to end US gold purchases.

The current situation that the world now faces is not a major war—although with Iran we certainly cannot dismiss that risk—but rather, democracy's tendency towards fiscal profligacy. *The central thesis of this book is that universal suffrage democracies exhibit a long-term tend toward the socialization of risk and massive unsustainable levels of debt and unfunded entitlement liabilities, and this situation will inevitably lead to defaults broadly defined.* Money printing and the destruction of their currencies is one obvious solution for governments. Quantitative easing has to be viewed as money destruction. *Quantitative easing* is just a fancy name for irresponsibly printing high-powered fiat money out of thin air. Its rationale is demand management boosting in the face of a deflationary recession, but its long-run effect will be inflationary nevertheless.

Now for some good news. An odd byproduct of all this is that the so-called advanced economies really can't afford another major war. The United States announced that it will no longer plan to fight a two-front set of wars. Historically, countries have been broke *after* wars, not before. There's a silver lining in every cloud. No pun intended. As alluded to earlier, if the US had a war with China, would it have to borrow the money from China to finance the war?

Are We Really in Deflation?

Disinflation is usually defined as a decline in the rate of inflation. Deflation defined simply means an actual negative CPI.

If you believe the official numbers, the world is definitely in disinflation. The rate of deflation is coming down almost everywhere (except India). One of the justifications for quantitative easing is that the advanced countries are supposedly now tending toward deflation. No question that this is true in most countries in the real estate sector. And no question China, Japan and other Asian countries with their mercantilist industrial policies have created global overcapacity in some industries. And no question, global deleveraging has squashed demand. The world economic activity overall is recessionary or very close to it.

But are the advanced countries really experiencing deflation? Only Japan, is the answer. Otherwise, the answer is "not yet." Take the Eurozone. Inflation year over year is up 3 percent. Go back to 1900—a randomly chosen central year in the days of the gold standard— and tell someone that 3 percent is no big deal. They would be shocked. But it's the trend that counts. And disinflation is the trend.

In *Monetary Regimes and Inflation,* Peter Bernholz examined the statistics of the cost of living for Britain, Switzerland, France, and the United States. No upward trends can be found between 1750 to 1914.[8] Today's record of disinflation would be classified as unacceptable inflation during the heyday of the gold standard.

Whether the Western countries actually have deflation remains to be seen. But so long as the pressure is downward, fixed income securities will be in a favorable environment. This will be discussed in Chapter 7.

Measuring Inflation—Are the Numbers Really Higher?

In most countries, it is governments that publish the inflation numbers. In all countries it is in the governments' interest that inflation numbers come out lower rather than higher. Some governments— Argentina currently comes to mind—flat out cheat on this. But governments don't have to cheat. In putting together price indexes, there are choices on this where either choice is intellectually respectable. Governments have a bias in favor of honest choices that are lower rather than higher. (The same argument can be made for most macro government statistics including the monthly employment numbers.)

Once again, the devil is in the accounting details. Measuring inflation is not as simple as it sounds. For example, should commodity and house prices be included in the inflation measure? Also, how should we account for quality improvements in computers and autos and the like? And how about stock and house prices? Money-created bubbles show up in unpredictable places. And what about central banks' favorite habit of subtracting out food and energy price increases—the very things consumers worry about the most—and coming up with a usually lower "core" rate of inflation? You can't eat a computer.

The world's central banks argue they can print all the high-powered money they want right now without any near-term inflationary consequences. They dismiss increases in food and energy prices as due to transient factors such as the weather or wars, and not their money printing. Not everyone would agree with this.

As mentioned, governments everywhere have an incentive to publish *lower* rates of inflation. In Argentina, you can get fined for publishing inflation numbers that differ from the artificially low generally-accepted-as-fraudulent government numbers.[9] In the United States, government-published inflation numbers are used to index Social Security payments and interest payments on Treasury Inflation-Protected bonds (TIPs). There are a host of legitimate technical questions regarding the calculation of inflation. Honest people can differ, but there is plenty of wiggle room for a less than disinterested party (i.e., governments).

Let's look a little closer at the United States. As of May, the US Consumer Price Index for All Urban Consumers (CPI-U) was up only 1.7 percent year over year. But the methodology for computing the CPI-U was changed in 1980 and then again in 1990. An advisory service called the Shadow Government Statistics (SGS) computes May CPI-U as up 9.3 percent and 5 percent (approximately), year over year, respectively, using 1980 and 1990 methodologies.[10] Quite a difference!

Frankly, although I read SGS analysis every month, I really haven't a clue as to which methodology is right. But neither did the Germans in 1914–1923 who were living under accelerating inflation and really didn't know exactly how bad things were. But I am convinced that globally, the year-over-year CPI, whatever its true reading, is going down. Disinflation is a reality.

Even accepting that the official CPIs may be understated, I believe the world is in a giant deflationary trap whereby debt, including sovereign debt and unfunded entitlement obligations, are way above their borrowers' ability to repay. Economic growth will be slow or nonexistent until the debt and the obligations are repudiated. In addition, the global economy is experiencing substantial oversupply in the area of industrial commodities and manufactured goods. The one "benefit" of all this supposedly is the current low rate of inflation. But if government-reported inflation numbers understate the true rate of inflation and inflation is really higher, that argument goes out the window. Stagflation would be a better word.

The legendary economist Irving Fisher postulated that the long-term yield on a (risk-free) bond should be the real rate of interest plus a premium equal to the expected rate of inflation. Right now, investors are receiving no such yield. Right now, people are buying US government debt as a place of refuge, regardless of yield. Woe to the world since the US 2012 elections did not go to the US conservatives; the market may suddenly decide its place of monetary refuge is no longer US government debt. Assuming the US rate of inflation is higher than that reported in the official numbers, at current rates, investors in US government bonds are already the victims of inflation default.

You may ask after reading this chapter why people would trust fiat paper money at all. I would ask the same question. Two answers can be given. The first is simply its convenience. Commodity moneys like gold coins are bulky and not convenient for commerce and industry. The public seems willing to put up with a small amount of inflation as the price of the convenience of paper money. The second is the historical amnesia that characterizes the bulk of the population. German hyperinflation? The average person might answer, "When was that?" At least until recently, the quickest way to bore MBA students was to talk about things like past bubbles and inflation. Unfortunately, in the 2000 bubble, many of the smartest MBA/money managers were doomed to repeat the history they had ignored.

A Default

In the United Kingdom, millions of workers have lost a pension battle with the government in what could be called "default with statistics." This is a default, as we see it, thanks to a government playing with inflation statistics.

The default relates to Work and Pensions Secretary Iain Duncan Smith's decision to use the consumer price index (CPI) instead of the normally faster-rising retail price index (RPI) to measure price increases influencing pension upgrades. The UK courts have now ruled that Mr. Smith's decision was proper.

The unions say the CPI choice will see the value of pensions cut by up to 20 percent. The courts said otherwise. I won't bother repeating the courts' legal reasoning here. I will only say, expect more of this.

Of course, from an investor's point of view, this type of "default" is in his or her interest—unless, of course, he or she is also receiving the pension.

Notes

1. Ralph T. Foster. *Fiat Paper Money; The History and Evolution of Our Currency* (Berkeley, CA: Foster Publishing, 2010). Readers need to be careful with Foster since he does not use the now conventional pinyin transliteration system for historical Chinese names.
2. Ibid., 6.
3. Ibid.
4. Ibid., 22.
5. Constantino Bresciani-Turroni, *The Economics of Inflation: A Study of Currency Depreciation in Post War Germany,* (Hesperides Press, 2006), 23.
6. One very good book on this is Adam Ferguson, *When Money Dies, The Nightmare of Deficit Spending, Devaluation and Hyperinflation in Weimar Germany* (New York: Public Affairs, 2010).
7. The "bible" for statistics on post–WWI German inflation is Constantino Bresciani-Turoni's *The Economics of Inflation—A Study of Currency Depreciation in Post War Germany* (London: George Allen & Unwin Ltd., 1937).
8. Peter Bernholz, *Monetary Regimes and Inflation: History, Economic and Political Relationships* (United Kingdom: Edward Elgar Publishing, 2006).
9. Juan Foreo, "Fight over Argentina's Inflation Rate Pits Government Against Private Economists," *The Washington Post* (October 31, 2011). www.washingtonpost.com/world/americas/a-quiet-battle-over-argen tinas-inflation-rate/2011/10/29/gIQAEiUjYM_story.html.
10. John Williams, "Shadow Government Statistics, Analysis Behind and Beyond Government Economic Reporting," Shadow Government Statistics, American Business Analytics & Research, LLC (December 22, 2010). www.shadowstats.com/.

An Overall Assessment of the Current Investing Scene

If all the economists were laid end to end—that's where they belong.

—Unknown

I've painted a pretty glum picture for investors in advanced Western countries. There are so many unknowns. This is the first time in history that all the major central banks have printed high-powered money without restraint. The downside from this is unknown. At the same time, major advanced democratic countries of the world are in fiscal crisis and are undergoing a massive debt deflation. The international monetary system is malfunctioning and has been a major source of global bubbles. The euro is a major source of instability. Unlike in 2008, we have no history to rely on. The outlook is so scary because several quite different scenarios are possible.

The most likely near-term scenario is for further debt deflation in the advanced Western countries, which doesn't end until the unfunded entitlements and sovereign debts are defaulted on. Global oversupply of manufactured goods and commodities is a second near-term deflationary force. Despite all the money printing, accelerating inflation is not a near-term threat.

But there is one event that could have changed everything. That was the 2012 US presidential and congressional elections. If the fiscal conservatives had swept and along with them supply-side remedies and government spending cuts, then the long-term outlook would have brightened. Well folks, that didn't happen. Unfortunately, the victory of Obama and the Democrats could bring irreparable economic damage to the United States. The Obama administration and Democratic Senate, with the wind of their reelection at their backs, will favor more government spending, higher taxes, financial repression, Luddite environmentalism, and increasing dependency of underperforming groups on the government. After WWII the US, with its Marshall Plan, Bretton Woods international monetary system, United Nations, and its magnanimous treatment of the war's losers, put the world back together. Can the US do it again or, as so many have argued, is it a spent force for which bankruptcy is inevitable? Keep in mind that sound long-term reforms could be painful in the short term.

Let's summarize what seems likely in the coming years.

The Bad News

1. There is a greater-than-average possibility of another major global crash in equity prices. This would be the result of continued debt deflation and economic recession in the advanced Western countries and China. And now, although it sounds partisan, the victory of Obama in the United States.

2. Deflation/disinflation rather than inflation is the investment reality of the near term. Debt deflation and global oversupply of goods and services in a recessionary environment will exert downward pressure on prices.

3. Advanced-country central banks will continue quantitative easing in a futile attempt to revive their economies via high-powered money printing. Macroeconomic demand management has been a failure but is something governments and economists will never give up. The global high-powered money printing is likely to have minimal effect on stimulating aggregate demand until the deleveraging is over.

4. If there is no major demand for credit, the high-powered money created in quantitative easing will just sit in the central banks as excess reserves and inflation will not be a problem. But like a sword of Damocles, it will hang over the global economy.

5. A relative slowdown in China as years of capital misallocation by the state sector will result in a lowering of total factor productivity and economic growth. China as the future engine of global growth is overrated. China's reliance on exports will be a negative in a global environment of recession and near recession.

6. A near-term continued budgetary crisis will occur in India due to populist spending measures and failure to undertake structural supply-side reforms.

7. There will be a coming massive default on advanced-country government debt and entitlement obligations, default being defined broadly.

8. In Europe, overindebtedness, excesses of socialism, and government involvement in the economy will intersect with the design flaws of the euro, prolonging the euro crisis.

9. Advanced-country governments will raises taxes to avoid default. Investors will be targets.

10. Advanced-country governments will make a concerted effort to impose various forms of financial repression including penalties on holding alternative moneys such as gold and possible restrictions and/or punitive taxes on promising foreign investments in countries not burdened by excess debt.

11. An unfavorable demographic situation will push worker/beneficiary ratios downward.

12. Environmental and water problems will continue, particularly in Asia.

The Better Washington Does, the Worse the Country Does, So Buy Washington, DC, Real Estate?

Americans have always been very proud of their capital city with its expansive parks, monuments, and public buildings. Those things are nice, but think about it. The better Washington does as a city is probably inversely correlated with how well the country does. President Obama campaigned on the idea that he would reduce the influence of lobbyists and insiders in Washington. Ha! In fact, the presence of lobbyists and their fellow travelers in Washington is not a function of presidential speeches but, rather, the size and influence of the government in economic life. If the government is a major decision maker in an industry through tax policies and regulations, then the private sector from that industry has to be in Washington to defend its interests.

(continued)

(Continued)

The fact is that under Obama the federal government has expanded massively and is likely to expand further. Regulations for the environment, finance, energy, health care—the list goes on. The new regulations have flowed copiously from the bureaucrats' PCs, and because of Obama's reelection, they will keep coming. All this has been a bonanza for Washington, DC, whose growth has dramatically outperformed that of the rest of the otherwise sickly US economy. The army of federal workers has grown, the army of lawyers and lobbyists to "enlighten" them has grown, and many firms, including those in the technology and media space, have found it useful to locate in the Washington, DC, area. If the government is the big player in a market, the private sector has to engage the government. It has to be there. According to futurologist Joel Kotkin, "California may have Facebook, Google, and Apple, but Washington has federal agencies, the defense establishment, a growing media sector, and the lobbying industry to feed upon." According to Kotkin, Washington "thrives as the marketplace for the collusional capitalist state that has been growing for decades . . ."

So since President Obama was reelected, buying Washington real estate might be a good idea. *Mal de muchos, Consuelo de tontos,* it is said in Spanish. "The bane of many, the advice of fools." If the government grows, it is the rest of the country—who don't live in Washington but pay the taxes—who will be the fools.[1]

The Good News and Some Long-Term Trends (Which Are Mostly Good News)

1. There is always the hope that governments would take a turn toward fiscal responsibility. With the reelection of President Obama and the overall loss by conservatives, this hope now becomes dimmer for the United States. I believe the 2012 election was a game changer and the wrong guys won the game.

2. New types of moneys, including gold-backed currencies, will be introduced that would be immune from government debasement. This would be combined with the reorganization of the international monetary system. All of this is postcrisis, of course. So it's years off.

3. Technological progress will accelerate as a fundamental part of human evolution. This is the driving force behind Schumpeterian creative destruction and productivity increases in advanced countries. Biotechnology, Internet-based technologies, and agriculture are areas of investment interest.

Unfortunately, Luddite attitudes by electorates and governments can slow this process.

4. Globalization, which benefits the human race as a whole, will continue, although there will be losers as with technical progress. Still, globalization is a positive sum, not a zero sum game.

5. There will be a major positive shift in the world energy equation whereby technological breakthroughs of fracking and horizontal drilling have opened up vast new potential supplies of natural gas and oil around the world. Dependence on the volatile Middle East will be reduced and the perceived need for unproductive "green" energy investments will be reduced. Energy will not be a constraint on global economic growth longer term. The one caveat here is whether the extreme environmentalist program of the Obama administration can significantly arrest the development of the energy potential of the United States.

6. Economic growth in countries in Asia and Latin America that formerly were classified as underdeveloped will continue.

7. In advanced countries, aging populations will have special needs. There's a silver lining in every cloud. The ratio of workers to retirees may be becoming less favorable but the geezers will also be a growing market. One example is dietary supplements, which, however useless, may prove to be in great demand from senior citizens seeking eternal life.

The Unknowns

1. When and if will the markets finally deny access to governmental borrowings by the "core" advanced countries (i.e., the United States, Japan, and Germany)? My best guess is that this could happen not far beyond the 2012 elections, as the market senses the entire budget process is more taxes and more spending. I have to admit, however, that there are no signs of this happening yet.

2. What effects will zero-interest-rate policies and quantitative easing have on the allocation of capital? Central bank "price controls" will inevitably have negative fallouts.

3. Will the United States embark on another major war? This could hasten the coming fiscal crisis for the United States and the global financial system. The Iranian situation is

particularly worrisome and complicated. Even if hostilities are not initiated by the United States, it is likely the United States will become involved in a major way. To be fair, on this point Obama might be less likely to start a war than Romney, whose high-testosterone demeanor and seeming inflexibility on China were a little unsettling.

4. When will inflation replace the current debt deflation? In my opinion, that day is further off than many think.

5. What will emerge on the other side of the coming crises? Will a renewed emphasis on free-market principles be the result, or will the advanced countries find themselves in an economic death spiral of ever-higher taxes, more regulations, civil unrest, and unfavorable demographics? This question is particularly important for the United States, which has served as the engine of growth and center of innovation for the entire world.

6. Will the East Asian countries abandon or at least modify their mercantilist economic models?

7. Will major wars interrupt the advance of human progress and disrupt the investment environment, as they have so often in the past?

Supply-Side Reforms Must be Enacted

I have made a strong case against overreliance on demand-side management, be it monetarist or Keynesian. Future reforms of the economic systems, outside those in the monetary sphere, should be broadly defined *supply-side* or *structural* reforms. Countries that embark on supply-side/structural reforms are long-term buys. The current fiscal austerity reforms coming out of Europe right now involving higher taxes and little meaningful reduction in government or government regulations are not the reforms we are talking about. They are wealth destroyers.

Supply-side/structural reforms would include the following (perhaps after the American elections this becomes an unattainable wish list):

1. *Simplification of the tax code and reduction in taxes.* A flat tax is the ideal. Austerity programs which increase taxes and their complexity are economy destruction programs.

2. *Removal of the myriad of work related, environmental, and gender restrictions on labor.* These restrictions vary by country but they are pervasive. Note the adjoining sidebar regarding labor regulations in Italy. These regulations are worse than Ayn Rand's worst nightmare.

3. *On the energy front, particularly in the United States, addressing energy dependency.* This would include getting rid of the regulatory barriers inhibiting the production of oil and gas and eliminating the subsidies currently being doled out by the federal government to unpromising and frequently environmentally destructive "alternative" energy sources such as wind power, which reportedly has taken a huge toll on bird populations. The United States with Canada has the potential to be the next Saudi Arabia of energy. But right now, the Obama administration is holding up the creation of new facilities for LNG export, has effectively blocked the Keystone pipeline, which would allow the shipment of Canadian oil to the American Gulf Coast, has greatly slowed the drilling of offshore oil in the Gulf of Mexico, has prevented the drilling for more oil and gas on federal lands, and has prevented the further drilling for oil in Alaska. The Obama administration has carried on a war against conventional energy sources including oil, gas, and coal, which in the United States, thanks to new technologies, are in great abundance. But the United States is not the only offender. Germany, which has been powered very efficiently and safely by nuclear facilities, has now decided to close these nuclear facilities and substitute for them unproven, unreliable, and expensive alternative energy sources. Germany is putting its own economy and that of Europe at risk with this decision.

4. *Regarding food, an approach based on science and facts.* This approach should prevail over the Luddite approaches based on irrational fears and nonscience. This is particularly true in Europe, where in my opinion the psychological and guilt hangovers from the massacres and genocides of the twentieth century have given Europeans an irrational fear of both technology and any kind of risk. Genetically modified food overall is banned in Europe, despite one study after the other finding no ill health effects. I think the Europeans subconsciously fear that some kind of genetically modified Hitler is

going to pop out of a Monsanto corn stalk. I don't want to be dogmatic about this, but most studies that I am aware of do not show organic produce to be healthier than produce grown by technologically efficient conventional methodologies. I would agree that the organic movement has made a useful contribution in raising sensitivities concerning the excessive use of pesticides. But the world population has now hit seven billion and is likely to add another billion or two before declining birthrates reverse this trend. Technology, including genetically modified food, has dramatically increased agricultural productivity. From what I have read, so-called organic farming has been proven to be far less productive in terms of output per acre. If the world had to live on only organic produce, the acreage that would be need to produce this would probably require the destruction of large amounts of as-yet-untouched wildlife habitats in the world and would dramatically increase the cost of food.

5. *On the international front, reduction of tariff and nontariff barriers and a recognition that globalization is part of technological acceleration and offers nonzero sum benefits to all mankind.* This, of course, assumes that the international monetary system is not distorted where one or more countries can set their exchange rates below market to encourage exports. This is not the case today, and thus reform of the international monetary system is really a supply-side/structural reform.

6. *Regarding health care and finance, market-oriented solutions.* The massive regulation-centered approach of the Obama administration promises that the heavy hand of bureaucracy and regulatory minutia will effectively consign to stagnation two major areas of the American economy.

Economic Delusion Italian Style—Mario Monti's "Growth Decree" versus 40 years of Labor Regulations

Italian Prime Minister Mario Monti has issued a new "growth decree" to revive Italy's stagnant economy. Among other things, the 185-page plan proposes loans for corporate R&D, tax credits for businesses that hire employees with advanced degrees, and reduced headcounts at select government ministries. It even envisages some privatizations.

Will Monti's plan solve Italy's economic problems? Doubtful. Italy, like all the southern European countries, has tied up its businesses and entrepreneurs into a labyrinth of bureaucratic knots. The knots are unbelievably detailed and costly and would discourage any normal person from ever considering becoming an entrepreneur in Italy.

For example according to newspaper reports:

1. The entrepreneur must pay at least two-thirds of his (or her) employees' social security costs.
2. After employee 16 is hired, it becomes virtually impossible to dismiss any employee.
3. Once employee 11 is hired, the entrepreneur must submit a report to the national authorities outlining possible health and safety hazards to which employees are subjected. This exhaustive report touches on things like work-related stress, gender and racial problems, measures taken to prevent risk, and so on.
4. After employee 16 is hired, then come the unions, and their many representatives, all of whom must be consulted on company decisions.
5. After employee 16 is hired, the next employee must be disabled. (I don't know if Italians game the system by self-mutilation.)
6. After employee 51 is hired, at least 7 percent of the workers must be disabled.

I could go on. The point is that the social welfare philosophy and resulting regulations that pervade Western Europe—especially the South—constitute an incredible weight on the economy. This weight has been imposed by well-meaning politicians over time who have no appreciation for, nor understanding of, how private businesses or markets work.

Frankly, I cannot see making major investments in Europe until it dawns on Europe how a market economy really works. I am an optimist deep down. I believe one day that the supply-side or structural reforms will be undertaken. Europe, after all, is filled with well-educated, intelligent people. They can't be stupid forever.

Taxation—Americans versus Everybody Else

In the years to come, we can expect not only increases in taxes but patriotic guilt tax trips from politicians. Don't pay attention to these. Why should investors feel a special moral responsibility to pay for generally wasteful government spending and debt that they were opposed to in the first place?

An obvious investment strategy for investors everywhere is to move money to jurisdictions in which taxes are low or nonexistent and not likely to rise dramatically. This is easier said than done and depends on the tax regime prevailing in an investor's home country. Taxation of capital gains and interest income is not consistent across countries.

There are many illegal ways to avoid taxes. This book is not recommending any of these, although it seems very obvious that tax policies in most advanced countries are extremely burdensome and counterproductive in an economic sense. Raising these taxes is the wrong policy. But the law is the law. Tax revenue departments in most countries are becoming more and more aggressive in enforcing their tax laws. The United States is taking a global approach to tax evasion by pressuring other countries to turn in Americans who keep money abroad to avoid American taxes.

Virtually all advanced Western countries tax their resident citizens on income on investments made abroad. However, in most countries if the investor becomes a nonresident of his home country then foreign income is not taxed. So one solution followed by many wealthy investors is to move abroad but retain their home country citizenship.

Americans do not have this option. The United States embraces a global tax policy for individuals whereby Americans are liable for taxes on foreign income whether or not they reside in the United States. Thus, investing and living abroad for Americans does not legally reduce their tax burden. Americans must move abroad and take the extra step of acquiring new citizenship and renouncing their American citizenship. On financial grounds, this step makes a lot of sense for wealthy American investors. Still, this is not a practical option for the majority of American investors and is a complicated technical and legal subject that we will not dwell on further here.

It is also true that most Americans would regard giving up citizenship as unpatriotic and disloyal. If things get really bad, expect this attitude to change. Capital, both financial and human, will go to where they are most wanted. When France under Louis XIV revoked the Edict of Nantes in 1685, talented French Protestants (Huguenots) moved out of France to more hospitable places like England and Holland. A devastating economic blow was dealt to France by this self-destructive act. Similarly, in the late fifteenth century Jews were driven from Spain and Portugal, thus depriving those countries of another valuable and talented group. Will the United States, with punitive taxation, deteriorating educational institutions, and protectionist campaigns against outsourcing drive out its financial and human capital? Come to think of it, will the French President Hollande, with his 75 percent income tax proposal on high earners, once again drive France's talented people out?

We are already seeing this phenomenon of tax-oriented migration on an internal level in the United States. There has been a continuous move out of people and businesses from high-tax states like California, Illinois, and New York to lower-tax states.

Recent "reforms" in the United States have seen the introduction of burdensome reporting requirements for taxes on Americans with assets abroad and on financial institutions dealing with Americans. Americans may find it difficult in some countries to find financial institutions that will deal with them at all. Longer term, certain financial institutions may decide to special in American customers and their special reporting problems.

Note

1. Joel Kotkin, "The Expanding Wealth of Washington," *Forbes*. (March 19, 2012). http://www.forbes.com/sites/joelkotkin/2012/03/19/the-expanding-wealth-of-washington/print/

7

Investment Survival in the Age of Defaults

Resolve not to be poor: whatever you have, spend less. Poverty is a great enemy to human happiness; it certainly destroys liberty, and it makes some virtues impracticable, and others extremely difficult.

—Samuel Johnson

Now comes the hard part—how to preserve your wealth in the coming crisis.

Caveat: If the Obama proposals to significantly increase taxes on dividends and capital gains go through, this would be a huge negative for the US and possibly all global markets.

I will start with a disclaimer. Cataclysmic events don't happen often, and when they do most pundits are taken by surprise. I read lots of authors and get lots of newsletters on investing. I am continuously amazed at the certainty these authors have regarding the investing future, particularly since they don't usually agree with one another and, looking back, their mistakes are plentiful. The "illusion of knowledge," as historian Daniel Boorstin put it, is very dangerous. But it sells books.

Wall Street, on average, tends to be cautiously optimistic. Sell-side Wall Street economists, strategists, and analysts are not paid to be pessimists. If they are too optimistic and wrong, they are forgiven. If they are too pessimistic and wrong, they are fired.

OK. Here's my version of a disclaimer. Investment forecasting can be hazardous to your fiscal health. But investors don't have a choice. They must do it anyway. Buy and hold equity strategies for the US have worked over the very long run. But who lives that long? Periods of dramatic underperformance—like 1929–1933 and 1966–1981—are not rare. And other less fortunate countries—like Japan and Germany, which suffered crushing defeats in wars—offer more somber histories. And peacetime Japan from 1991 until the present has not been good for buy and hold equity investors either.

So let's begin with a forecast of asset classes that may outperform in the coming years.

Asset Classes for Investment Survival

What follows is not the typical laundry list of stocks or alternative investments to buy. And it is certainly not a short-term trading guide. Rather, it is an assessment of what asset classes might preserve wealth and what long-term trends might offer opportunities in what looks like a difficult investing environment in the years to come. Some of these assets may be relatively cheap right now. Some may be expensive. I don't want to get into a discussion about price-to-earnings ratios (PEs) or current valuations or whether near term the global markets are ready to go up or down. This book is not about whether the United States will have a double-dip recession in 2013(the odds do favor this) or whether China will have a hard or soft landing.

2008 showed that when the markets panic—and no doubt, some panics do lie ahead—the markets throw even the best stocks out the window. Timing is for the reader to decide. Sophisticated investors may want to consider hedging activities such as selling out-of-the-money calls on stocks they own. What follows below is a discussion of longer-term trends and investor strategies in an environment of sovereign debt defaults (broadly defined) and predator governments desperately seeking funds any way they can get them.

Cash

Let's start out with the first asset every portfolio should have some of—CASH. There are so many uncertainties. Some cash, it seems to me, is advisable. It's just common sense. Investment advisers don't usually recommend cash, especially in a zero-interest-rate environment. Why pay someone to invest your money in something with a zero return?

But what kind of cash?

Cash 1 (Dollars, Euros, Pounds)

For this discussion, we define Cash 1 as cash or near cash investments in dollars, euros, or pounds. In many ways, Cash 1 seems like the logical asset choice for investors whose home currencies are the dollar, the euro, or the British pound. A major financial crisis will arrive when the core advanced countries like the United States have trouble funding their debt. Markets as they did in 2008 may crash around the world. Then with all your cash you can start buying and pick up bargains. A simple strategy: stay in cash until that day arrives. (Although nobody's going to ring a bell and tell you when that day is.)

The problem with that is that cash—whether it's dollars, euros, or British pounds—in nominal terms earns near zero. And in the United States and other countries that trivial return is taxed! Check out your favorite money market fund. In real terms—that is subtracting out current CPI inflation and the tax insult—cash earns a negative return. Cash, to some extent, is a bet on deflation.

Government statistics ex-Japan in the major countries show current CPI inflation running between 2 and 3 percent on an annual basis (3 to 4 percent in the case of the United Kingdom). Making for an even darker picture, central bankers around the world are openly wishing for *higher* inflation. Nevertheless, if Japan is our near-term future, then deflation is a possibility.

If inflation persists, the longer you hold Cash 1, the more you lose. Just to take the opposite side of my own recommendation, Table 7.1 gives some idea of how quickly the losses build up in terms of real purchasing power. $1,000,000 in year zero drops to $940,900 in three years assuming 3.0 percent inflation and 0 percent interest rates, but ignoring taxes. Holding cash with 0 percent interest rates and 10 percent inflation (remember the 5 percent to 9 percent that Shadow Government Statistics calculates for the US CPI under older methodologies) would be downright catastrophic, as Table 7.1 shows. If the crisis is five years out, people waiting in Cash 1 will be even poorer when the big day comes. When a central banker says he has an inflation target of 2 percent or more, with today's near-zero interest rates he's telling the holders of his currency—consider it a product that he is in charge of—that he wants them to *lose* money by holding his product.

Of course, what the table doesn't show is if we had actual *deflation*. Then, in terms of real purchasing power, holders of cash would experience an *increase*. In a deflationary or near deflationary

Table 7.1 Cash Loss of Purchasing Power $1 Million

Inflation	Year 0	Year 1	Year 2	Year 3	Year 4	Year 5
1%	$1,000,000	990,000	980,100	970,299	960,596	950,990
2%	$1,000,000	980,000	960,400	941,192	922,368	903,921
3%	$1,000,000	970,000	940,900	912,673	885,293	858,734
4%	$1,000,000	960,000	921,600	884,736	849,347	815,373
10%	$1,000,000	900,000	810,000	729,000	656,100	590,490

environment, holding cash in US dollars may be the best conservative strategy.

Investors in cash are fighting with bankrupt predator states. The various monetary interventions (i.e., QE1, QE2, and QE3; LTRO; Operation Twist II), are funding these states. They have reduced the cost of paying interest on government debt even as the total amount of government debt continues to rise. They are manipulating investors to take risks they might not otherwise take. The monetary interventions are distorting the cost of capital, increasing the role of government in the economy at the expense of the private sector, and possibly setting the stage for big inflations in the future and impoverishing the investor class.

But there's one more problem. If the crisis does come, your dollars and euros and pounds may depreciate against gold and against other currencies whose countries don't have a huge debt crisis. So if you hold Cash 1, make sure you don't include those fiscally strong countries in your future travel plans. You won't be able to afford them.

OK, I've run through all the negatives. But it's still common sense. If the world is as unsafe and unsure as I think it is and the crisis doesn't drag on for ten years, you might be glad you had your cash.

Note we've left the Japanese yen out of what we call Cash 1. The Japanese have huge foreign exchange reserves and are running zero to slightly negative CPI inflation. Ignoring the practical difficulties for non-Japanese, holding cash in yen, at the moment anyway, carries less risk than the Cash1 currencies. In fact, for Japanese investors, holding cash near term has been a *smart* decision. Again, as has been argued, most observers, particularly Western observers, are clueless about Japan. Japan is supposed to be collapsing as we speak from a debt overload. But it isn't.

Cash 2 (Global Financial Centers)
But there are other cash alternatives. Who said you needed to keep all your cash in dollars, euros, or pounds? There are alternatives, if only to diversify partly out of the major currencies.

Ideally, we're looking for global financial centers for whose major business—finance—depends on the soundness of their currencies. If a country's major business is money, then it is more likely to take care of its money. You don't take the attitude of the Fed, the Bank of England, the ECB, and the Bank of Japan that there are macroeconomic "greater goods" that take precedence over the soundness of your currency.

What we want from Cash 2 countries is a safe place to warehouse money where the Cash 2 currencies appreciate against the deteriorating global reserve currencies, including the US dollar. If we can find assets in these financial centers that offer reasonable yields, so much the better.

My ideal Cash 2 financial center has a long list of positive attributes:

- As mentioned, a principal business of a Cash 2 financial money center must be money. Of course, as we will see in the case of Switzerland, there are no countries where the money business is the sole driver of national policy.
- The country will have a well-developed financial system including banks and a significant securities exchange.
- The country must be above reproach as far as fiscal soundness and debt ratios go.
- Its banking system must be rock solid with no Minsky-like bubbles weighing it down. In other words, the country's private and public sectors must not be in the throes of debt deflation as are the major Western countries.
- It must be wide open to the ingress and egress of foreign capital.
- It must have a long-established legal tradition favorable to the protection of capital.
- It must have complete flexibility in managing its money, should there be widespread weakening of the major reserve currencies including the US dollar, the euro, and the Japanese yen.
- Corruption should not be a major problem.
- Its populace should be well educated and reasonably happy (no racial, ethnic, or caste strife). The money business is a *knowledge* industry.
- Populist urges should be under control.
- Finally, there must be a reasonable expectation that the country's currency will hold its value and even appreciate in a world where the major reserve currencies (i.e., the dollar and the euro) are losing value.

The list of countries that might qualify for Cash 2 is not a long one. Singapore, Hong Kong, and Switzerland are this book's recommendations. Stashing some of your money there or going long their currencies while waiting for the financial Apocalypse may be a good idea. There is one major risk. These global financial center economies are highly integrated into the global economy. If the global economy tanks in a major way, they will be hurt. But so will the rest of the world.

Australia and Canada are fiscally responsible countries with a lot of positives. But money (i.e., finance) isn't their main business. They are not finance-driven countries. Their dependence on commodities, energy, and China are near-term negatives. We'll put them in the Cash 3 category. Financially solvent countries like Chile may not welcome significant inflows of capital. Panama, definitely an emerging financial center as onerous US laws drive off Latin wealth management business, uses the US dollar and doesn't have a significant stock market. And, although things have improved significantly in Panama, it has a very checkered past as far as political stability goes. Dubai is an emerging financial center but it is still recovering from its huge real estate hangover. And Dubai, located in the Persian Gulf with Iran only a little more than a nine iron away across the Persian Gulf, is not in the happiest neighborhood.

There are a number of ways for individual investors to get their money into these Cash 2 countries. Of course, they can always fly there and enjoy life as they open their accounts. But the global economy provides lots of options. Even Americans get a break. Local banks may not want to deal with them but a number of American brokerage firms are now offering the ability to trade foreign stocks on line and will allow clients to carry cash balances in foreign currencies. ETFs exist to go long the majority of currencies (and, thus, short the US dollar). American brokerage firms will include all foreign transactions placed through them in their annual 1099 IRS form for Americans. Presumably, similar services are available in other non-US countries.

For those readers unfamiliar with the following three Cash 2 countries, the following is a brief description:

Singapore
Politics and History For some people, Singapore is a sticky, tropical, authoritarian state that whips its citizens when they are bad, gags the press, and bans chewing gum.

Caricature to be sure. But I would say—with tongue only partly in cheek—that even this caricature should pique the serious investor's attention. After all, who wants to deal with a banker who chews gum? Singapore is not Venice Beach (California) and hopefully never will be. And yes, Steve Jobs probably wouldn't have liked to live there. Although Edward Saverin, a Facebook cofounder who nowadays is more of a *rentier* than creator like Jobs or Facebook CEO Mark Zuckerberg, has taken Singaporean citizenship. Perhaps Singapore's vaunted Changi Airport should have a sign—*Give me your rich, your persecuted capital, yearning to be free.*

Singapore is well on its way to becoming the Switzerland of Asia. It welcomes foreign capital and the wealthy people of the world. It is becoming a major money management center for the new wealth of Asia. The visitor is impressed by Singapore's ultramodern skyline, which now includes the iconic Marina Bay Sands towers. Marina Bay Sands is one of two casino/entertainment/integrated resorts that now attract visitors to the city-state. Only Dubai and Abu Dhabi can rival Singapore for architectural daring. The ultramodern skyline by the way coexists with a number of well-preserved colonial era buildings. All of this in a garden-like tropical setting as Singapore promotes itself as "The Garden City." Which indeed it is.

This is a highly literate, wired country. English is the lingua franca and the language of finance, business, education, government and law. But thanks to the government's bilingual educational policies and the country's multiethnic makeup (as of 2011 74.1 percent Chinese, 9.2 percent Indian, 13.4 percent Malay), Mandarin, Tamil, and Malay are also official languages and are widely spoken as well.

One reason, by the way, that the print media is controlled is to avoid interracial strife. The policy has worked, as the race riots of the 1960s have been replaced by a general respect and camaraderie among Singapore's various groups. (Recently, when a PRC Chinese couple objected to a Singaporean Indian neighbor's kitchen's curry smells, it seemed like the entire nation rose up to support the Indian neighbor's right to cook with curry and thus perfume the neighborhood with its olfactory charms.) The Reverend Al Sharpton, the notorious and outspoken African American leader in the United States, would have a short career in Singapore. Singapore is a meritocracy, and racial quotas and race baiting are taboo. The contrast with Malaysia, with its bumiputra policy of racial quotas favoring Malays, could not be more acute.

The economic numbers contrasting Singapore and Malaysia favor Singapore more every year.

Singapore is a parliamentary republic with a Westminster system of unicameral parliamentary government. Singapore has been run since independence in 1966 by one party, the People's Action Party (PAP). The PAP takes a very technocratic, nonpopulist approach to governing, and frankly, it has done a damn good job. Elections are held regularly and, yes, the electoral structure and the print media are moderately "tilted" in the PAP's favor. But there is no voter fraud, and if the electorate really wanted to kick the PAP out, they could. In fact, in last year's general election, the PAP had a tough fight. Accusations that Singapore is a dictatorship are gross exaggerations. The winds of populism (unfortunately, in our opinion) have infected parts of Singapore's younger population that doesn't remember the struggles of earlier years. But the next election is probably four years off. James Madison would probably like Singapore.

Singapore as a former British colony has inherited a British-based legal system and the English language. For a brief period 1963–1965, Singapore was part of the Federation of Malaysia. But due to Chinese–Malay rivalries, it was kicked out. Lee Kwan Yew, Singapore's leader and the man who could be regarded as the founder of modern Singapore, openly cried on television when this happened. He saw a bleak future for his little island, devoid of resources and industry. But MM (Minister Mentor), as he has been more recently called, was wrong. Singapore has boomed. People and brains are more important than resources. MM would cry again if he were told today that Singapore suddenly was back in Malaysia.

Finally, there is the subject of small. Singapore is a tiny city-state with a population, including foreigners, of 5.2 million. It is not too much of an exaggeration to say that everybody knows everybody else. Unlike in the big semi-socialist Western countries, where dictums issued on high for the entire country result in endless economic inefficiencies, one size can fit all in such a small place. Information does flow on a person-to-person level. Feedback, a necessary ingredient in economic efficiency, happens informally in small places.

Parenthetically, the Singapore model, contrary to the occasional statements of admiring leaders from China, does not scale.

It works because it is small. China is too big to adapt the Singapore model, at least not without extensive modifications.

We think that small is a good antidote to democracies' fatal attraction of populism. When countries are small, people can appreciate firsthand the stupidities of government. They instinctively know that they, the local people, must pay for everything their politicians so graciously give them.

The other antidote to populism is culture. Singapore's core culture is Confucian Chinese, which stresses obedience to authority, conformity, hard work, and study. Just what you want in a banker. Just what an investor wants in an electorate.

Economic Structure   Singapore is a major banking center and shipping nexus. Shipping and banking originate together. The latter is necessary to support the former. Its key location on the Straits of Malacca and now its centrally located modern airport give it a major presence in logistics. Its banks rode through the 2008 crisis without a hitch, as they did through the 1998 Asian crisis. Nonperformers are not a significant problem, and the super prudent Singapore government and prudent banking practices have made sure that nonperformers are not a problem.

Singapore, by the way, is not just in the money and shipping businesses. Almost 12 million tourists visited Singapore in 2010. Health care and biomedical sciences are also important. The recent addition of casinos—*integrated resorts,* as they are officially called in Singapore—helps alter Singapore's traditional image of being dull and, in the case of Marina Bay Sands, offers some spectacular architecture.

Singapore is also an educational center. Singapore has a goal of establishing itself at a *global schoolhouse,* enrolling 150,000 foreign students by 2015. Education is a key industry for knowledge intensive money. Singapore's bilingual educational policy—particularly the emphasis on English/Mandarin capabilities for its ethnic Chinese population—is perfectly suited to the needs of knowledge industries such as the global money business. Table 7.2 shows a quick summary of Singapore statistics.

The reader will view these figures and notice that the sovereign debt/GDP ratio is quite high and is quoted on a gross basis. So why am I recommending this country? The angel, in this case, is in the details. Singapore, as far as is known, has zero foreign sovereign

Table 7.2   A Quick Summary of Singapore Statistics

General Government Gross Debt/debt/GDP	107.6%
General Government Expenditure/GDP	17.6%
Current account/GDP	21.9%
GDP per capita (US dollars)	$49270
Consumer price inflation	5.25%
Unemployment rate	2.03%
Official Reserve Assets (US dollars)	$244 billion
Population	5.3 million

Sources: IMF-2011 data

debt. It generally runs a significantly positive primary budget surplus. But there apparently are three reasons for Singapore's official gross public debt figures to be high. First, Singapore has a compulsory retirement scheme called the Central Provident Fund (CPF). All citizens and permanent residents contribute to the CPF. The government issues debt, which the CPF purchases. So far, this sounds like just another potentially bankrupt social security system. But there's a big difference. The government then borrows the money raised via issues of nontradable Singapore Government Securities and puts it into two sovereign wealth funds, the Government Investment Corporation (GIC) and Temasek. GIC invests all its funds abroad. Temasek invests in Singapore companies and in foreign companies. The whole process could use more transparency—for example, it's not clear if some of Temasek's investments in government-controlled Singapore corporations are profitable—but overall, the system is totally different from Western pay-as-you-go systems that fund their own governments. Although the IMF doesn't publish a net sovereign debt/ GDP number for Singapore—it is curious that it does not—it seems clear that Singapore's net number is way below the gross number of 100.8 percent.

Second, roughly 60 percent of public companies in Singapore reportedly have majority government ownership. These companies are not necessarily unprofitable but their debt is added to overall statistics of government borrowing.

Third, Singapore sells some government paper to offer liquidity in the local money market.

The Singapore Dollar   Being small brings its own set of problems vis-à-vis global capital flows. If the world "discovers" Singapore, like Switzerland (to be discussed) too much cash will flow in thus endangering local export industries. The money business may be Singapore's most promising business but it is not the only business.

The Singapore dollar is managed by the Monetary Authority of Singapore (MAS) against an undisclosed basket of currencies. The country's large foreign reserve position combined with its current account surplus and relative large foreign reserves suggest that the currency is a sound bet on a long-term basis. Right now, the markets seem to still put Singapore in the "risk-on" category. Great news for investors who think Singapore doesn't really belong in this category.

Nevertheless, Singapore is currently running a CPI inflation rate in the 5 percent area. This is higher than the current rates in the deflationary West. The country's high level of reserves, combined with this higher inflation rate, suggest that the Sing dollar could be allowed to appreciate further.

Some Singapore Investment Suggestions   The risks for Singapore are its position in the entire global economy. Singapore is a child of globalization. Singapore is sensitive to economic events in China, the United States, and Europe. But we are not recommending Singapore stocks per se. We are recommending Singapore as a place to put cash and ride out the global storms. The reward, hopefully, will be a solid currency that appreciates as the Western currencies fall on hard times.

Conservative investors can park cash in Sing dollars and earn whatever meager interest rates are currently available and—sooner or later—own an appreciating currency.

For those who wish to take on more risk, there are some alternatives. One is Singapore REITs (Real Estate Investment Trust). Singapore has its own thriving stock exchange, and it is the home of a number of REITs. Unless there is a total collapse of the global economy and a massive global credit squeeze as in 2008, Singapore REITs offer reasonably attractive returns with a reasonable level of safety. Of course, vacancies are likely to rise in the coming months. With Singapore REITS you get returns currently of 5 to 7 percent in Singapore dollars plus you are long Singapore dollars. Again, there is the risk that in the event of a major global crash, Singapore

REITs will decline in price as vacancies rise and rents decline in a major way.

A second, riskier alternative would be to buy shares in Singapore banks. Singapore banks are relatively well capitalized and carry reasonable dividends. They are not the large global banks; later in this chapter it will be explained why those should be avoided. Remember, the "raw material" of a bank's business is money. The Singapore dollar, in our opinion, will hold its value if the dollar and the euro suffer a major decline.

Switzerland
Politics and History   As we said, Singapore is becoming the Switzerland of Asia. Switzerland, on the other hand, already is . . . Switzerland. Too bad everybody knows this. An investment is always less attractive when everybody knows about it. And in an age of massive global capital flows, Switzerland's virtues almost become liabilities when the entire world, including ourselves, want to put money there and/or buy its currency. Highly prosperous Switzerland is synonymous with banking, sobriety, and a rock-solid currency.

Switzerland restores our battered faith in democracy, as this is one country that is fully democratic and fiscally responsible. You can carp about Singapore's authoritarian side, but no such objections have been leveled at Switzerland. In fact, its federal canton system actually has features of direct democracy that would probably make James Madison cringe. Switzerland is living proof that our theory that the fatal attraction of populism will inevitably undermine functioning democracies is not *always* right. Thank goodness.

The similarities between Switzerland and Singapore are amazing. Both are small. Both have conservative, core cultures. Like Singapore, Switzerland is multiethnic and multilingual with German-speaking Swiss at 65 percent, French 20 percent, Italian 7.5 percent, and Romansh 0.5 percent. English is not a Swiss official language but it has widespread usage in Switzerland and to some extent serves as a link among the various ethnic groups. As is Singapore, Switzerland is a meritocracy and there are no downtrodden minorities demanding special treatment and more government services. The core culture is conservative and thrifty—in this case German-based, as opposed to Singapore's Chinese Confucian. And French-speaking Geneva, it will be recalled, was the home of "fun-loving" John Calvin. This author can personally remember dining in Geneva and a dinner companion being berated by the waiter for not finishing her cheese. The spirit of John Calvin lives on!

Both Switzerland and Singapore require adult males to serve in the military. Both countries feel they need a strong military to discourage larger and, at least in the past, sometimes unfriendly neighbors. As we have argued, nobody likes money men, especially rich ones. In Switzerland's case, the unfriendly neighbors were Germany, both under Kaiser Wilhelm II and later Adolf Hitler, and Italy under Benito Mussolini. The Nazis had a plan, never executed, called *Operation Tannenbaum* to invade Switzerland.

Switzerland's educational system is world renowned. The university system is known for its research in the medical and science area. Several major pharmaceutical companies, including Novartis and Hoffman-La Roche, are based in Switzerland. The Global Competitiveness Report (GCR), a yearly report published by the World Economic Forum, in 2011–2012 ranked Switzerland as number one in the world. Singapore was number two! (Hong Kong, which we will discuss in the next section, was number eleven.)

Economic Structure   Switzerland's financial sector plays a central role in its economy with regards to labor, the creation of value, and tax revenue. The financial sector is responsible for roughly 12 percent of the gross domestic product and employs 6 percent of the workforce. Furthermore, this sector contributes to approximately 10 percent of the country's income and corporate tax revenue. Switzerland's general stability accounts for its international reputation as a preferred provider of financial services. Important competitive advantages are, for instance, its political constancy and the stability of its currency. Switzerland also plays a leading global role in asset management: roughly one third of all private assets invested abroad are managed by Swiss banks. Table 7.3 shows a quick summary of Switzerland statistics.

As can be seen, the numbers shout out financial prudence, low debt, and wealth. Switzerland's statistics are consistent with its image.

The Swiss Franc   The Swiss franc, like gold, has been seen as a traditional refuge against monetary instability. As can be seen from the chart below, the monetary base of Switzerland virtually flatlined from 2002 to 2008. The Swiss franc has a record of constant appreciation against the euro and the dollar. Inflation has centered in the zero area.

Table 7.3   A Quick Summary of Switzerland Statistics

General Government Net Debt/GDP/GDP	25.9%
General Government Expenditure/GDP	33.4%
Current account/GDP	10.5%
GDP per capita (US dollars)	$83072
Consumer price inflation	.23%
Unemployment rate	3.92.84%
Official Reserve Assets (US dollars)	$479.8 billion
Population	8.0 million

Sources: IMF-2011 statistics

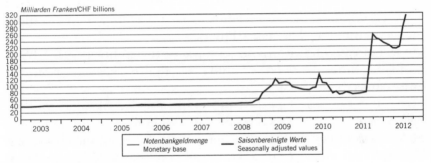

Figure 7.1   **Monetary Base**
Source: Swiss National Bank

But on September 6, 2011, the Swiss did something very un-Swiss. In response to an avalanche of incoming funds fleeing the euro crisis and pushing up the Swiss franc, Switzerland effectively devalued its currency and pegged its currency to the euro at SF 1.20 = 1 euro. The SNB had concluded that the rise in the franc had put Swiss industries in an intolerable position. The SNB threatened to buy "unlimited" quantities of foreign currency to push down the value of the franc. The money business had to take a back seat to the rest of the economy. But after this announcement and the SNB began buying currencies, the monetary base leapt upward. The SNB, the world's paragon of monetary virtue, had just done its own quantitative easing. See Figure 7.1.

The franc peaked in August 2011 as the market began to react to comments from the Swiss that a peg might be coming. Investors who bought the Swiss franc in August could have been down as much as twenty five percent. For the moment, investors, who had looked to the Swiss franc as a refuge in perilous times, were handed huge losses. The Swissy, as the franc is sometimes called, had tanked big time.

So why should anyone consider parking money in Swiss francs or going long the currency? Several reasons can be given in response to this. First, the worst in terms of currency depreciation is probably behind us. Second, the Swiss tradition of financial soundness, low government involvement in the economy—all the things that made it number one in the GCR report—have not gone away. This intervention was not a Keynesian Bernanke type of stimulus. It was almost a "wartime" response to an external event. Third, it seems inconceivable that on a long-term basis the Swiss franc's fate will be tied to the euro. Unless of course the euro transmogrifies into the New Deutschmark.

In the case of Switzerland, because of the troubles with UBS in particular in the 2008 crises, unlike Singapore we would avoid the Swiss banks themselves.

Hong Kong
Politics and History   Put money into an entity that since 1997 has been part of authoritarian still officially communist China? Isn't that crazy? Maybe not.

Hong Kong became a British colony in 1840 and was returned to China in what is now called the Handover in 1997. Hong Kong operates under a "constitution" called the Basic Law hammered out in negotiations between the British and the Chinese prior to the Handover. The Basic Law guarantees to Hong Kong basic freedoms including freedom of speech, English common law, property rights, and its own currency and banking system. "One country, two systems" is the operating principle and is guaranteed to stay in place for at least fifty years. The English language has an official status along with Chinese and is used in the courts, the financial sector, and the university system (but not unfortunately by the majority of taxi drivers). Contrary to the prognostications of the gloom and doomers at the time of the Handover, China has lived up to its agreement with the British and indeed the Comrades have respected the Basic Law.

Western visitors to Hong Kong have a hard time noticing much change since the Handover in 1997. Hong Kong has the freest media in Asia. You have to have a visa and fill out forms when you go from Hong Kong to China, as if you were entering a separate country. You can be annoyed by Falun Gong devotees in Hong Kong just as you can on the streets of New York. Judges still wear wigs and Hong Kong's frenetic nightlife continues in full swing. The colonial era names remain in place as, for example, Victoria Harbour is still Victoria Harbour (except it is gradually disappearing thanks to its being filled in to create more buildable land. But that's another story). Contrast this with India, where, for example, the venerable Prince of Wales Museum in Mumbai (itself formerly known as Bombay) has been renamed the Chhatrapati Shivaji Maharaj Vastu Sangrahalaya.

The Western press, including the local soft-left English-medium *South China Morning Post,* is constantly complaining that Hong Kong does not have universal suffrage. The departed British, who never introduced universal suffrage in Hong Kong themselves, have been among the loudest complainers. But James Madison might not complain. People worried in 1997 that the Peoples Liberation Army (PLA) would come marching in and turn off Hong Kong's free market lights. But that hasn't happened. The PLA regiment that is stationed in Hong Kong has remained quietly and decorously in its barracks, unlike some of the British lads stationed in the city in pre-Handover days who were known to occasionally misbehave on Friday nights while enjoying the dissolute pleasures of the city's nightlife.

Hong Kong *has,* however, been invaded since 1997. Not by the PLA but by an "army" of populists who, if they had their way, would introduce a European-style welfare state and replace Hong Kong's traditional and highly successful noninterventionist free market policies. It seems to be of no interest to them that Europe is going broke. Already, a minimum wage law has been put in place. Bankruptcy-envy is a phenomenon that the good Doctor Freud should investigate. But so far overall Hong Kong's semi-democracy has managed to hold off the populists. Hong Kong now has a Legislative Council consisting of seventy representatives. Thirty-five are elected by universal suffrage from what are called geographic constituencies. The other thirty-five are elected in what are called functional constituencies. In a somewhat-opaque process, in those constituencies the representatives are elected by electors from professional associations.

The head of Hong Kong's government is called the chief executive (the nefarious colonial term "governor" departed with the British). The Chief Executive (CE) is elected by a 1,200 member Election Committee that resembles in a vague way the American Electoral College in its early days. Critics say the Election Committee as well as the professional associations are dominated by wealthy individuals who yield to Beijing's wishes. They are right. But from James Madison and investors' point of view, this might not be such a bad thing. Beijing nowadays worries more about how to help its citizens get rich rather than imposing revolutionary doctrine. Louis Vuitton and Chanel have replaced Marx and Engels. Beijing has promised to give Hong Kong universal suffrage. Look for Beijing to procrastinate on that.

Economic Structure   Finance accounts for over 25 percent of Hong Kong's economy, with international trade and tourism next. Long gone are the low-wage factories, which have migrated to China and elsewhere. (Because this happened so fast in Hong Kong, it left an older, poorer population of ex-factory workers behind. This is a problem that the populists have exploited.) With the increasing wealth of the Mainland Chinese and their obsession with Western brands, along with the fact that there are no tariffs on imports into Hong Kong, the visiting comrades have turned Hong Kong into what might be called the Great Mall of China. Selling European luxury brands to an ever-increasing number of Mainland tourists has become big business in Hong Kong.

Hong Kong is one of the great financial centers of the world, along with London and New York. Banking, stock and derivatives trading, money management—Hong Kong does it all. The fact that the Hong Kong dollar has been one of the world's predictable and reliable currencies has been a major attraction in making Hong Kong a major financial center and IPO center. Table 7.4 shows a quick summary of Hong Kong statistics.

Table 7.4 shows an economy that is fiscally prudent and with low government involvement but, like Singapore, with a current rate of inflation in the 5 percent year over year area. The question

Table 7.4   A Quick Summary of Hong Kong Statistics

General Government Gross Debt/ /GDP	33.83%
General Government Expenditure/GDP	20.3%
Current account/GDP	5.3%
GDP per capita (US dollars)	$34,259
Consumer price inflation	5.3%
Unemployment rate	3.4%
Official Reserve Assets (US dollars)	$244 billion
Foreign reserves per capita (US dollars)	$41633
Population	7.1 million

Sources: IMF-2011 data

again needs to be asked why Hong Kong is running higher inflation rates than the United States and Europe. This takes us to the Hong Kong currency.

As with Singapore, locally the massive debt deflation is not operative as it is in the West. As far as is known, the banks and government regulations have been very stringent as far as down payments on mortgage loans go. The excesses that characterized the United States in 1996 are absent. Mortgage delinquencies at the local banks are currently running about 0.01 percent. Excess money creation by the Fed spills over into Hong Kong and, unlike the current US situation, does bring inflation.

Future of the Hong Kong Dollar   The Hong Kong dollar is a unique animal in the world of international finance. At an official target ratio of HK 7.8 dollars to US 1 dollar, it is pegged via a currency board mechanism to the US dollar under a system known as the Linked Exchange Rate. This system requires both the stock and flow of the monetary base to be fully backed by foreign reserves. This means that any change in the monetary base is fully matched by a corresponding change in foreign reserves at a fixed exchange rate.

The net result is that technically Hong Kong does not have a central bank and its monetary policy, as it were, is determined by the Federal Reserve and the flows of capital in and out of the territory. The peg has come under fire in recent years because of what is regarded as an irresponsible monetary policy followed by the US and the increasing importance of the Chinese economy to Hong Kong.

Critics point to the fact that the current peg only dates back to 1983 and could be changed again. The following history of Hong Kong exchange regimes shows that on this point they are right. As can be seen, the peg has not been changed often but it has been changed.

1863–1935	Silver standard with silver dollars as legal tender
1935–1967	Linked to sterling at one pound = HK $16
1967–1972	Linked to sterling at one pound = HK $14.55
1972–1973	Linked to US dollar with US$1.0 = HK $5.65
1973–1974	Linked to US dollar with US$1.0 = HK $5.085
1974–1983	Free float
1983–present	US$1.0 = HK $7.80

Critics have argued that relatively high rate of Hong Kong inflation suggests that the Hong Kong dollar is undervalued. Raising the value of the currency would limit inflation. At least one prominent money manager in New York publically predicted in 2011 that the peg would be altered and the currency revalued after the new CE took over on July 1, 2012. So far he has been wrong.

There is no doubt that sooner or later the peg will be changed. *But in our opinion it is unlikely to be changed in the very near future.* Suggestions that the Honky dollar, as it is sometimes called, be pegged to the renminbi are off the mark. The renminbi is not fully convertible. For technical reasons alone pegging to the renminbi at the moment is not practical. Moreover, China has only recently arrived as a major player on the international scene. It does not have a long-term track record in terms of monetary stability. And China has further to go in terms of the rule of law. Pegging to the renminbi would be dangerous and impractical at this time.

Suggestions have also been made that Hong Kong adopt the Singapore system of setting the value of the Hong Kong dollar against an undisclosed basket of currencies. But what would be gained by this? Singapore's and Hong Kong's rates of inflation are similar. Moreover, eliminating the peg would move the exchange rate front and center and would politicize its level. To some extent, this unfortunately is already happening in Hong Kong. Singapore has been run by one party that has exercised firm control and can withstand populist heat. Hong Kong's politics are still in the formative stage. This is a highly technical area, and one that the public is not likely to fully understand. There are great advantages in having the value of the Hong Kong dollar on "automatic" pilot, as it were. And Hong Kong's role as a major IPO center in particular depends on the issuers being able to have confidence in the value of the funds they are raising.

Right now, the US dollar is a place of refuge in the global economy. The US elections, in theory, could bring a major change in fiscal policy. But that looks doubtful now. Hong Kong should not think about changing the peg until and if it becomes clear that the United States cannot reform itself.

Investment Strategy   Parking some money in Hong Kong dollars can be a good idea. Since the Honky dollar is currently pegged to the US dollar, the fate of the US dollar is your downside risk. For foreign nonresident holders of Hong Kong dollars, it doesn't matter what Hong Kong's inflation is. Unless of course you want to live in or visit Hong Kong. Only the US rate of inflation matters. If the US dollar goes into the abyss, then Hong Kong will surely have to think about ending the peg. Then the chances are the Hong Kong dollar will be revalued against the US.

Meanwhile, like Singapore, there are some local REIT names available for those who wish to take additional risk and earn a reasonable yield. The same risks apply to Hong Kong REITs as they do to Singapore. There are also a number of Hong Kong real estate companies but, as most of these now have major positions in China, we would avoid these.

Hong Kong also has a sound banking system. But we would avoid the Mainland banks as well as HSBC. Several other banks in Hong Kong that are local in nature (plus Standard Chartered) and carry yields may be worth a look.

Cash 3: The Resource Twins—Canada and Australia

Canada and Australia will be considered together since they have so much in common. Many have recommended these countries as a good short-term place to park capital and thus avoid the perils of holding US dollars. They could be very wrong even though the longer-term picture for these countries is bright.

I just don't buy into the long-term commodity/resource scarcity story. The current world slowdown, particularly in China, is highly negative for commodities in the near term. Longer-term commodities will underperform in real terms because of ever-advancing technology. Unfortunately, today commodity/resource plays are China plays. And China has overinvested in a number of resources/ commodities and is slowing down. Unlike the Sing and Honky dollars and the Swissy, on a near-term basis the Aussie dollar and the Loonie (as the Canadian dollar is infelicitously called) are unlikely to outperform the US dollar.

As mentioned, there's no gainsaying that Canada and Australia are attractive on a long-term basis. It is tempting to include New Zealand in this discussion as well. But the white/Maori divisions in that country represent a complication not present in Canada and Australia, Australia isn't called the "lucky country" for nothing, and Canada would be lucky too, if it weren't for its lousy weather. They may not be such great places to park cash near term while waiting for the United States in particular to work through its coming budget crisis but they may great longer-term investments. Both might be great places to look for investments after the world is further into the big crisis that is currently unfolding.

Both Canada and Australia are former British colonies and as such have inherited democracy, the English language, British common law, and a respect for property rights and the rights of individuals. Both are predominantly European-origin countries without the populist threat of numerically important downtrodden minority groups demanding extra levels of government services (the English–French divide in Canada seems to be slowly disappearing). Both have enormous land areas relative to modest populations. The land areas are brimming with natural resources and, in the case of Canada, energy. Both have well-educated, intelligent populations well suited to competing in a global knowledge economy. Both are attracting high-quality Asian immigrants and, in the case of Australia, Asian students. (Australia may be about to acquire a new round of high-quality Greek immigrants as well.) And, as the accompanying numbers show, in terms of fiscal ratios like net sovereign debt/GDP, both have run reasonably conservative fiscal policies. The European disease, socialism, hasn't totally infected these countries.

Tables 7.5 and 7.6 show a quick summary of Canada and Australia statistics. One major difference from Singapore, Switzerland, and Hong Kong: These countries' foreign reserves are multiples of those for Canada and Australia. Considering their much smaller populations and size, it brings out my point that the Cash 2 countries

Table 7.5   A Quick Summary of Canada Statistics

General Government Net Debt/GDP	33.1%
General Government Total Expenditure/GDP	42.7%
General Government Structural Balance/GDP	–3.6%
Current account/GDP	–2.8%
GDP per capita (US dollars)	$50,496
Consumer price inflation	2.9%
Unemployment rate	7.5%
Official Reserve Assets (US dollars)	$66.321 billion
Population	34.4 million

Sources: IMF-2011 data

Table 7.6   A Quick Summary of Australia Statistics

General Government Net Debt/GDP	8.1%
General Government Total Expenditure/GDP	36.4%
Current account/GDP	–2.2%
GDP per capita (US dollars)	$66,371
Consumer price inflation	3.4%
Unemployment rate	5.3%
Official Reserve Assets (US dollars)	$45.416 billion
Population	22.4 million

Sources: IMF-2011 data

are in a sense global banks. Places to hold cash. Australia and Canada in many ways are better places to look for long-term investments.

Fixed-Income Securities

It seems almost a contradiction. The central banks are printing high-powered money with wild abandon, government budgets are out of control, and most of the governments of the advanced countries have unsustainable debt loads. Yields should be rising. Fixed income should be the last place anyone would want to look. Especially dollar fixed income.

But in fact, the opposite is true. Global supply exceeds global demand for tradable goods. The huge debt loads are forcing a retrenchment of spending, including that of government. The current buzzwords are *deflation/disinflation,* not *inflation.*

Advanced-country bond markets around the world currently divide up into two groups. First, there are countries under market attack, such as Greece, Italy, Spain, Portugal, Ireland, and even France. Second, there are those countries not under market attack—the United States, Japan, Germany, and even the United Kingdom.

Owning fixed-income securities in the latter group of countries seems like a sensible strategy so long as deflation/disinflation is in the air. It seems clear that of this group the United States will be the "last man standing." A market attack on the United States will bring on a global financial Armageddon. Then you want to get rid of all your fixed-income securities.

Will anyone ring a bell that Armageddon is here? I doubt it. The US elections, however, could have been the bell ringer. It is interesting that the election of Francois Hollande in France has not rung a bell—yet. Hollande is pursuing an anticapitalist, anti–supply-side strategy including higher taxes on the "rich" and a reduction of the retirement age. One would have thought Hollande's election would have brought about a collapse in French bond prices. It hasn't happened—yet.

Now here are two thoughts. We associate higher levels of government debt and governmental defaults with inflation. Is it possible that government bond yields could rise to punitive levels as governments totter into bankruptcy while the overall economic environment continues to be one of disinflation? The near term forces of deflation including massive oversupply of many commodities and goods as well as debt deleveraging remain in place. In fact rising government bond yields and disinflation has already happened in Southern Europe. And would the yields on non-government bonds—particularly those of solid global corporations—trade below those of government yields?

That's the problem for investors now. We have no history, no example of massive government (inflationary) money printing conflicting with massive global deflationary forces.

European Equities

Not much to say here except AVOID for now. But not forever. As far as Europe goes, longer term, who knows. Europe is populated by intelligent, well-educated people. But they have been infected with socialism and populism. Can they rid themselves of this disease and enact real supply-side/structural reforms? Or will all of the intelligent and productive Europeans simply stop working (or leave), as they did in Ayn Rand's *Atlas Shrugged?*

Europe has some great global companies especially in Germany, the United Kingdom, and France. They just happen to be headquartered in the wrong place. The legendary Mexican mogul Carlos Slim is already investing in Europe. Slim learned his investing from his father who began buying property in Mexico City in the height of the Mexican Revolution. People are always referring to the famous Barron Rothschild quote (although they never specify *which* Barron Rothschild) that investors should be buying when there is blood in the street. The Slims literally followed that advice. But for mere mortals, with regard to Europe, better to wait.

As far as European sovereign debt goes for the weaker countries, yes there will be opportunities—but not for amateurs, and not yet.

What about American TIPS?

A comment on Treasury securities adjusted for inflation. The United States version of these is called TIPS—Treasury Inflation Protected Securities. Great concept. I don't like TIPS for two reasons:

1. Near term, it's deflation/disinflation, not inflation, that investors have to worry about.
2. When and if the inflation comes, as discussed, you cannot trust government CPI numbers. The temptation for governments to cheat on the CPI will become overwhelming. By cheating on the CPI, the US government can save money on TIPS and also Social Security. I am not enthused about TIPS for that reason, although intellectually TIPS make sense for an inflationary era.

Gold—Don't Get Carried Away

There are three ways to look at gold. The first is simply as an inflation hedge. In this view, gold is sort of an index of commodity prices. Here gold may be ahead of itself. For example since the gold link was terminated in 1971, CPI inflation index has risen 567 percent. From its $35 per ounce official 1971 price, gold has moved up roughly 4,600 percent. While the choice of beginning price is somewhat arbitrary in this calculation since the official price in 1971 was below market, the likelihood is that on a pure inflation basis, gold is currently overvalued. Moreover, in a period of near-term debt deflation in the advanced Western countries and Chinese slowdown as we are now in, gold as a commodity is likely to decline in price. No question if hyperinflation is on the horizon, gold will rally. But not yet. As mentioned, deflation, or at least a lack of significant inflation, is our near-term future.

Comparisons with the past for gold can be misleading. When gold was the center of the monetary order, it was the anchor, the constant. Of course, gold held its value. Today it performs no such role. In periods of financial stress when in theory people should be buying gold, they are sellers as they need liquidity. In periods of global expansion, gold becomes an attractive asset to hold. Many people argue that quantitative easing is releasing high-powered money into the system, which will then chase gold. I don't see it that way. I think the high-powered money created is just sitting in the central banks as excess reserves. Debt deflation is a powerful force. Of course, the high-powered money won't sit in the central banks forever.

A second way to look at gold is an attractive alternative asset and store of value for central banks and investors in a time of loss of confidence in the dollar and the euro. Under this view gold might play some role in a new international monetary system or as the basis for one of several future alternative currencies. A lot has been written about this. Under this view, gold presumably would have a higher value than under the first view but it is hard to come with some kind of valuation formula for this. Moreover, all of this, while it makes for interesting intellectual discussions, is somewhat "mushy" as an investment strategy. Despite what many believe is illogical, the dollar today is strong and the euro has held together. So long as the dollar and the euro hold together, gold will not be the refuge that its supporters believe it should be. A breakup of the euro could cause a rush into gold as an alternative. That would be bullish for gold. But I do not think the euro will break up. Yes, longer term, the ECB's money printing will be inflationary. But not now as Europe careens into a recession.

The third way to view gold is to assume the classic gold standard will be revived. In that case, there would be a huge shortage of gold at current prices. Depending on what kind of gold standard would be adapted (e.g., full or partial backing for checking and currencies), a great deal more gold would be required. Since the supply of physical gold is highly inelastic, the only way to increase the supply of gold in monetary terms would be to increase its price by several multiples of where it is today. Most gold bugs implicitly assume a gold standard restoration. They are anticipating a monetary cataclysm to force this change. I would answer, maybe someday but not yet.

But remember from our discussion on the price-specie flow model. The gold standard doesn't work if central banks can create high-powered money out of thin air in addition to holding gold. Frankly, it seems unlikely central banks will give up this power. Nobody needs a phony gold standard, and that's what it would be if central banks still had money creation powers. Government demand management is considered a divinely appointed duty by modern economists, central bankers, politicians, and indeed electorates. They are not going to let go of that.

So buying gold in hopes of a restoration of a pure gold standard seems like a long shot. The gold standard would be wonderful, but it's not likely to happen. The fatal attraction of populism makes it unlikely that democracies will ever allow a return to the classic gold standard. *I am torn between a fundamental view that the historically successful gold standard should be restored vs. the unlikeliness that such an event would ever happen.*

Keep in mind that David Hume's price-specie flow model is *not* an investment scheme. It is an economic system with gold at the center. It equilibrated automatically the entire global system of trade. Surplus countries and deficit countries would be brought back into balance. Hume wasn't a gold bug in the sense the term is used today. He wasn't urging his followers to go out and buy gold. The classical gold standard is not a get-rich scheme. Restoration of this system will, in theory, bring about a major one time capital gain for gold holders. If the system is not restored, no capital gain.

As argued in the previous chapter, the more gold goes up in price and the more people are seriously considering giving gold a renewed monetary role, the greater risk of confiscation and/or punitive tax treatment of gold by governments whose monetary monopoly is threatened. Never forget Franklin D. Roosevelt's 1933 Executive Order 6102. This forbade the hoarding of gold coin, gold bullion, and gold certificates within the continental United States, thus criminalizing monetary gold by any individual, partnership, or corporation. Ironically, Roosevelt made it illegal to own gold about the same time the Twenty-First Amendment made it legal to drink liquor. The majority of the country was more pleased by this latter action than displeased by the former.

Note that the government of India—desperate for money any way it could get it—recently doubled the import duty on gold. After huge protest and a twenty-one-day strike by jewelers, most of this tax increase was rolled back. OK, the government of India is not exactly a model of good governance. But the message is clear. Gold can be an easy target for governments.

One justification governments give when they institute measures to discourage their citizens from holding gold is that they want to redirect funds into "productive assets." That's what the Indian government said. What could be more productive for citizens than an asset like gold, which provides a store of value for their own savings? Doesn't that fill a consumer need as much as a computer or a bag of potato chips? Providing a store of value is something government-issued depreciating fiat money generally does poorly or not at all.

Commodities/Resources—Not a Simple Story

My view of continued deflation/disinflation followed by inflation later makes for a complicated story. During the inflationary period commodity prices will rise, but we are not there yet. Near term, further weakness is likely to be exhibited in the commodity sector.

Longer term, my preference is not to buy commodities themselves but rather to buy the companies that make commodities more plentiful. Technology always comes along to enable a supply increasing response to higher commodity prices. We have seen this recently with horizontal drilling and fracking suddenly appearing to make oil and natural gas more abundant. The same in the agricultural sector, where genetically modified food and biotechnology have the potential to increase food output. The world's not going to run out of anything. Technology will always come to the rescue. Commodity booms always reverse. This leads to a preference for companies in the oil service and oil and gas infrastructure sectors, the biotech sectors and in the mining equipment sectors. As mentioned, the greatest risk to companies in these sectors is mindless and exaggerated environmentalism and related Luddite movements.

Of course in a period of hyperinflation, in *nominal* terms commodity prices are likely to spike upward.

Selected Big-Cap Nonfinancial, Global Companies

This asset class would include tech and nontech companies. It is attractive longer term because it has a significant chance of preserving wealth in a variety of economic environments. Here's why:

1. *Exposure to globalization.* Globalization is a major factor driving global wealth creation and the Western global companies have the products the world wants. Starbucks for example is today a China story as Las Vegas Sands. The products and the technology may come from the West but the demand is global. While Western governments may have been wasting money and making promises they couldn't keep, Western companies have transformed themselves into global players with products that are in demand in the faster-growing non-Western world.

2. *Exposure to technology.* Globalization is really the product of technology. Technology makes globalization possible. As we have argued, technology is now driving human evolution and the key to increased productivity in a modern economy. Globalization is the product of technology. No airplanes, no fiber optic cables, no computers, no propeller-driven ships equals no globalization. You don't have to buy tech companies specifically to get technology. Global companies are massive users of technology.

3. *Ability to stand up to bankrupt governments.* In the German hyperinflation large industrial companies did relatively well. They got special deals from the government and banks. The large global companies today have the financial means to protect themselves against future depredations by desperate politicians and to deal with the onslaught of regulations that has arisen from the growth of governments and the crash

of 2008. They are going to lose some battles, but compared to the smaller companies, they will have a better chance. Smaller companies in the advanced countries may find themselves choking in a sea of taxes and regulations. There is a certain economy of scale in coping with regulations. Big companies can afford the lawyers and accountants. It's a misallocation of resources from society's viewpoint, but that's the way it is.

4. *Long-run survivability.* Again going back to the German hyperinflation, the stocks of the big industrial companies recovered after the hyperinflation was over. You may have some bad moments with the big cap stocks but in the long run, if they don't survive, society doesn't. Big cap stocks may turn out to be a better alternative for wealth preservation than gold.

Again, without actually picking stocks, I would like to review some areas to look for in global companies. First is technology, particularly American technology companies. This is what America does best. When it comes to pure tech, better to own an ETF or mutual fund on a long-term basis. Yes, you would rather own the next Apple or Microsoft. But who knows which company that is. And when tech companies stumble, the results can be ugly. Nokia is an example. To repeat, technology is driving human evolution and human progress. Telecommunications, computer technology, nanotechnology, biotechnology all fall under this category. The big global companies will do relatively well. The small tech companies are for specialists.

Second, there are the companies that cater to the consumer sector in the emerging markets. All those billions of *nouveux riche* ex-third-world consumers are filled with lust for Western products. Anyone doubting this should spend some time in Hong Kong and watch the hordes of Mainlanders line up behind velvet ropes at Louis Vuitton or Chanel stores. Or go to Macau and see how in one decade the gambling business has gone from a sleepy backwater to doing five times the volume of Las Vegas.

Third is agricultural stocks. As mentioned, while birthrates are collapsing almost everywhere, the world's population is likely to add at least another billion or so people to the current seven billion. And they don't want to eat rice anymore. As people get rich, they want meat and fish. And cows eat corn. Lots of it. Note

I am not *not* forecasting an agricultural commodities price boom, although ag prices will have their bubbles. What I am saying is that technology is going to have to increase agricultural output. Organic farming is not going to do the trick. (In fact, because of its substantially lower productivity per acre and unsubstantiated health benefits, it could be argued that organic farming is environmentally harmful. But that's another story.) The Monsantos and the Syngentas of the world are going to be needed to feed the world.

One point worth noting here. The United States, with its freedom of expression and information, sophisticated financing system, and superb higher educational institutions, has been the center of world technology development. It is no accident that Apple, Microsoft, Google, Facebook and so many other tech firms are American. Steve Jobs would have been crushed if he had grown up in China. It would be a global tragedy if in the coming crises a tax-hungry, regulation-infatuated US government undermined this.

Large Global Banks—Avoid

From an investment point of view, there are several fundamental realities concerning banks that exist in virtually every country.

First, large banks will not be allowed to go bankrupt and they won't be allowed to take risks and earn high rates of return. Governments won't allow these banks to take risks since the governments will have to pay if, as in 2008, the risks turn out badly. I cannot argue with this government logic, by the way. If governments are going to socialize the risks, then governments should socialize the profits as well. Or, to put it another way, bank risks should be limited and bank capital should be enhanced to protect the governments from losses. *Unfortunately, on a long- and short-term basis this makes for a rather unattractive equity outlook for global commercial banks.* For a global bank, if it's too big to fail, then it's too big to sail. (OK. That phrase isn't quite memorable but think of a better one.)

The failure of Lehman Brothers in 2008 and J.P. Morgan's recent huge derivatives losses are two signature events. Regarding Lehman Brothers, the American regulators followed the free market, Austrian School prescription and allowed Lehman to go bankrupt. It was as if one hundred years of populist thinking and an ever-greater government role in the economy was suddenly forgotten. But not for long. The American officials quickly lost their nerve as they feared in horror that the entire global financial sector was lined up to go down next. Maybe after the financial sector completely crashed a new and better one like a phoenix would rise from the wreckage. But US Treasury Secretary Hank Paulson wasn't going to take the chance and find out. I think he knew quite correctly that the American people—indeed, the entire world—did not want him to take that chance. We'll never know what might have been. The Austrian school economists can write all they want. The global public and the economics intelligentsia have a closed mind on this subject.

Ramsey MacDonald, a now-forgotten British Labour Prime Minister in the dismal 1930s, once said that the financial sector is the nervous center of capitalism. No modern elected government anywhere can allow its financial sector to have a nervous breakdown.

So Who Needs Capital?

The author (Peter Treadway) can remember vividly one experience from his days in the 1980s as a savings and loan and government-sponsored entity (GSE) equity analyst on Wall Street. I was visiting a savings and loan CEO in San Diego. This particular institution had very little in the way of capital and an aggressive policy of making high-risk loans. Its CEO was a PhD in economics who had a way of letting investors and his fellow thrift industry executives know that he thought he was smarter than they were.

At any rate, I pointed out to him that his company needed a big capital boost. He laughed and, after pointedly telling me what he was about to say was not for quotation, condescendingly informed me that as an economist I should know that the government was his capital and it was stupid for him to raise any more. His company's strategy was to borrow at government-insured rates in his branches and then make whopping spreads on his high-risk loans. This would give his company a handsome return on its miniscule capital. He and his staff, of course, knew how to originate risky loans safely, since they were smarter than everyone else.

A year or so later, his institution was closed by the authorities because his high-risk loans had massive default rates. Hubris is fatal in the world of finance, where there are no certainties and most participants are in the higher IQ brackets.

Actually, as I looked back his strategy wasn't stupid at all. Banks don't need capital if the government is going to bail them out and take the losses. "Heads we win, tails they (governments) lose." He had just gotten a little too greedy.

But how do regulators draw the line between preventing global banks from taking undue risk and totally stifling initiative and innovation among these institutions? All of this keeping in mind that government's implied guarantee to the large banks creates a major case of moral hazard. If the government is going to pick up the losses, why, bank managements may ask, not take more risks on less capital? Of course, that is what happened over the years.

Various approaches have been suggested to curtail big bank risk. The so-called Volker rule is one. Under this rule, big, publicly guaranteed commercial and investment banks shouldn't be allowed to engage in speculative or nonhedged proprietary trading since the government has to pick up their losses if they lose. But then we have the spectacle of J.P. Morgan announcing a multibillion-dollar loss on what it considered a hedged trading investment. J.P. Morgan is considered by many to be the best run of all the large American banks. Its CEO Jamie Dimon is considered to be the most gifted bank executive, perhaps, in the world and one to rival the original J.P. Morgan himself. But here we have J.P. Morgan stumbling in a most egregious manner. And its gifted CEO proclaiming before Congress that he doesn't really know what the Volker rule is. Of course Dimon was being disingenuous. The Volker rule, named after former Fed Chairman Paul Volker, supposedly prohibits banks from using depositors' money to engage in speculative activities. What Dimon was really asking was "how do you draw the line between a normal bank hedging of its books and proprietary trading? Jamie Dimon before Congress essentially said he could not. Maybe nobody can. The Dodd–Frank bill (discussed below) includes the Volker rule, but the regulations on this have yet to be issued.

Over the years, large commercial banks gave the public an illusion that they were safe and protected by their governments. The banking crisis in 2008 shattered this illusion. The large global banks are now subject to tougher oversight by all bank supervisors. Governments and central banks realize that global banks are no longer their friends. These banks took high risks, distributed handsome bonuses to their star employees, and paid good dividends to their international shareholders. However, they came back to their governments to ask for support after serious losses.

A second approach to mitigating bank risk are the Basel III requirements. Bank supervisors realized the risk of commercial banks in the 1980s, when they implemented Basel Accord (known as Basel I). This bank supervisory standard linked capital to asset risk. Ultimately, the Basel I and later Basel II standards were failures. Basel or no, banks have gone down in every Western country, thus far (with the exception of hapless Lehman, which wasn't technically a bank and therefore not under Basel) bailed out in one form or another by their regulators.

In 2008–2010, Basel III was developed by central banks via the Basel Committee. Two simple words can summarize Basel III: *higher equity*. Banks must have higher equity requirement to support their high-risk activities. The equity requirement in Basel III is around three times what is required in Basel II. Basel III becomes effective in 2013–2018. In this five-year period, all the banks, regardless of large size or small size, need to issue new equity to support their operation. *Investors will have to be more patient if they want to buy bank stocks. There will be an enormous supply of new equity in the coming years.*

Still, in view of what has happened in Europe and the looming sovereign debt crises in all the advanced countries, the entire Basel approach could be viewed as regulatory stand-up comedy. Government bonds are treated as risk-free assets, requiring little or no capital. As it turns out, in Europe today government bonds are frequently the riskiest asset banks can own.

An additional regulatory negative piled on to the US banks is the Dodd–Frank bill, or to call it by its proper name, the Wall Street Reform and Consumer Protection Act. Passed in 2010 with the Volker rule and many of the Basel III rules included, its sponsors were none other than Representative Barney Frank and Senator Christopher Dodd, the two congressional leaders right at the top of the Fannie/Freddie legislative rogues gallery.

It would seem that the primary purpose of this bill is to tie up all banks with enough regulatory requirements so as to make the fulfilling of these requirements banks' primary activity. Bankers who spend their time filling out government forms and worrying about being politically correct won't have time for mischief making in the derivatives markets! Many of the requirements in the Dodd–Frank bill have nothing to do with banking but satisfy America's insatiable need to protect women, consumer, and minority groups via government regulation.

I believe this bill will eventually be judged to be as harmful in its economics as was the Community Reinvestment Act, about which this book spoke earlier. The Dodd–Frank bill will add to banks' cost of doing business and inhibit innovation. There's an irony here. The larger banks can deal with regulations better than the smaller banks. There are economies of scale in hiring lawyers and accountants to deal with the unproductive task of complying with burdensome regulations. The too-big-to-fail big banks will benefit on a relative basis as compared to the "small-enough-to-die" small banks. In the future, talented young men and women aspiring to a career in banking will major in law and human relations, not finance.

It is interesting that one of the most disastrous regulatory decisions of the last decade rarely gets mention. In 2004, the Securities and Exchange Commission vastly liberalized the limits on leverage for the major American broker dealers. Goldman Sachs, Morgan Stanley, Merrill Lynch, Bear Sterns, and Lehman Brothers were allowed to increase their leverage by a quantum leap. And by 2008, they had done just that. What so many observers don't seem to care about was that the government *had* sufficient power to regulate the financial system. But, in the case of the major brokers and also in the case of Fannie Mae and Freddie Mac, the government *failed* to use the powers that it already had. What America needed to regulate its financial system was a government with integrity and brains and not corrupt politicians who then went on to pass the giant legislative atrocity called the Dodd–Frank bill.

Many observers have also argued that the big banks are just too big to be managed well. This may be true, but I think it's something for the market, not the regulators, to solve. The major corporations of the world get bigger and more global every day. Banks who service them have to be big and global as well. It may be that some of the functions of the big global banks should be divided up. Some of these functions, including derivatives and other types of proprietary trading, can be done by non-banks. This is already happening. Many Wall Street analysts are calling for breakup of the big banks on financial grounds. Fine. If the market thinks it's a good idea, let the big banks split themselves up. This is one area where regulators should not tread.

A second important factor and potential negative for banks is money. A bank's raw material is money. This book has spent a lot of time worrying about the possibility of inflation over the long-term as the result of current central bank policies. Banks can have real problems if inflation comes, especially if it is unexpected. Mess with a country's money and you are messing with a country's banks. But right now, with the central banks holding short rates at zero, you don't need a Harvard MBA to be a banker. Borrow short, lend long.

A *third negative factor regarding the big global banks is regulatory/ legal.* This factor became more prominent as this book went to press. The Standard Chartered case for me, at least, was a shock. The big global banks look to be the perpetual victims of what I would call "the bank protection business." Bankrupt governments can now help themselves to bank profits, since bank regulations are now so complex and arcane that there is always grounds for a good lawsuit. The recent hold-up of Standard Chartered is just another chapter in what has become a very familiar pattern. Somebody sues a bank for something and rather than fight in court, the banks settle and essentially pay a protection fee so they can keep doing business. In the past in the United States, the banks have had to pay from time to time on alleged discriminatory lending practices by such organizations as the notorious ACORN (Association of Community Organizations for Reform Now). Thus, the banks were sued for underlending to minorities and then overlending after the 2008 crisis. The Community Reinvestment Act (CRA) in particular has been a useful tool for activists and their allies in government to extort money from ever-eager-to-comply bank managements.

Now things have gone international. HSBC and Standard Chartered are being accused of money laundering. They are, of course, paying up as fast as they can write the checks. The initial bravado exhibited by Standard Chartered's CEO Peter Sands quickly evaporated when he was faced with the possibility of losing his bank's New York license, guilty or not. "Your money or your life," is not a pleasant choice when someone has a gun held to your head. Peter Sands proved to be no Jack Benny.

There are five unpleasant realities facing banks that make them easy targets for activist and governmental extortion:

1. *Historically, people dislike lenders, a feeling that has intensified since the 2008 financial crisis.* Banks are held solely responsible for the crisis. If accused, banks are guilty even if proven innocent. Regarding the 2008 crisis, the contributory role of Chairman Greenspan's Federal Reserve, which fed the housing bubble with super low interest rates, is too complicated for the public to understand. Even more complicated was the

role of the international monetary system and the undervalued Chinese exchange rate, which required reinvestment of
excess Chinese dollars in the United States. The same goes
for Fannie and Freddie, the two mortgage monsters that
bought or guaranteed so many of the junk mortgages
that were written. Forgotten also is the disgraceful role of the
Fannie/Freddie congressional supporters including Frank
and Dodd.

2. *US banking laws and regulations are so byzantine and complex as
   to make it possible for anyone just out of law school to build a case
   against them for some alleged infraction.* The Dodd–Frank bill,
   when the enabling regulations are finally written, will offer a
   cornucopia of vehicles for eager regulators, activists, and fellow travelers with grievances to sue the banks.

3. *The US Constitution specifically prohibits the enactment of ex post
   facto laws.* Thus, a person or bank cannot be punished for an
   act that is a legally a crime today but was not legally a crime
   when the act was committed. But the Founding Fathers
   didn't count on regulators who apparently have never heard
   of ex post facto prohibitions when interpreting regulations.
   For example, one set of regulators gives approval to a particular practice and informs the banks that its practice is legal.
   Later, this practice becomes politically unacceptable and, lo
   and behold, a new set of regulators comes in and punishes
   the banks for following this practice, which previously had
   been tolerated. I suspect, although I obviously cannot prove,
   that something like this is going on with Standard Chartered,
   HSBC, and also the LIBOR problem.

4. *Never forget that the bank regulators represent entities, in this case
   the federal and state governments, which are now broke.* Standard
   Chartered according to some reports is going to have to
   shell out some $1.0 billion in fines. This is a nice piece of
   change to be divided between the federal government and
   the always near-bankrupt state of New York. Reportedly, the
   regulators are eyeing a whole host of global banks for similar regulatory action. The regulators haven't had so much
   fun since the cigarette company settlements. I'm an economist. For me, it's axiomatic. When money talks, people listen.
   Oh well. Chairman Ben Bernanke holds short-term interest
   rates at zero, the banks borrow at zero, lend longer term, and

make the spread. Then the regulators and the activists move in with their lawsuits and take their cut. The risk is that the regulators and activists get greedier and greedier with each successful suit.

5. *Don't be surprised that the United States is pushing its weight around and asserting extraterritoriality.* It has the economic muscle, and other countries will cave in and grovel before the American regulators and tax authorities. Once-independent Switzerland is an example. Might always makes right, or as Chairman Mao less gently put it, "All power flows through the barrel of a gun." And indeed the United States is not alone with regard to this type of behavior. The big and the strong always push around the small and the weak. As China's Foreign Minister Yang Jiechi recently pointed out in the context of China's disputes with its smaller neighbors regarding disputed mini-islands, "China is a big country and other countries are small countries and that is just a fact." Global banks have to face the fact that the US regulators are their primary regulator and that Uncle Sam is their uncle.

Equities from Selected Emerging Markets

The emergence of so-called emerging markets has been a major financial theme in recent years. Spreads on emerging market bonds have narrowed dramatically, fiscal houses have been put in order in many though not all countries and globalization has been a boon to untold millions of people in poorer countries around the world. The acronym "BRICs"—Brazil, Russia, India, China—has become a symbol of the new wealth that is being created. Symbols are important. Enthusiasts for Indonesia and South Africa and even Turkey have tried to get their countries' names somehow incorporated into the BRIC acronym.

Advanced country investors should allocate part of their funds to these new markets. But keeping the following in mind:

1. With all the new wealth creation, there still is tremendous volatility in emerging market stock markets and significant chance for underperformance. In 2011, emerging markets did significantly *underperform* US markets. In the nineteenth century the United States went from an economically

unimportant (though a very important political experiment) at the beginning of the century to the world's foremost industrial power by the end of the century. A civil war and some big bubbles and busts including those in 1837, 1873, and 1890–1893 punctuated this advance along the way. American states defaulted in the 1840s and again after the Civil War. Investors at times had a very rough ride.

2. Developing country markets aren't a secret anymore. Once upon a time, legendary investor John Templeton made his fortune by going around the world picking up bargains in stocks that nobody in the West ever heard of. Those days are over.

3. Not all emerging markets are alike. The acronym BRIC in a way does a disservice to investors because for example it implies the four countries are alike. They definitely are not. Or that they have achieved high institutional or legal standards. They definitely have not. (In one way the BRICs are alike, or at least three of them. Out of 50 countries ranked for ease of doing business by Bloomberg, Russia, India, and Brazil ranked 48, 49, and 50, respectively. The BRICS held up the rear! China, which is not known for its corporate governance, surprisingly was 19.)

4. Living and investing in a globalized world has one disadvantage. Interconnections among the world's economies means there is going to be significant correlation among all the markets. That means in case of a global meltdown there may be no place to hide.

5. At the present time, most emerging market companies are not global and are not on the cutting edge of technology. Their home countries are catching up with the advanced countries. Their technology has been imported from advanced countries. *Tropicalization* is one irreverent term for this phenomenon. Emerging market firms do not have global brands. This, of course, will change with time. But right now, with only a limited number of exceptions, they are one country investments so that analyzing these companies requires a macro view on the countries themselves.

6. For most investors, given that emerging market companies are smaller and home country oriented, it often will pay to invest in ETFs and mutual funds, which are country or region specific.

A Review of the BRICs

China

China and India have a combined population of almost 2.5 billion people. You have to have a view on both to invest in emerging markets. Both countries are not simple stories. We've already discussed the flaws in these countries' economic models in Chapter 3. Starting with China, we would say the following are general rules:

- Expect a significant downturn in the Chinese economy this year. *Perhaps all Chinese stocks should be avoided near term.*
- Longer term, stick to Chinese consumer stocks. The Chinese model has to change from emphasis on investment to a greater consumer orientation. The Chinese people are hungry for a better life. They are not the big savers as is always portrayed, provided the right goods are available and they have a middle-class income.
- Consider companies that cater to Chinese consumers that are located in Hong Kong or Macau. The gambling sector comes to mind.
- Avoid Chinese majority state-owned companies. They are run for government objectives (more specifically, the ruling Communist Party) rather that market-determined objectives without real profit-making goals in mind. Their profits are an illusion in most cases, a product of subsidized borrowing rates from government controlled state-owned banks. Managements can be removed or changed at the whim of the Communist Party.
- Only buy genuine private-sector companies or ETFs and mutual funds whose portfolios are dominated by private-sector Chinese companies. These private-sector stocks trade in New York, Hong Kong, and Singapore.
- Avoid the Chinese export sector. The Chinese mercantilist export model has reached a dead end.
- Avoid Chinese banks. The case against them is well laid out in *Red Capitalism* by Frazer and Howie, which is actually required reading for anyone seriously thinking about investing in Chinese banks or China in general. Chinese banks are a gaggle of Fannie Maes. Chinese banks follow government policy and make massive loans to government entities. Then later, the government bails them out. This is a business?

- Avoid the Chinese real-estate sector. This is too intertwined with the banking system and government policy.
- Take care on corporate governance. Look for things like quality auditors, respected foreigners on company boards, the extent of insider ownership, and trading and up-to-date functioning websites in English. (One major turnoff for Chinese companies is websites that are not up to date.) Unfortunately, many of the better Chinese private companies have convoluted capital structures involving offshore structures, which were set up to get around certain Chinese laws regarding raising capital abroad.
- *To invest in China, look at Southeast Asia and the ASEAN countries. Especially Singapore, Thailand, Malaysia, and the Philippines.* That's where the Chinese tourists will be going. (They will be going to Myanmar too but Myanmar doesn't have a stock market yet.) The region will also benefit from increased trade with China. My number one pick in Southeast Asia, after Singapore, is Thailand, which actually is about 30 percent Chinese in its ethnic origins. (You get the Chinese work ethic combined with the famous Thai smile) Korea is also another China play.

Au Revoir La France—Bonjour Hong Kong: Welcome to the New Huguenots

The following is an excerpt from the *Economist*. It seems there has been a small exodus of French professionals from France to Hong Kong. Are these the new Huguenots, fleeing fiscal persecution in this case?

"Last summer Jean-Pascal Tricoire, the chief executive of Schneider Electric . . . moved to Hong Kong to run the company from Asia . . . Schneider Electric's official headquarters, and tax domicile, remains in France. But with only 8% of annual turnover in France these days, the firm's eyes are on the rest of the world."

"An Inconvenience Truth." *The Economist.* (March 31, 2012). www.economist.com/node/21551461.

India

India from an investment point of view can be summarized in one phrase. Great companies, terrible government.

India is a frustration for investors. India has some of the best companies and managements in the world. India, unlike China, allows a free flow of information. India has a tradition of intellectual freedom and creativity, superior corporate governance, a world-class scientific elite and the use of English as the primary medium of corporate communications.

But as mentioned, as the world's largest democracy, India is as vulnerable to the fatal attraction of populism as the advanced Western countries. Government expenditure is misdirected to welfare type rather than infrastructure expenditures. India's inflation remains high, in part, because of government-imposed bottlenecks and lack of infrastructure. One reform after the other gets thwarted by state governments and vested interests. Government-run companies like the railroads and Air India continue to drain the government coffers with their appalling and chronic losses.

As mentioned, you cannot understand India and ignore its caste system. Many modern Indians don't want to talk about it. They argue that it is rapidly disappearing and that the British exaggerated its importance. Maybe so. But the caste system has been a core feature of the dominant Hindu religion. India's private companies are run by talented, well-educated, generally higher-caste professionals. But India's democracy more and more is dominated by the less-educated, lower-caste groups who look to the government to equalize a playing field that has been unfairly balanced against them for over a thousand years. These lower castes have a legitimate grievance. But investors can't be social workers. Fairly or unfairly, the upper castes are where you find the Indians loaded with talent. Moreover, India has had a tradition of Nehruvian socialism that, while intellectually discredited in some circles, still maintains a powerful hold on the country's political process.

Investors who are surprised at India's occasional irrational antipathy to foreign investors need to be aware of Indian history. The country was essentially run by a foreign multinational, that is, the British East India Company, for roughly a hundred years up until the assertion of full British Imperial authority in 1858. Old memories die hard.

Another point about India should be understood. The Republic of India today is but a (substantial) fraction of the Imperial Raj under the British. Raj India included today's India, Pakistan, Bangladesh, and, from an economic point of view, Sri Lanka (Ceylon), Myanmar (Burma), Nepal, and Bhutan. Anyone with even the most cursory knowledge of economics would clearly see the tremendous advantages of a free trade arrangement among these countries. But India's trade with its neighbors is extremely small. Politics, of course, is the reason. Post–independence Indian relations with its immediate neighbors has, shall we say, been less than cordial in most cases. Any opening up in the trade area would be a tremendous boost for the GDPs of India and its neighbors. That's a no-brainer.

Indian stocks have rallied in 2012, much to my surprise. The talk of reform is once again in the air. But we've heard this before. There is still a good chance that India is headed for another foreign exchange crisis. I would be cautious regarding Indian stocks.

Brazil

Brazil, it used to be said in Latin America, "is the country of the future and it always will be." For the last few years, people stopped saying that as it looked like a new and fast-growth Brazil was emerging. In my opinion it's a little early to start breaking out the champagne for Brazil.

Brazil, like India, has great companies with great professional managements. Brazil also has an inheritance of welfare state socialism—more the Continental Europe variety as opposed to the Nehruvian form (assuming there really is a difference). But it all amounts to the same thing—a hungry government looking to please its poor underclass rather than investors.

And Brazil has another similarity with India. Brazilian society can be divided by race as India is divided by caste. Over 50 percent of Brazil now is non-white, the bulk of African descent. The contrasts between the white/Asian groups where the professional, managerial class comes from and the non-white Afro Brazilians are stark using the usual metrics of education and family income. The level of race consciousness is not at the same level as caste consciousness is in India (or race consciousness in the United States), but it is there. (White) Brazilians make a big deal about how they are color blind and not like Americans. But most of the race mixing in Brazil occurred in colonial days when there was a shortage of white women.

The fact is that Brazil fits our model perfectly. It is just one more democratic country where there is a fatal attraction of populism that is made worse by a tradition of socialism. In Brazil's case, it is also made worse by a visible division of the population into two groups, the Afro Brazilian group clearly at the bottom of society and potentially demanding more in the way of government services.

Brazil had its balance of payments and debt crises in the 1980s and 1990s. It is not a sovereign debt risk now. Brazil has made amazing progress in the fiscal area. But real interest rates in Brazil have been kept very high, and inflation is running stubbornly above 5 percent. Brazilian GDP growth rates never approached the GDP growth rates of the high fliers of India and China.

For years, Latin Americans complained that they were "exploited" by the advanced countries of the world that bought Latin American commodities at cheap prices and then reexported these commodities back to Latin America in the form of higher-priced manufactured goods. Argentine economist Raul Prebisch, sometimes called the "Keynes of Latin America," was the intellectual spokesman for these complainers. But then came the rise of Asia. Asia, especially China, vacuumed commodities out of Latin America, thus pushing up commodity prices and giving a huge boost to all Latin American economies including Brazil's. Suddenly Latin Americans were happy to be exploited and people began talking about the new Latin America and the new Brazil.

Unfortunately, with the gradual slowdown of China and the coming foreign exchange/ balance of payments crisis coming for India the world commodity boom may slowdown. And so will Brazil and Latin America.

I am not excited about the overall near-term prospects of the general Brazilian stock market. Since Brazil is not facing a sovereign debt crisis and Brazilian interest rates are relatively high, opportunities may be available for the purchase of *real* denominated bonds though this is not for amateurs. And I would be the first to admit there are some really great Brazilian companies. But, as with India, I am cautious.

A Note on South Africa

South Africa of late has been lobbying to be included in the BRIC category. I don't see this at all. Yes, the transition to majority rule has gone much better than anyone expected. Nelson Mandela will be remembered as one of history's great men. But if the United States, India, and Brazil have race/caste problems, South Africa has them by some quantum multiple. The white (and to some extent Asian population) constitutes the managerial/professional class in South Africa. Its standard of living and educational/skill level is far above that of the majority African population. The African population harbors significant resentments due to the years under Apartheid. It is estimated that some 10 percent of Boer (whites of Dutch descent) farmers and their families have been murdered since the transition to majority rule. A far-reaching program of affirmative action favoring the African population has been implemented. Although statistics are hard to come by, it is estimated that some 20 percent of the white population has emigrated since the transition to majority rule in 1994. And anyone watching the TV reports of black South African miners being gunned down by police cannot help but conclude that underlying tensions in the country are massive.

When I worked on Wall Street, I seem to remember the CEO of my firm (Sandy Weill) saying that the company's real assets got on the elevator every evening and went home. The challenge was making sure that they came back in the morning. South Africa's real professional assets are getting on the elevator and not coming back. South Africa's future may be more like Zimbabwe than Singapore or Thailand.

The Russian Federation

Russia is a country well in transition from a centrally planned communist disaster to a genuine market economy. I like Russia for the long term, although near term Russia needs to work its way through its current political crisis and move away from the bad behavior of its authoritarian past.

I may be crazy, but here's what I like about Russia:

1. The country has been to hell and back economically, starting with the Communist years of 1917 and the repudiation of Czarist debt, the immense devastation of WWII, the collapse of the Soviet Union, the financial crisis of 1998, and the botched privatization program. Russian history in the twentieth century may seem like a bad dream, but the good news is the worst is behind the country and many lessons have been learned.

2. Having overdosed on the extreme version of the welfare state and populism—Communism—the fatal attraction of populism has less of an appeal in Russia. This factor may be further reinforced by Russia's ringside seat at the debt debacle underway in Western Europe. Unlike many other countries, the race/caste problems are not significant in Russia.
3. Russia is a major repository of oil and many industrial commodities. Although this ties Russian stocks to the roller coaster of commodity prices, we think longer term Russia can at least partially escape from this dependency.
4. Russia has a significant and growing expertise and presence in information technology.
5. The macroeconomic numbers look good for Russia. GDP, assuming the rest of the world is not in recession, has the potential to grow at least 5 percent. General government gross debt/GDP is roughly 12 percent of GDP, and foreign reserves total a comfortable $510+ billion.

The risk with Russia is that the bears could turn out to be right. The bear case for Russia is that the country is run by gangsters and that to keep the populace from complaining too much, the country recently under the reelected Putin has lurched into an orgy of government expenditures and populism.

Note

1. Carl Walter and Fraser Howie, *Red Capitalism: The Fragile Financial Foundation of China's Extraordinary Rise* (Hoboken, NJ: John Wiley & Sons, 2011).

APPENDIX A

A Quantitative Approach to Sovereign Risk Assessment

Michael C. S. Wong

Previous chapters consider economic history and economic trends to predict sovereign risk. To monitor and manage sovereign risk exposure, many banks and fund houses mostly rely on mechanical tools to risk rank countries and set their exposure limits. Some simply consider external ratings from different sources and some apply econometric techniques to build shadow models that replicate expert opinions. This appendix will summarize the general practices on modeling sovereign risk and discuss their major weaknesses. Although these institutions have their own models and tools to predict risk, the European sovereign debt crisis in 2009–2012 demonstrates that these models all fail. Sovereign risk assessment can be in the forms of letter grades, ranks, probability of default, high-medium-low, or other ordinal scales. In a broad sense, these outputs on credit risk measurement are the results of some models, which are all about data, variables, procedures, measurements, and methodologies. A model can be an expert model, a scorecard model, a checklist model, a statistical model, or a hybrid one. Will there be any accurate models to predict sovereign risk? Is there any way to improve the model performance? These questions will be addressed in this appendix.

Measuring Sovereign Risk

Sovereign risk does not have a clear-cut definition. Some relate sovereign risk to the inability of a country to fulfill its debt obligations, such as formal defaults or rescheduling of sovereign debts.[1] Some simply link it to political instability, economic stability, implementation of exchange control, sharp depreciation of exchange rates and etc. These factors can be major concerns of foreign direct investments.[2] This wide range of risk definitions arise from various uses of sovereign risk analysis. Global banks are generally required to conduct their country risk analysis, assessing the business risk of their overseas branches and setting limits on international counterparties and borrowers. Institutional investors usually have mandates to guide their choices of investment products. For instance, pension fund managers tend to look for high-quality sovereign debts to invest. Portfolio managers and hedge fund traders may apply sovereign risk analysis to trade sovereign bonds and credit default swaps, build their investment portfolios, or set their expected portfolio returns.[3] They would care more about the changes of sovereign risk rather than actual defaults because assets prices are sensitive to sovereign risk.

How Do Banks Assess and Manage Sovereign Risk?

Many commercial banks engage themselves in international lending and sovereign bond investment. Also, they set up overseas branches to deal with both domestic and foreign clients. Country debt crises, currency crises, and/or exchange control crises in emerging economies did lead to bankruptcy or severe credit loss of some European and North America banks in the past. Hence, country risk management is always a key issue in banking supervision in advanced economies. Bank supervisors usually have guidelines issued on country risk analysis. These guidelines mostly stress the importance of country risk management and require that relevant process of risk analysis be in place. However, there is no solid scope on what the banks should do. The US Federal Reserve publishes a paper summarizing how US banks conduct their country risk and manage their country risk.[4] This paper provides a good summary of related practices. The following are some observed practices mentioned in the paper:

- All banks have country risk management programs. Most of the programs are centralized at their headquarters.
- Country risk management is integrated with credit risk management.
- Responsibility for country risk management generally lies with either a senior country risk officer or a high-level country risk committee.
- Some banks have established procedures to deal with deteriorating country risk situations.
- Banks mostly consider the following risk profiles for country risk assessment: internal analysis of political/economic/ social issues and risks prepared by country risk officers or international economists; external analysis prepared by rating agencies or consultants; and officer call memos. No multinational or regional bank relies entirely on external country risk analyses.
- Most banks assign formal country risk ratings. Their risk ratings cover a broad definition of country risk, including transfer risk and local currency/indigenous risks.
- Most banks apply country risk ratings to all types of credit and investment risk exposures, including local currency lending.
- Most banks integrate country risk ratings with their commercial credit risk rating system. For instance, country risk ratings establish a ceiling for commercial credit risk ratings (i.e., the borrower's commercial risk rating cannot be better than the country risk rating for its country of domicile).
- Most banks apply a "top-down" approach to allocate country risk limits. Some large banks use "value-at-risk"[5] limits for foreign trading accounts. Some banks consider percentage of capital to set ceilings for individual countries.
- Almost all banks report country risk limit exceptions to executive management. Many also report exceptions to the board of directors or its committee.

Are Banks Good at Sovereign Risk Assessment?

Sovereign risk assessment procedures are obviously in place in commercial banks. These banks are regarded as finance and risk experts. However, the history of banking crises and cases of bank collapses tell that these experts are mediocre in analyzing and managing risk. Large US banks suffered serious loss from the Latin America debt crisis in the early 1980s. Asian banks and global banks were severely injured from the Asian financial crisis in the late 1990s. In the early 2010s, European banks are the victims. Are these experts serious in their risk analysis? Is sovereign risk very difficult to predict?

One important group of variables in sovereign risk analysis is economic fundamentals. Most forecasting models are based on recent economic fundamentals. These models may work very well for short-term economic forecasts, such as one-year-ahead forecasts. More importantly these models may work well only for economic expansions. Previous studies on OECD or IMF economic forecasts show that these forecasts tend to have systematic errors and bias.[6] Biases come from overestimating growth rates during slowdowns and recessions and underestimating growth rates during recoveries and booms. Predictive errors are also observed on inflation forecasts. Forecasters tend to overstate inflation in low-inflation periods and understate inflation in high-inflation periods. Evidence also shows that the one-year-ahead forecasts of IMF are irrational.[7] Stekler (2008) finds that economic forecasters fail to predict recessions in advance and that forecasts longer than 12 to 18 months might not be valuable. What is wrong with these professional economists and the tools they apply?

Many economists like to build econometric models to predict the future. The models generally assume stable relationship among variables. A model built with 20-year data tends to provide statistically-reliable coefficients. However, a 20-year data set mostly includes the data from economic good times, and the model derived from this data set does not help predict worst-case scenarios. In addition, economic fundamentals sometimes do not have stable relationship. When some unusual incidences break out, those models tend to lag behind the reality.

One source of unpredictability of sovereign risk is attributed to international capital mobility and international trade. International capital flows facilitate speedy contagion of sovereign crisis.[8] The crisis in Europe can trigger international investors to sell their assets in Asia. It is because they anticipate international trade will soon be weakened and export-oriented economies will likely get troubles. The Asian financial crisis in 1997–1998 is an interesting lesson. A crisis that occurred in Thailand quickly caused trouble in South

Korea, although Thailand and South Korea have a gap in geographic distance, economic development, and political structure. Under a panic atmosphere, one may find it hard to make sensible predictions. Cash suddenly becomes king. Predictive models totally fail in stressed conditions.

OECD and IMF have built their large team of economists to make forecast. Still their predictive forecasts are under fire. One cannot expect banks will do it better than the OECD or IMF. In practice, many banks simply collect external sovereign risk ratings and their major inputs. In 2009, Blankfein, the chairman of the Goldman Sachs Group, said that too many financial institutions and investors simply outsourced their risk management and that the banking industry relied too heavily on ratings agencies to assess risk. He named such issues as a "systemic lack of skepticism." The survey evidence of the Federal Reserve reveals that the ratings provided by leading credit ratings agencies (CRAs) are a major input of banks' internal sovereign risk assessment. Given limited resources for internal economic forecasts, banks' outsourcing risk analysis to CRAs is cost-effective to analyze risk. Another possible reason for heavy reliance on the ratings of CRAs is the behavior of conformity. Social psychologists find that human beings are inclined to match their attitudes, beliefs, and behaviors to group norms. If major CRAs assign "A" to a country, a bank analyst will find it embarrassing and troublesome to propose a different credit grade. If the analyst is more conservative than the CRAs in risk assessment, frontline people, such as credit marketers or financial traders, will likely give the analyst some trouble. The frontline people all want higher risk limits and more transactions. It seems that CRAs become the final voices on sovereign risk assessment. Whether these voices are reliable is controversial all the time.

Common Practices of Credit Rating Agencies

This section briefly summarizes how CRAs generally conduct their sovereign ratings and discusses the methodological issues of their practices. A working paper of IMF published in 2002 provides comprehensive discussion on the sovereign ratings methodologies of S&P, Moody's, and Fitch.[9] These CRAs assess both governments' issuer/obligor risk and government debt risk. Some focus on predicting probability of default (PD) alone. Some consider expected loss, which is a combination of both PD and loss rate given default.

Sovereign ratings business grew especially fast in the mid-1990s. Before the 1990s, S&P and Moody's provided sovereign ratings mainly on industrialized countries. In 1990, each of the two CRAs rated 33 to 35 countries. In 2000, S&P and Moody's included many emerging and transition economies into their ratings portfolios. The number of sovereigns covered by either of the two CRAs increased to 108. Around 40 percent of their sovereign ratings belonged to speculative grades.

Sovereign creditworthiness is always a subjective opinion because it cannot easily be verified with statistical data. Sovereign defaults rarely take place. Without a sufficient number of defaulted cases, analysts find it hard to build statistical models on sovereign risk. Therefore, the CRAs establish procedures to assign their sovereign ratings via debates in a rating committee. Responsible analysts first make ratings recommendations. Then a rating committee confirms or adjusts the recommendations. To assure consistency of the sovereign ratings, recommendations are mostly based on an agreed upon checklist of risk factors. A country is sometimes assigned to a peer group for comparison. The CRAs also visit a country by holding meetings with senior officers of the country's central bank and government. The information collected via the meetings is used for making ratings recommendations. The checklist of risk factors varies among the CRAs. It is usually a long checklist of questions or scoring items. Economic fundamentals, political fundamentals, government budget situations, export situations, manpower quality, and so on are usually included in the checklist.

It seems that the CRAs have done comprehensive work on sovereign risk assessment. However, they are frequently criticized for their failures to predict financial crises and sovereign defaults. For instance, they fail to downgrade entities when a crisis breaks out, and fail to upgrade entities when the crisis is over.[10] Recent debates on CRAs mostly focus on their conflict of interest. They collect fees to provide ratings and may thus become more lenient in assigning ratings. Cornaggia, Cornaggia, and Hund (2012) show that revenue generation and rating standards are inversely correlated in a leading CRA. Poon (2003) also finds that, all other factors equal, unsolicited ratings, in which information subscribers pay fees, tend to be more stringent than solicited ratings, where the issuers pay fees. Both of these two studies demonstrate the presence of a conflict of interest in CRAs.

Can the Models of CRAs Be Replicated?

The ratings conclusions of CRAs are always considered to be mysterious. Many doubt whether analysts of the CRAs are able to score the long checklist of questions with related professional standards and internal consistency. Many of the questions rely on subjective judgments. If the same questions are given to an analyst many times, it is likely that the analyst will provide inconsistent answers. If the questions are debated in a group, the final decisions will be biased according to social psychologists. In a group environment, decision makers likely conform their views to the majority's opinions. Also, the majority's final judgment will likely be polarized, either more aggressive or more conservative than the original average opinions.

Regardless of the many variables or inputs for decision making, statisticians believe that expert judgments can be finally predicted with a small number of essential independent variables. It is because many economic variables are highly correlated and can be easily predicted by a combination of other economic variables. Some analysts try to replicate expert opinions by building shadow models. In these models, the dependent variable is the expert's decision and the independent variables are factors and variables highly resulting in the expert decision. The use of the shadow model to judge credit risk has become a common practice after the confirmation of Basel II on using an internal-ratings based approach to compute bank capital requirements. CRAs also develop their shadow models on sovereign risk, counterparty risk, and corporate credit, and sell these models to banks and corporations.

Through building a shadow model, one can easily identify those important factors shaping a professional's judgment. António Afonso (2002)[11] provides an easy-to-understand shadow model to predict sovereign risk. It is based on regression analysis on S&P and Moody's sovereign ratings. In a typical regression analysis, an analyst identifies a dependent variable (or a Y-variable) and some independent variables (or X-variables). The X-variables should explain the Y-variable in both statistical and economic sense. The relationship between the variables will be in a linear form, such as:

$$Y = a_0 + a_1 X_1 + a_2 X_2 + \cdots + a_n X_n + \text{error term}$$

where:

$X_1, X_2, \ldots X_n$ are the X-variables and Y is the Y-variable.

Table A.1   Sovereign Ratings of S&P and Moody's in June 2001

Country	Ratings S&P	Moody's	Country	Ratings S&P	Moody's
Argentina	B	B2	Lithuania	BBB−	Ba1
Australia	AA+	Aa2	Luxembourg	AAA	Aaa
Austria	AAA	Aaa	Malaysia	BBB	Baa2
Barbados	A−	Baa2	Malta	A	A3
Belgium	AA+	Aa1	Mexico	BB+	Baa3
Belize	BB	Ba2	Mongolia	B	
Bolivia	B+	B1	Morocco	BB	Ba1
Botswana	A	A2	Netherlands	AAA	Aa2
Bulgaria	B+	B2	Norway	AAA	Aaa
Canada	AA+	Aa1	Oman	BBB	Baa2
Chile	A−	Baa1	Pakistan	B−	Caa1
China	BBB	A3	Panama	BB+	Ba1
Colombia	BB	Ba2	Papua New Guinea	B+	B1
Costa Rica	BB	Ba1	Paraguay	B	B2
Cyprus	A	A2	Peru	BB−	Ba3
Czech Republic	A−	Baa1	Philippines	BB+	Ba1
Denmark	AAA	Aaa	Poland	BBB+	Baa1
Dominican Republic	B+	B1	Portugal	AA	Aa2
Egypt	BBB−	Ba1	Qatar	BBB+	Baa2
El Salvador	BB+	Baa3	Romania	B−	B3
Estonia	BBB+	Baa1	Russia	B−	B3
Finland	AA+	Aaa	Senegal	B+	
France	AAA	Aaa	Singapore	AAA	Aa1
Germany	AAA	Aaa	Slovakia	BB+	Ba1
Greece	A	A2	Slovenia	A	A2
Hong Kong	A+	A3	South Africa	BBB−	Baa3
Hungary	A−	A3	Spain	AA+	Aa2
Iceland	A+	Aa3	Suriname	B−	
India	BB	Ba2	Sweden	AA+	Aa1
Ireland	Aa+	Aaa	Switzerland	AAA	Aaa
Israel	A−	A2	Taiwan	AA+	Aa3
Italy	AA	Aa3	Thailand	BBB−	Baa3
Jamaica	B+	Ba3	Trinidad & Tobago	BBB−	Baa3
Japan	AA+	Aa1	Tunisia	BBB	
Jordan	BB−	Ba3	Turkey	B−	B1
Kazakhstan	BB	Ba2	UK	AAA	Aaa
Korea	BBB	Baa2	EUA	AAA	Aaa
Kuwait	A	Baa1	Uruguay	BBB	Baa3
Latvia	BBB	Baa2	Venezuela	B	B2
Lebanon	B+	B1			

Table A.2   Transformation of Ratings to Numeric Orders

S&P	Moody's	Numeric Order
B−	B3	1
B	B2	2
B+	B1	3
BB−	Ba3	4
BB	Ba2	5
BB+	Ba1	6
BBB−	Baa3	7
BBB	Baa2	8
BBB+	Baa1	9
A−	A3	10
A	A2	11
A+	A1	12
AA−	Aa3	13
AA	Aa2	14
AA+	Aa1	15
AAA	Aaa	16

CRAs may develop a magically long checklist to score the risk of a country, while a regression model analysis mostly includes 3 to 10 X-variables only. Sample size, number of defaulted cases, correlation and so on highly affect the number of X-variables to be finally included.

Afonso (2002) considers sovereign ratings of Moody's and Standard and Poor's in June 2001 and transforms the ratings from letter grades to numeric order. Table A.1 provides the ratings collected. Table A.2 summarizes the transformation results.

After some statistical procedures, Afonso identifies the six essential variables most relevant to the sovereign ratings. These variables include:

(+) GDP per capita

(−) External debt (with respect to exports)

(+) Economic development (developed country or not)

(−) Default history in 1975−2001

(+) Real growth rate (3-year average)

(−) Inflation rate (3-year average)

The "+" and "−" signs suggest the direction of association. Those countries with high external debt, default history and high inflation rates tend to have high sovereign risk and worse sovereign ratings. Those with high GDP per capita, the status of advanced economy, and a high real GDP growth rate tend to have lower sovereign risk and better sovereign ratings. Briefly speaking, the above six variables can replace the long checklist of questions that CRAs apply to make their sovereign ratings. GDP per capita indicates nationals' earnings power and the stability of tax revenue. High external debt is problematic if a country fails to generate income via exports or attract foreign direct investments. Developed economies tend to have higher political and economic stability. Default history reflects behavioral tendency. High real growth rates indicate economic stability. High inflation rates likely generate economic and political instability. These six explanatory variables appear to make economic sense.

Can this model be useful to predict the European debt crisis in 2009–2012? Obviously, it is far from satisfactory. All the defaulted European countries are advanced economies, with similar inflation rates and without any default history in the past 15 years. According to this model, the defaulted countries should have a high score. This explains why the two CRAs failed to predict the European debt crises in the period.

Quantitative Models on Sovereign Risk

The Alfonso study is just an example of many similar quantitative models. Quantitative analysts may build their models with different dependent and independent variables. Linear statistical models, such as multiple regression, logistic regression and discriminant analysis, are commonly used to find out association among variables. Some researchers may apply nonlinear and neural network models to study their linkages. Nonlinear models may provide better predictive power but may provide less convincing economic sense for understanding the relationship. In addition to CRAs' ratings, the dependent variables may include credit spreads and bond yields. Variables in these sovereign risk models can include the following:[12]

Dependent Variables

CRA ratings

Government bond yield spreads

Government bond yield over LIBOR

CDS prices of sovereign debts

Change in the net position in US direct investment

Dummy = 1 if currency value drop by 10% in one month

Dummy = 1 if currency value drop by 40% in one month

Dummy = 1 if default takes place

Dummy = 1 if loan rescheduling takes place

Debt-related Independent Variables

Average value of debt rescheduling

Debt-service payment to exports ratio

Amortization to debt service ratio

Capital inflow to debt service ratio

Short-term external debt to exports ratio

Interest payments to exports ratio

Amortization to total debt ratio

External debt to reserves ratio

Medium-term plus long-term bank debt to short-term bank debt ratio

Undisbursed credit commitments to total bank debt ratio

Unallocated credits to total debt ratio

Use of IMF credits to IMF reserves (quota) ratio

Interest rate on private loans

Loan duration

Medium- and long-term debt to bank debt ratio

Interest rate on all debts

Loan value

Net external debt to exports ratio

Narrow net external debt to exports ratio

Net public sector external debt to exports ratio

Gross external debt to GNP/GDP ratio

Debt service difficulties (dummy = 1 when a country ask some of its creditors for debt relief and 0 otherwise)

Interest to GDP ratio

Government debt held domestically to GDP ratio

Gross external debt to exports ratio

Value of external debt rescheduling

Net external liabilities to exports ratio

Net interest payments to exports ratio

Number of external debt rescheduling

Net borrowing to current account receipts ratio

Other Independent Variables

GNP/GDP per capita

Savings/GDP (%)

Net resource transfer to GDP ratio

Investment to GNP/GDP ratio

Growth rate of real GDP

Growth rate of per capita GDP/GNP

Growth rate of real investment

Unemployment rate

Inflation rate

Indicator of economic development (dummy = 1 if the country
    is classified as industrialized by IMF)

Reserves (excluding gold) to IMF quota ratio

Reserves to GNP/GDP ratio

Rate of change of inflation

Difference between GNP and GDP growth rates

Reserves variability

Outward orientation index

Rate of devaluation

Log population

Income distribution index

Accumulated arrears to long-term debt ratio

Agriculture share in GDP

International reserves to debt outstanding and disbursed ratio

Savings investment ratio

Long-run multiplier

Growth rate of OECD countries

Residuals (domestic)—unluckiness

Budget surplus (deficit) to GDP ratio

Primary balance to GDP ratio

Government revenue to GDP ratio

Government spending to GDP/GNP ratio

Current account receipts to GDP ratio

Current account balance to exports ratio

Current account balance to current account receipts ratio

Reserves to imports ratio

Import to reserves ratio

Current account balance to GNP/GDP ratio

Export variability

Export growth rate

Imports to GNP ratio

Import growth rate

Net FDI to GDP ratio

Net investment payments to exports ratio

Same as the study of Afonso (2002), similar quantitative models mostly identify only four to six essential independent variables. Maltritza, Bühna and Eichlera (2012) provides a summary on the samples and variables of various sovereign risk models. The authors also added some of the latest ones. Table A.3 shows the results.

From these two summary tables, we can easily find reasons why analysts failed to predict the sovereign crises in 2009–2012. All these models reflect human wisdoms in understanding and predicting sovereign risk. However, these models are based on sample data from 1970–2000, in which sovereign crises of developing/emerging economies are the dependent variable. There is nothing related to the sovereign crises of industrialized economies.

Obviously, the global economic landscape changes very fast. Old wisdom tells us industrialized economies are safe and new economies are risky. After the global crisis in 2008, many emerging

Table A.3   Studies with Bond Spreads, Ratings, or Crisis as a Dependent Variable

Study	Sample	Dependent Variables	Independent Variables Identified	Developing Country Status	Past Default Record
Afonso (2002)	June 2001, 81 countries	Bond spread or credit ratings	GDP per capita, External debt, Stage of Economic development, Default history, Real growth rate, Inflation rate	Yes	Yes
Arora and Cerisola (2001)	1994–1999, 11 countries	Bond spread or credit ratings	Risk-less interest rates, Debt service ratio, Ratio of total debt to GDP, Ratio of reserves to GDP, Ratio of reserves to GDP, Ratio of reserves to imports		
Bernotha, Hagenb, and Schuknechte (2012)	1993–2009, 15 countries	Bond spread or credit ratings	Fiscal imbalance, Issuer's relative bond market size, Difference of debt-to-GDP outstanding, Difference of the projection (12-month ahead) deficit to GDP, Difference of debt service payment to total revenue		
Cantor and Packer (1996)	September 1995, 45 countries	Bond spread or credit ratings	External debt, Stage of economic development, Default history	Yes	Yes
Detragiache and Spilimbergo (2001)	1971–1998, 69 countries	Crisis as dummy	Ratio of short-term debt to total, Ratio of total debt to GDP, Ratio of reserves to GDP, Overvaluation of the currency, Share of credits from multilateral creditors on total debt, Openness of the economy		
Edward (1986)	1976–1980, 13 countries, 167 bonds	Bond spread or credit ratings	Debt to output ratio, Gross investment ratio, Debt service ratio, Maturity		
Eichengreen and Mody (1998)	1991–1996, 55 countries, 1033 bonds	Bond spread or credit ratings	Ratio of debt to GDP, Debt Service Ratio, Dummy for rescheduling, (10 year) risk-less US interest rate, Private placement, Israel dummy, Supranational, Public or private issuer, Currency(DM/Yen), Latin America dummy, Ratings of Institutional Investor	Yes	

Author	Sample	Crisis measure	Variables	
Feder and Just (1977)	1965–1972, 30 countries	Crisis as dummy	Debt Service Ratio, Ratio of import to reserves, Ratio of debt repayments to total debt, Per capita income, Ratio of capital inflows to debt repayments, Growth rate of real exports	
Frank and Cline (1971)	1960–1968, 26 countries	Crisis as dummy	Debt Service Ratio, Ratio of imports to reserves, Ratio of debt repayment to total debt	
Hilscher and Yves Nosbuschm (2010)	1994–1997, 31 countries	Bond spread or credit ratings	Volatility of terms of trade, Changes in the terms of trade, Years since last default variable, VIX index, Debt/GDP, Reserve/GDP	Yes
Kamin and von Kleist (1999)	1991–1997, 304 bonds	Bond spread or credit ratings	Debt Service Ratio, Ratio of total debt to GDP, Ratio of reserves to imports; Ratings of S&P and Moody's, Maturity, Currency dummy (Yen, Non USD), Time dummies	
Lloyd-Ellis, Mckenzie and Thomas (1989)	1977–1981, 27 countries	Crisis as dummy	Growth rate of exports, Ratio of long-term debt to total debt, Ratio of short-term debt to total debt of banks, Ratio of bank deposits to disbursed credits, Ratio of reserves to IMF-Quota	
Manasse, Roubini, and Schimmelpfennig (2003)	1970–2002, 47 countries	Crisis as dummy	Ratio of short-term debt to reserves, Ratio of debt services to reserves, Ratio of current account balance to GDP, Interest rate on US treasury bills, Growth rate of GDP, Dummy for inflation rate above 50%, Dummy for past defaults, Index of political freedom, Dummy for years with presidential election	Yes
Mayo and Barrett (1977)	1960–1975, 45 countries	Crisis as dummy	Ratio of credits to exports, Growth rate of consumer prices, Ratio of reserves to import, Ratio of imports to GDP, Ratio of gross capital formation to GDP, Ratio of IMF quota to imports	

(Continued)

Table A.3 (Continued)

Study	Sample	Dependent Variables	Independent Variables Identified	Developing Country Status	Past Default Record
Min (1998)	1991–1995, 10 countries, 482 bonds	Bond spread or credit ratings	Debt Service Ratio, Terms of Trade, Growth rates of exports and imports, Current account balance, Ratio of debt to GDP, Ratio of reserves to GDP		Yes
Mulder and Perrelli (2001)	1992–1995, 23 countries	Bond spread or credit ratings	Debt over exports, Default history, Fiscal balance, Output growth, Inflation, Investment ratio to GDP, External current account deficit		
Rowland and Torres (2004)	1998–2002, 16 countries	Bond spread or credit ratings	Economic growth, Ratio of debt to exports, Ratio of debt service to GDP, Ratio of reserves to GDP		
Rowland (2004)	July 2003, 50 countries	Bond spread or credit ratings	GDP per capita, Economic growth rate, Inflation rate, External debt ratio, Debt-service ratio, International reserves, Openness of the economy	Yes	
Saini and Bates (1978)	1960–1977, 25 countries	Crisis as dummy	Growth rate of consumer prices, Growth rate of money supply, Current account balance to exports, Growth rate of reserves		
Sargen (1977)	1960–11976, 44 countries	Crisis as dummy	Debt service ratio, Inflation, Export growth, growth rate of money supply, Real GDP growth rate, Deviations in purchasing power parity		

Source: Maltritza, Bühna and Eichlera (2012) and the author.

economies have demonstrated strong and stable economic growth. In terms of GDP ranking, many emerging economies have been among the top 30 in the world after the crisis. It is very true that previous models are deficient in predicting sovereign risk in such a fast-changing economic environment. Analysts may find it hard to get robust indicators about sovereign risk over time.

Banking System Stability and Sovereign Risk

Many attribute the root of the sovereign debt crisis in 2009–2012 to banking system stability. Banks invested in toxic assets and got hurt. Governments bailed out banks and got serious financial burdens. Governments in the advanced economies did not have the bailout experiences like they did in 2008–2012. No previous sovereign risk model has considered this factor as an independent variable. Also, indicators on banking system are not often included in commonly used sovereign risk models. The crisis in 2008–2012 pinpoints that sovereign risk and the risk of the sovereign's banking system are indispensable. The question is whether we can assess which banking system is more vulnerable and whether such vulnerability would result in sovereign crises. Table A.4 provides risk measures of the banking sector of 29 regions and countries. The ratios in the tables are the average measures in 2002–2006. They can be regarded as risk measures of a banking system before the global financial crisis in 2008–2012. These ratios are further illustrated as follows:

Bank capital to assets ratio (%): This measures the financial leverage of the banking system and the ability of banks to absorb loss. A lower ratio means a higher degree of vulnerability of the banking system.

Bank liquid reserves to bank assets ratio (%): This measures the liquidity of the banking system and the ability of banks to deal with the liquidity crisis. A lower ratio means a higher degree of vulnerability of the banking system.

Bank nonperforming loans to total gross loans (%): This measures the quality of credit assets of banks. A higher ratio means a higher degree of vulnerability of the banking system.

Domestic credit provided by banking sector (% of GDP): This measures the leverage level supported by banks of a country. A higher ratio means higher risk of the banking system.

Table A.4   Average Risk Measures of 29 Regions and Countries in 2002–2006

Country Name	Average ratio in 2002–2006				
	Bank Capital to Assets Ratio (%)	Bank Liquid Reserves to Bank Assets Ratio (%)	Bank Nonperforming Loans to Total Gross Loans (%)	Domestic Credit Provided by Banking Sector (% of GDP)	Domestic Credit to Private Sector (% of GDP)
United States	9.9000	0.0072	0.9600	218.9588	188.5903
European Union	6.7100	0.0289	2.3600	125.8784	111.2274
Portugal	5.9400	0.0026	1.9000	143.3422	140.4337
Ireland	5.2000	0.0121	0.8200	139.7868	139.9530
Italy	6.8800	0.0093	6.0000	104.5669	86.6386
Greece	6.3400	0.0276	6.2400	100.8685	72.2557
Spain	7.2400	0.0119	0.8800	146.3332	131.3483
Austria	4.9000	0.0117	2.8000	125.1905	109.4731
Belgium	3.0400	0.0162	2.3200	106.8371	74.9763
Bulgaria	10.2600	0.1211	2.4400	33.4408	33.4214
Cyprus		0.0589		193.2427	210.5462
Czech Republic	5.5000	0.3228	4.9200	45.5189	34.6363
Denmark	5.8400	00605	0.6200	169.9893	162.5418
Estonia	9.7600	0.0742	0.3800	60.7716	61.7311
Finland	8.9300	0.0215	0.4000	71.8383	68.7944
France	5.2400	0.0129	3.9400	107.8867	91.2592
Germany	4.2400	0.0135	4.5000	138.4870	113.7889
Hungary	8.4000	0.1156	2.6200	59.8655	46.0975
Latvia	8.0600	0.0611	1.1400	59.2281	55.8466
Lithuania	8.9000	0.0932	2.3000	32.7041	31.7266
Luxembourg	4.8200	0.0213	0.3000	113.8444	119.3126
Malta	13.8667	0.0332	4.4000	132.0754	107.9612

Country Name	Average ratio in 2002–2006				
	Bank Capital to Assets Ratio (%)	Bank Liquid Reserves to Bank Assets Ratio (%)	Bank Nonperforming Loans to Total Gross Loans (%)	Domestic Credit Provided by Banking Sector (% of GDP)	Domestic Credit to Private Sector (% of GDP)
Netherlands	3.8000	0.0112	1.5800	167.4735	155.8439
Poland	8.1400	0.1058	15.1200	38.5258	29.1764
Romania	9.8400	0.6357	5.4500	18.2896	17.0769
Slovak Republic	7.7400	0.4367	4.4800	47.1163	35.0677
Slovenia	8.3200	0.2947	3.7400	57.1475	50.0118
Sweden	4.9400	0.0038	1.1600	112.0691	104.1858
United Kingdom	7.1400		1.7800	154.4766	152.5272
75th percentile	8.5250	0.0964	4.4200	139.7868	131.3483
25th percentile	5.2300	0.0121	1.0950	59.2281	50.0118

Source: World Bank database

Domestic credit to private sector (% of GDP): This measures the leverage level of the private sector of a country. A higher ratio means higher leverage and higher risk of the banking system. Basel III, the international banking regulation, considers this ratio as an input to compute countercyclical buffer.

The bottom two rows of Table A.4 show the 75th percentile and 25th percentile of each average ratio. In the first two columns, those ratios below the 25th percentile are considered to be high risk. In the last three columns, those ratios above the 75th percentiles are considered to be high risk. We wish that these risk classifications would help evaluate sovereign risk. Those high-risk ratios are shaded in gray. Do the high-risk classifications tell the risk? Obviously, the Netherlands have four high-risk ratios. The next are the United States and Portugal. Each of them has three high-risk ratios. These ratios of the banking sector fail to tell us which countries would be riskier in crisis. The United States and the Netherlands are of higher risk but their sovereign risk remains low in 2008–2012. Portugal has its sovereign risk well predicted by these ratios. In general, it is difficult for analysts to conclude that these ratios help predict sovereign risk.

Both economic variables and banking-sector ratios demonstrate their limitations in predicting sovereign risk. One simple reason is that risk does not have a single route or a single set of explanatory variables. However, when risk comes, the market quickly responds. The next section will introduce some market indicators that may help predict risk. These indicators may not tell the rationale of risk but will simply tell you the arrival of risk.

Market Indicators on Sovereign Risk

Many finance textbooks claim that market prices reflect fundamental values. This is based on the well-known efficient market hypothesis (EMH). EMH assumes that rational expectations of analysts should be fully channeled to market prices. Research on behavioral finance suggests that market prices may be irrational, such as overreacting to good news or bad news. Therefore, market sentiments are not equal to rational expectations. If negative sentiment on a country continues, this will trigger panic selling in its capital market, depreciation of its currency, international capital outflows, and the collapse of its banking system. This section will introduce several market-price indicators that measure the market sentiment on sovereign risk. Market prices immediately integrate market sentiments and move much faster than economic variables and predictions based on economic variables. It must be noted that market prices could overreact.

Volatility Indexes

The well-known volatility index is the VIX in the United States. It measures the expected 30-day volatilities of the S&P 500 index. The VIX is computed with calls and puts prices on the S&P 500 index, and is generally regarded as a panic index. In finance theory, volatility measures market risk. Higher risk in stock market prices can suggest higher business risk, higher credit risk, and higher economic risk. Figure A.1 displays the VIX in 1990–2012:

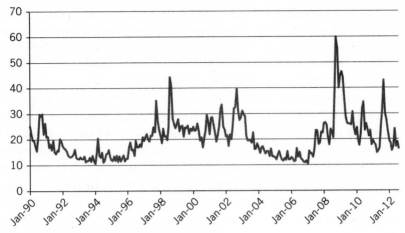

Figure A.1   Volatility Index of S&P500 (%) 1990–2012

Source: Yahoo! Finance

From the graph, the VIX ranges mostly between 10 and 30 percent in 1990–1997. The index jumps above 30 percent in 1997 and above 40 percent in 1998. These two big jumps are related to Asian financial crises. Then, in 2001, 2002, 2008, and 2011, the index jumps respectively above 30 percent. In general, VIX = 30% appears to be the first ceiling of the panic index in normal conditions. VIX > 30% is usually linked with crises, market crashes, panics and asset bubble bursts. Therefore, panic means VIX > 30%. The highest VIX in 1990–2012 is 60 percent. Analysts may simply classify panic severity with the following scale:

Mild panic: VIX = 30% to 40%

Severe panic: VIX = 40% to 50%

Highly severe panic: VIX: 50% or higher

A panic in the stock market easily triggers off crises in financial systems. Investors stop investing; lenders stop lending; corporations suffer from liquidity shortfall; and, banks do not trust their counterparties. Even though panic may last for several months, its impacts could last for twelve to twenty-four months.

The volatility index is a simple measure on panic sentiment. When a country has its volatility index staying higher than 30 percent, analysts should have a procedure in place to review sovereign risk exposures and to reset limits. Volatility index moves much faster than any economic variables. It tells us the market sentiment rather than the facts recorded. When the index stays higher than 40, 50, or 60 percent, one may simply set ceilings of sovereign ratings that correspond to these thresholds. Higher panic severity generally results in higher economic uncertainty or a higher degree of crisis. Most economic crises are solved eventually. It is just a matter of time. Before the end of a crisis, asset prices remain volatile and credit risk remains high. Sovereign ratings as a risk management tool is to evaluate the level of uncertainty involved. With sovereign ratings, investors rebalance their global portfolios, banks adjust their credit, sovereign and counterparty risk limits; corporations adjust their trade credit limits. They provide signals for investors and economic agents to allocate their resources. The above simple rule based on volatility index can supplement the inadequacy of known sovereign risk models that mostly ignore market sentiment and fast-changing macroeconomic relationships.

Historical Volatilities

Volatility indexes are available in economies where stock index futures and options are actively traded. For economies without a stock index option market, analysts can apply historical volatility to rank the market risk of each country. This information may become one input for the final sovereign risk analysis. Table A.5 summarizes the annualized stock market volatility of 36 regions/countries in the pre-crisis period (2005–2007) and the crisis period (2008–2012).

The gray-colored cells in the table indicate the countries among the top 15 of market risk of the period. In 2005–2007, Iceland, Ireland, Greece, and Italy were at the top of this list. These economies remain at the top of the list in the crisis period. Both Spain and Portugal are excluded from the top list in both the periods. The correlation between the volatility of the two periods appears to be very high. Most top-listed countries in the pre-crisis period remain as the top-listed in the crisis period.

Analysts may consider time-series data of historical volatility to track changes in risk. Figures A.2 and A.3 show the annualized volatility of two groups of countries. The volatility is obtained by standard deviation of the recent 12-month returns multiplied by $12^{0.5}$. The first group includes countries of higher sovereign risk, such as Greece, Iceland, Ireland, Italy, Portugal, and Spain. The

Table A.5   Annualized Stock Market Volatilities of OECD Countries

Country	Annualized Stock Market Volatility	
	2005–2007	2008–2012
Iceland	20.55%	42.70%
Luxembourg	14.41%	31.53%
Greece	14.16%	30.94%
Estonia	18.38%	30.53%
Turkey	21.38%	28.52%
Hungary	19.27%	27.72%
Austria	13.91%	27.54%
Czech Republic	14.43%	26.97%
Ireland	13.37%	26.11%
Norway	15.95%	24.65%
Italy	10.26%	23.73%
Poland	17.45%	23.19%
Non-OECD Member Economies	17.00%	23.15%
Netherlands	11.56%	22.88%
Denmark	12.04%	22.85%
Finland	11.43%	22.62%
Germany	11.23%	21.79%
Spain	10.09%	21.45%
Euro area (17 countries)	9.97%	21.06%
Sweden	13.21%	20.22%
France	10.36%	20.16%
Korea	15.26%	20.03%
Japan	14.66%	19.96%
United States	8.45%	19.93%
Belgium	11.09%	19.86%
Portugal	10.79%	19.71%
Slovenia	16.17%	19.12%
Mexico	15.78%	19.03%
Israel	12.43%	18.85%
United Kingdom	8.46%	17.44%
Canada	9.94%	17.28%
Switzerland	10.02%	16.53%
Australia	9.62%	16.51%
Chile	10.86%	16.11%
Slovak Republic	10.32%	14.99%
New Zealand	9.48%	12.21%

Source: OECD Data

NB: The volatility is based on standard deviation of monthly returns multiplied by 121/2. Those gray-colored cells indicate "among top 15 of the period."

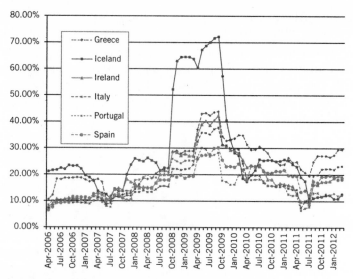

Figure A.2   Annualized Volatility of Countries of Higher Sovereign Risk
Source: OECD Database

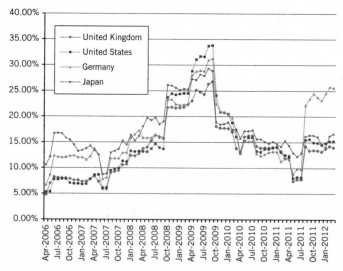

Figure A.3   Annualized Volatility of Countries of Lower Sovereign Risk
Source: OECD Database

second group includes countries of lower sovereign risk, such as the United Kingdom, the United States, Germany, and Japan. Iceland had its volatility going higher than 40 percent in October 2008. Greece and Ireland had their volatility higher than 40 percent in

April 2009. All the members in the high-sovereign-risk group hit 30 percent in 2008–2010. In the low-sovereign-risk group, both the United States and Germany hit 30 percent in the crisis period. None of the members in this group have volatility higher than 35 percent.

With the time-series data, analysts can develop simple rules to monitor sovereign risk and set sovereign risk limit. An example of such rules follows:

Volatility > 30%: review the sovereign risk limits

Volatility > 40%: downgrade sovereign ratings and reduce sovereign risk limits

Credit Default Swap (CDS)

Credit default swap is a derivatives contract that helps investors ensure against the downside risk of government bonds. Bonds are generally priced by considering a number of risk factors, such as interest rate risk, credit risk, and liquidity risk. Suppose that two bond issuers issue bonds of the same maturity and specifications. One is a risk-free issuer and the other one is a risky issuer. Investors may want to swap the cash flows between these two bonds. Such a swap also includes the swap of the risk ownership. The one who swaps to the risk-free bond will enjoy the safety of the risk-free bond but will give up the higher yield from the risky bond. The one who swaps to the risky bonds will bear the credit migration risk and default risk of the risky bond but obtain a high yield. Normally, if all the factors are equal, the cost of the swap will be the present value of all differences in cash flows. The CDS market computes a fixed annual interest spread between the two bonds, which is known as the CDS price. The present value of all credit spreads will be the total swap cost. In simple terms, the CDS is the credit spread between a risk-free bond and risky bond. The CDS prices differ across different maturities. If the CDS market is actively traded, the CDS price can be considered a good tool to reflect market sentiment in sovereign risk. However, the CDS market may not be actively traded. When government bonds in a country are not actively traded, the CDS on the country likely becomes illiquid and their prices will likely become subject to manipulation. In normal economic periods, many government bonds are actively traded. However, in crisis periods, some high-risk government bonds will be totally illiquid and their CDS prices may jump quickly.

Table A.6　Credit Ratings, Maturity, and Spreads in 1997–2003

Grade	Maturity and Credit Spread (in basis point)	
	1–3 years	3–5 years
AAA	49.5	63.86
AA	58.97	71.22
A	88.82	102.91
BBB	168.99	170.89
BB	421.2	364.55
B	760.84	691.81

How to judge sovereign risk from CDS prices is a key issue? Amato and Remolona (2003) provide summary statistics on credit spreads in 1997–2003. This period may cover a full economic cycle. Therefore, the spreads are long-term average or full-the-cycle spreads. Table A.6 shows the credit spreads associated with different grades and maturities.

In the crisis period between 2008 and 2012, many criticized those several leading CRAs for their reluctance to downgrade ratings in the early stage and their eagerness to downgrade ratings in the later stage. However, the CDS prices may have told the reality. In the period between December 2010 and June 2011, the two-year CDS prices of Portugal and Ireland mostly stayed between 400 and 600 basis points. This indicates that their risk was close to BB-rated entities according to Table A.6. They rose above 700 basis points from July to September of 2011. This implies the risk of B-rated entities shown in Table A.6.

The CDS market is not a liquid market in crisis periods. Therefore, CDS prices may easily overreact to bad news. However, analysts find it hard to believe that an A-rated bond generates a BB-rated credit spread or that a BBB-rated bond generates a B-rated credit spread. Credit analysts should immediately review the current sovereign ratings of a country if the CDS of the country shows a big gap against the reasonable level of the current ratings.

Integration between Shadow Models and Market Indicators

Shadow models are based on our knowledge of economic relationships and statistical estimations of related coefficients. If the relationships or coefficients change, the shadow models will be paralyzed. Debates among analysts can adjust quickly to fast-changing economic

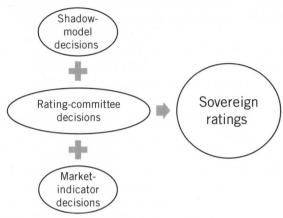

Figure A.4   Sovereign Rating Decision-Making Model of CTRISKS

environments. This approach works well when the analysts are rational and smart enough to analyze the economic environments. Unfortunately, many institutions do not have sufficient manpower to conduct their own rational analysis and debates. Market indicators do not make any assumptions on underlying relationships. They just indicate relative market sentiment. The sentiment may be irrational sometimes. However, panic sentiment itself can have threatening impacts on the market. Relative sentiment is able to adjust quickly to new economic relationships, such as civil wars, natural disasters, rapid changes in international relations, and so on. Currently, CTRISKS, a credit ratings agency licensed in Hong Kong, applies a hybrid model to reach their sovereign ratings decisions. In its decision process, some expert opinions are formed first. Then, a shadow model is built with expert opinions and some selected observed economic variables. Meanwhile, market indicators are collected. Both of these sources of information are presented to a rating committee for discussion. Figure A.4 summarizes this hybrid model.

Managing Sovereign Risk

All risk management is based on risk analysis. Risk grades should determine risk-taking decisions, risk limits, and other risk mitigation actions. There is no 100%-accurate predictive model in the world. Models that work well in 1970–1990 proved to be unsuccessful in 1990–2010. Economic infrastructure, international capital movements, financial product innovations, and so on keep changing. Models can tell what would happen if history repeats itself. When the world really changes, models will be inadequate. This is known as model risk. In this case, market indicators may provide better corrections on model inadequacy. However, market indicators cannot easily tell what will happen in five years. Are there any models or indicators that can tell us what will happen five years later? Very likely, no. Market indicators only tell what would happen in the near term, such as in the coming 12 months. A hybrid decision model that combines past wisdom and latest market data will be better than either a shadow model or market indicators.

As long as a sovereign risk model is present, regardless of how accurate it is, the issue is how to manage sovereign risk. The basics could be as follows:

- Classifying countries in some risk categories
- Setting up sovereign risk limits on financial investments, direct investments, credit exposures, counterparty exposures in financial trading, trade credit exposures, supplier exposures, etc.
- Finding a way to integrate all exposures to a single country together
- Assuring no undue concentration of sovereign risk
- Identifying ways to mitigate sovereign risk if risk concentration is a must

Notes

1. See Hoti and McAleer (2004).
2. See Ghose (1988).
3. See Erb, Harvey, and Viskanta (1996).
4. See Federal Reserve (1998).
5. "Value-at-risk" is a measure of extreme loss amount at a confidence level.
6. See, for example, Fildes and Stekler (2002).
7. See Kirchgassner (1993).
8. See Hayes (1998).
9. See Bhatia (2002).
10. See Reinhart (2002).
11. See Afonso (2002).
12. This is based on the summary of Nath (2008) and the authors' inputs.

References

Afonso, A. (2002). *Understanding the Determinants of Government Debt Ratings: Evidence for the Two Leading Agencies, Department of Economics at the School of Economics and Management* (ISEG), Technical University of Lisbon, Working Papers 2002/02.

Amato J., and E. Remolona (2003). "The Credit Spread Puzzle," *BIS Quarterly Review* (December): 51–63.

Arora, V., and M. Cerisola (2001). How Does U.S. Monetary Policy Influence Sovereign Bond Spreads in Emerging Markets?, *IMF-Staff Papers, 48,* 474–98.

Bernotha K., J. Hagenb, and L. Schuknechte (2012). "Sovereign Risk Premiums in the European Government Bond Market," *Journal of International Money and Finance.* Available online 9 January 2012.

Bhatia (2002). "Sovereign Credit Ratings Methodology: An Evaluation," *IMF Working Paper* WP/02/170.

Cantor, R., and F. Packer (1996). Determinants and Impact of Sovereign Credit Ratings, FRBNY *Economic Policy Review* 2: 37–54. 27/42.

Cornaggia, J., K.R. Cornaggia, and J. Hund (2012). "Credit Ratings across Asset Classes: A ≡ A?" Available at SSRN: ssrn.com/abstract=1909091.

Detragiache, E., and A. Spilimbergo (2001). Crises and Liquidity—Evidence and Interpretation, *IMF-Working Papers* 01/02.

Edwards, S. (1986). "The Pricing of Bonds and Bank Loans in International Markets," *European Economic Review, 30,* 565–89.

Eichengreen, B., and A. Mody (1998). What Explains Changing Spreads on Emerging Market Debt: Fundamentals or Market Sentiment? *NBER Working Paper* 6408.

Erb, C. B., C. R. Harvey, and T. E. Viskanta (1996). "Political Risk, Economic Risk and Financial Risk." *Financial Analysts Journal* (Nov/Dec): 29–46.

Feder, G., and R. Just (1977). "A Study of Debt Servicing Capacity Applying Logit-Analysis." *Journal of Development Economics* 28 (42): 4, 25–38.

Federal Reserve (1998). "Common Practices for Country Risk Management in U.S. Banks." November.

Fildes, R., and H. Stekler (2002). "The State of Macroeconomic Forecasting." *Journal of Macroeconomics* 24: 435–468.

Frank, Ch., and W.R. Cline (1971). "Measurement of Debt Servicing Capacity: An Application of Discriminant Analysis." *Journal of International Economics* 1: 327–44.

Ghose, T. K. (1988). "How to Analyse Country Risk." *Asian Finance* (October): 61–63.

Hayes, N. (1998). "Country Risk Revisited." *Journal of Lending and Credit Risk Management* 80 (5): 61.

Hilscher J., and Y. Nosbusch (2010). "Determinants of Sovereign Risk: Macroeconomic Fundamentals and the Pricing of Sovereign Debt." *Review of Finance* 14 (2): 235–262.

Hoti, S., and M. McAleer (2004). "An Empirical Assessment of Country Risk Ratings and Associated Models." *Journal of Economic Surveys* 18 (4): 539–588.

Kirchgassner, G. (1993). "Testing Weak Rationality of Forecasts with Different Time Horizons." *Journal of Forecasting* 12: 541–558.

Kamin, S. B., and K. von Kleist (1999). "The Evolution and Determinants of Emerging Market Credit Spreads in the 1990s." *BIS Working Paper*, 68.

Lloyd-Ellis H., G. W. Mckenzie, and S. H. Thomas (1989). "Using Country Balance Sheet Data to Predict Debt Rescheduling." *Economics Letters* 31 (2): December, 173–177.

Maltritz, D., A. Bühn, and S. Eichler (2012). "Modeling Country Default Risk as a Latent Variable: A Multiple Indicators Multiple Causes Approach." *Applied Economics* 44 (36): 4679–4688.

Manasse, P., N. Roubini, and A. Schimmelpfennig (2003). "Predicting Sovereign Debt Crises." *IMF-Working Paper* 03/221.

Mayo, A. L., and A. G. Barrett (1977). "An Early Warning Model for Assessing Developing Country Risk." In S. H. Goodman (ed.) *Proceedings of a Symposium on Developing Countries' Debt Sponsored by the Export-Import Bank of the United States.*

Min, H. G. (1998). "Determinants of Emerging Market Bond Spread: Do Economic Fundamentals Matter?" *World Bank Policy Research Working Paper* 1899. 29/42.

Mulder, Ch., and R. Perrelli (2001). "Foreign Currency Credit Ratings for Emerging Market Economies." *IMF Working Paper* No 01/191.

Nath, H. K. (2008). "Country Risk Analysis: A Survey of the Quantitative Methods." *SHSU Economics and International Business Working Paper*, Sam Houston State University.

Poon, W. (2003). "Are Unsolicited Credit Ratings Biased Downward?" *Journal of Banking & Finance* 27 (4) (April): 593–614.

Reinhart, C. M. (2002). "Default, Currency Crises, and Sovereign Credit Ratings." *World Bank Economic Review*, Oxford University Press 16 (2) (August):151–170.

Rowland, P., and Torres, J. L. (2004). *Determinants of Spread and Creditworthiness for Emerging Market Debt: A Panel Data Study, Banco de la Republica de Colombia Borradores de Economia 00295.*

Rowland, P. (2004). *Determinants of Spread, Credit Ratings and Creditworthiness for Emerging Market Sovereign Debt: A Follow-Up Study Using Pooled Data Analysis,* Banco de la Republica de Colombia—Borradores de Economia 002336.

Saini, K. G., and Bates, P. S. (1978). "Statistical Techniques for Determining Debt-Servicing Capacity for Developing Countries: Analytical Review of the Literature and Further Empirical Results," *Federal Reserve Bank of New York—Working Paper* 7818. 30/42

Sargen, N. (1977). "Economic Indicators and Country Risk Appraisal," *Federal Reserve Bank of San Francisco—Economic Review* (Fall): 19–35.

Stekler, H. O. (2008). "What Do We Know About G-7 Macro Forecasts?" Working Paper No. 2008–009, Research Program on Forecasting, the George Washington University.

About the Author

Dr. Peter T. Treadway is an independent consultant and money manager. He is currently principal of Historical Analytics LLC. Historical Analytics is consulting/investment management firm dedicated to global portfolio management. Its investment approach is based on his combined top-down and bottom-up Wall Street experience as economist, strategist, and securities analyst. A regular letter titled *The Dismal Optimist* is produced for clients and interested readers. In addition, Peter has served as adjunct professor at City University in Hong Kong in the Department of Economics and Finance.

From 1965–2000, Peter had a distinguished career on Wall Street, and with major American financial institutions. For example, from 1978–1981, he served as chief economist at Fannie Mae. From 1985–1998, he served as institutional equity analyst and managing director at Smith Barney, following savings and loans and government-sponsored entities (GSEs). While at Smith Barney, he also served for a time as Latin American strategist and Latin American telecoms analyst. He was ranked as "all-star" analyst eleven times by *Institutional Investor* magazine.

Peter also serves as Chief Economist to CTRISKS Group, Hong Kong.

Peter holds a PhD in economics from the University of North Carolina at Chapel Hill, an MBA from New York University, and a BA in English from Fordham University in New York.

About the Contributor

Michael C. S. Wong is the founding president of CTRISKS, a credit-rating agency and risk-consulting firm based in the Greater China region, and an Associate Professor of Finance of City University of Hong Kong. He has advised more than 20 Asian banks on risk-process reengineering, risk-system development and risk-management strategies.

Dr. Wong is the Hong Kong regional director of Global Association of Risk Professionals and was a founding member of FRM Committee of the association in 1998–2002. He was granted a Teaching Excellence Award by the City University of Hong Kong and Doctoral Dissertation Award by the Chinese University of Hong Kong; and is included in the *Who's Who of Risk*. Prior to his career in academia and consulting, he had seven-year experience in investing banking. Dr. Wong graduated from University of Cambridge, University of Essex, and Chinese University of Hong Kong.

Index